THE WOLF CONNECTION

THE  WOLF
CONNECTION

WHAT WOLVES CAN TEACH
US ABOUT BEING HUMAN

TEO ALFERO

CREATOR OF WOLF THERAPY

ENLIVEN BOOKS

———

ATRIA

NEW YORK LONDON TORONTO SYDNEY NEW DELHI

ENLIVEN
ATRIA

An Imprint of Simon & Schuster, Inc.
1230 Avenue of the Americas
New York, NY 10020

First Enliven Books/Atria Books hardcover edition June 2019

ENLIVEN BOOKS / ATRIA BOOKS and colophon are trademarks of Simon & Schuster, Inc.

For information about special discounts for bulk purchases, please contact Simon & Schuster Special Sales at 1-866-506-1949 or business@simonandschuster.com.

The Simon & Schuster Speakers Bureau can bring authors to your live event. For more information or to book an event, contact the Simon & Schuster Speakers Bureau at 1-866-248-3049 or visit our website at www.simonspeakers.com.

Interior design by Silverglass Design

Cover art by Chris Perry's Wildside Galleries (upper photo) and Teo Alfero (lower photo)

Manufactured in the United States of America

10 9 8 7 6 5 4 3 2 1

Library of Congress Cataloging-in-Publication Data has been applied for.

ISBN 978-1-5011-9316-3
ISBN 978-1-5011-9318-7 (ebook)

To the Wolf Spirit that guides humanity,
and to all those who, knowingly or unknowingly, carry the
wolf message in their hearts and in their blood.

CONT

THE WOLF
CONNECTION

INTRODUCTION

The approach of a wolf—subtle, almost in slow motion, confident, and decisive, seeking connection on her or his own terms—can stretch time, open the heart, and awaken the soul. Her deep, unwavering amber eyes locked on you, seeing through you, have a disarming effect. In striking shades of white, brown, gray, and black, this perfectly engineered predator moves gracefully, effortlessly, each bone and muscle connected, alert, and in balance. Her massive paws spread over the ground with each step she takes toward you, projecting a wave of power that hits you long before she is near. Her almost imperceptible breath, noticeable only by the slight movement of her nostrils, somehow seems to merge with your own.

She initiates touch—her cold nose on your hand, arm, and face; the rough texture of her tongue invigorating, unnerving. The subtle vocalizations made in the back of her throat with her mouth closed—whines and grunting expressions of pleasure. You hear and feel her heart beating, or maybe it's your own. She emanates a wild, earthy smell, an ungroomed, fresh scent, nature's original design. As you run your fingers through the cold, coarse fur, the sunlight reveals intricate patterns of coloration and reflects silver, blue, and gold.

OPPOSITE: Neo approaching visitors during a program at Wolf Heart Ranch.
Photo by Chris Perry's Wildside Galleries.

Wolves have a heart-centered, awe-inspiring presence that is unforgettable and impactful beyond language. An encounter like this can awaken a dormant, primal memory within us, an echo from a distant time when we were more alert, connected to nature, awake, and alive.

Like wolves, humans are social beings. But unlike wolves, we often don't treat each other with the respect we all deserve. Rather, we create, intentionally or unintentionally, negative experiences for ourselves or for others, some of which can lead to temporary or lasting trauma. For that reason, dealing with other humans can be challenging.

Many people feel much safer with animals. That is why at Wolf Connection, the California sanctuary for captive, rescued wolves and wolfdogs that I founded in 2009, we create opportunities for people to find hope, healing, and personal growth in the company of wolves. There, men, women, and children of all ages, backgrounds, and walks of life have transformational experiences from their meetings with the thirty-two wolves of the Wolf Connection pack.

Early cultures around the world were aware of the power that emerges from our kinship with animals. Throughout time, we have encountered animals in dreams and in our waking life, known them as collaborative hunting partners, allies, guides, wise messengers, and even healers. Their importance is expressed in ancient ceremonies, attire, art, symbols, and legends. What we now refer to as animal-assisted therapy may trace its origins from the practice in ancient Greece (600 BC) of having incurably ill people interact with horses to lift their spirits. There are historical references to equine-assisted treatment modalities in Belgium in the Middle Ages. Animal interactions and activities to improve a patient's social, emotional, or cognitive function are described in eighteenth- and nineteenth-century European medical texts. Florence Nightingale believed that the presence of small pets improved mental health for patients, and Sigmund Freud noticed that when his dog was lying down in his office during therapy sessions, his patients were calmer and more receptive.

A direct, friendly interaction with almost any kind of animal releases serotonin, prolactin, and oxytocin, the feel-good hormones. Over the past few decades, numerous studies have examined the bonding processes and relationships between humans and animals. Extensive research has been conducted on the emotional, psychological, and even physical benefits of animal-assisted therapy (AAT), animal-assisted intervention (AAI), and animal-assisted education (AAE) with terminally ill individuals, and from children diagnosed with autism spectrum disorder (ASD) to people with neurophysical limitations.

Dogs, cats, horses, and farm animals are documented to have helped people in hospitals, prisons, youth camps, and schools to alleviate emotional and psychological afflictions. Spending time with animals, and caring for them, have helped people suffering from post-traumatic stress disorder (PTSD), from war veterans and concentration camp survivors to former gang members and abuse victims. The human-animal bond can offer a bridge to a higher level of functioning for people who do not respond positively to more traditional human-centered treatments.

Simply put, interacting, relating, and bonding with animals make us better, more compassionate, more loving and balanced humans. Animals can foster emotional security; they open our hearts and reconnect us with our ancestral, primal roots. They promote humane values and a sense of belonging to the natural world. They reduce our sense of loneliness and provide comfort. They help prevent cruelty, abuse, and neglect, not only toward animals, but also toward ourselves and other humans, and they create opportunities for motivational, educational, and recreational benefits that enhance our quality of life.

At Wolf Connection, we take this a step further by reclaiming the oldest human-animal relationship: the one we have with wolves.

FROM WOLF CONNECTION TO WOLF THERAPY

I never thought that exploring and cultivating the relationships between humans and wolves would become my life's work. But in the summer of 2009, I accepted the honor and responsibility of caring for a pack of sixteen rescued wolves and wolfdogs and witnessed the benefits of interacting with them firsthand. Not long after meeting these wolves, I myself felt more grounded, clear-minded, and confident. When the first volunteers came to help me, I could see that working with the wolves was helping them, too, in unexpected ways. They became better able to discern their moral and personal values, improve their communication skills, and enhance their overall ability to relate to others.

Soon I arrived at a compelling question: could we pair humans in need of emotional, psychological, and relational healing with captive, rescued wolves and wolfdogs to help each other heal? I founded a 501(c)(3) nonprofit organization, called it Wolf Connection, and began to develop the premise and foundation of the wolf-centered teachings and curriculum that ultimately evolved into the work described in this book. Drawing from biology, ecology, mythology, anthropology, coevolutionary history, behavioral sciences, and spirituality, we have created instructional techniques based on wolf behavior that can lead humans to greater self-understanding. This puts us in courtside seats to witness the miracle of the human-wolf connection every day.

There is no other organization like Wolf Connection. We rescue captive, often mistreated and abandoned wolves and wolfdogs and rehabilitate them to become ambassadors of hope among society's most vulnerable groups. The young men and women we serve are also often mislabeled and misunderstood, and may have experienced abuse, abandonment, or court-ordered separation from their homes and families. Many of the individuals who come to the Wolf Connection program have been unable to work through their problems with traditional interventions.

The most challenging and intensive part of working with people who have experienced trauma is to get them to open up and trust. At Wolf Connection we recognize that the process of receiving what can be gained from the wolves is individually paced and must be sensitively encouraged. When groups of troubled individuals first set foot at our Wolf Heart Ranch, they present a "wall." They are hurt, angry, resentful of society, and hostile toward life. Often they feel defeated. They are apprehensive about being in nature, and for some of them, this visit is the first time they've been outside of an urban environment. Yet even though they are shut off from other people and from the world around them, deep down they are eager to find a way forward.

Like many of our human program participants, wolves, too, have often been isolated and subjected to negative attitudes and adverse treatment because they were misjudged as "bad," "unwanted," "disruptive," or "a problem." Once our program participants interact with the wolves, a profound connection is established that can help them overcome obstacles. Their shared backstory establishes an almost instant alliance between the two species, a foundational trust that sets wolf and human on a mutual path of healing like the one that our ancient ancestors experienced with wolves.

Embedded in the Wolf Connection program are the lessons of the wolf's ways that I call Wolf Principles. They are a set of simple statements of character traits and intentions based on the behavior observed in the Wolf Connection pack as well as among wolves living in the wild. First Nations people in Canada and Native Americans in the United States have attributed many key features of their way of life to the adoption of behaviors they admired in wolf packs, such as hunting collaboratively for greater efficiency and organizing socially to improve survival and to support community members. The Wolf Principles are a practical application of what observing wolf behavior can teach us and, along with the Nine Realms of the Wolf, which are the areas of life, art, and science in which we encounter the wolf, they form a comprehensive modality I call Wolf Therapy.

Deep healing and bonding help us reclaim the joy and strength that are our birthright. *Photo by Chris Perry's Wildside Galleries.*

As the visitors get off the vans on the first day of the program, my team and I join them and circle up just outside the wolf compound. We ask everyone to remove their headphones, put away their phones, close their eyes, and remain silent to show respect for the wolves. They are then invited to silently ask permission to be in the wolves' home. At first, they fidget and joke nervously, but eventually they settle down, and as soon as they get grounded is when it comes: the deep, powerful HOWWWLLL of a pack of thirty wolves. And just like that, we have their attention.

What started with simple school assemblies and brief group visits to the sanctuary in 2009 have expanded into immersive field trips, multinight initiation camps, and a multidisciplinary Experiential Education and Life Redirection program. Initially, Wolf Connection was a program exclusively for youths in foster care. Over time, we have expanded our reach to serve youth from low-income neighborhoods and schools, and in probation with the juvenile system. We also serve military veterans, young adults in substance abuse recovery, ex-gang members, and individuals newly released from prison. In addition, we run cutting-edge leadership retreats for what is perhaps the most "at risk" population: corporate America. Prominent companies recognize the value in our method and come to Wolf Connection to recenter their teams and refocus their purpose.

While measuring effectiveness relies heavily on anecdotal records, an important benchmark of program success came out of a multiyear study by Claremont University graduate psychology students that evaluated self-reflection and insights, prosocial behavior, connectedness to nature, and personal growth in our prison diversion program. In every metric, participants demonstrated high emotional and behavioral engagement with and assimilation of our Wolf Principles, showing steady and significant improvement. Reinforcement of the measurable benefits of the program is critical as we expand the application of our work.

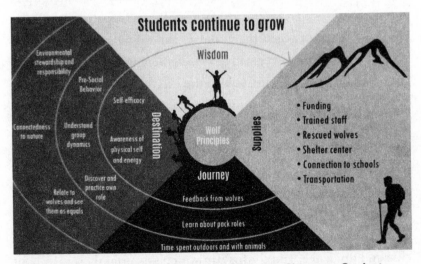

The Wolf Connection Program Model as described by Claremont Graduate University. *Courtesy of Claremont Graduate University Psychology Program.*

Wolf Connection programs are practical expressions of the ancient wolf-human bond that can transform the lives of people along socioeconomic, intellectual, and emotional continuums. With the help of these deeply intuitive animals, struggling youth and honor students alike, as well as affluent donors and community visitors experience traditional rites of initiation, life coaching and counseling, nature-based teachings, and self-mastery practices modeled by the wolves. The pack roles of alpha, beta, nanny, hunter, tracker, and omega are discussed in depth, as well as how wolf social dynamics can inform human interactions.

WHY WOLVES AND WOLFDOGS?

The lupine residents at Wolf Heart Ranch, home of Wolf Connection, are all rescued wolves and wolfdogs. They were bred in captivity and most of them were sold as pets and later mistreated, abandoned, confiscated by authorities in places where ownership is illegal, or relinquished to us by owners. Others come from even more dire situations, such as roadside attractions or fur farms. Wolves and wolfdogs are so beautiful, intelligent, intriguing, and captivating that some people mistakenly buy them as pets at breeding facilities across the country. But they do not make good pets because they are typically very challenging to handle. These animals and their immediate ancestors have been cut off from the wild for generations, so unfortunately, they are too accustomed to humans to be released into their natural environment. If we at Wolf Connection find them in time, we can help heal their physical, psychological, and emotional wounds so they can have a full and happy life under our care.

But why wolves for an intervention and therapeutic program?

Since the beginning, humans have turned to animals for medicine and guidance, and to this day we could certainly speak about the value of a close encounter with any large or small mammal—

and with many other animals, for that matter. However, the wolf is the first animal that humans ever associated with. We have lived alongside them for perhaps hundreds of thousands of years, so we share a unique connection that makes them especially suited to help us humans understand our past. Wolfdogs are a man-made creation—a mix of wolves and domestic dogs hopelessly caught between their wild, natural origin and an artificially created human world. This makes them a perfect mirror for a programmatic setting that can reflect the reality of most of us humans, who are often caught between our heart's desires and the frantic modern pace of our lives.

Wolves can help us recognize who we are, now, at our core, and, more important, where we are going and the future that is possible for us.

ONE STEP BEYOND FEAR: MIKO AND NINA

Nina, a mixed-race, gentle, and likable young woman, could not have anticipated the transformational experience that awaited her the day our Wolf Connection team visited the residential treatment home where she was staying. We were there to share the Wolf Principles. I was the program lead, joined by five handlers and five wolf ambassadors: Ayasha, our little "coy-wolf" with a huge personality; Beau, a large male who has taught resilience and redemption to many; Willow, a gentle, female gray wolf pup; loving and assertive Miko, our biggest and wildest female; and Maya, the alpha female who led Wolf Connection's pack until she passed away in 2017.

When we arrived, we unloaded the wolves from *Wolfmobile One*, a large four-by-four truck fitted with transport cages. The treatment staff who greeted us told us that they had six residents but that only five would likely participate with us. "Nina has rarely left her room since she arrived two weeks ago," a staffer said. "And she probably won't come out today."

Ayasha warming the hearts of program students. *Photo by the author.*

"Would it be okay if I bring one of the wolves into the house to meet Nina?" I asked. "I think it would make a difference. These animals can change people's lives in an instant."

"Sure," the director responded.

I chose Ayasha to be our ambassador, as she was the smallest wolf with us that day. I reasoned that little Ayasha would be the most inviting and the least intimidating at first sight in an indoor space. Ayasha and her handler followed me into the house, where I found Nina sitting at the bottom of the staircase that led to the second floor. At least she had left her room. In her midtwenties, Nina had a subtle beauty that was hidden by the timid way she met the world. She avoided eye contact, shy in the way that people are when they have been told over and over that they are a nuisance.

"Hi, I'm Teo," I said.

"I'm Nina," she responded meekly, looking at the wolf.

"This is Ayasha. Her name means 'little girl' in Cheyenne," I said.

Ayasha took a few steps forward and put her nose out to nuzzle Nina's face. Nina lit up right away, and she petted Ayasha on the neck.

"We have four more wolves outside. Do you want to come meet them?" I asked.

"Yeah, I'll come out," she said, as if it were no big deal. But it was.

Nina had been abused and abandoned as a child, and she felt overwhelming anger, resentment, and mistrust now as an adult. She had a phobia of open spaces and was uncomfortable in nature. Nina moved fearfully through the world, literally tiptoeing around the house, hopping from tile to tile, unable to step on the cracks in the floor for fear that doing so would cause some unknown harm. In an effort to numb her pain, she had turned to alcohol and drugs, until she decided to drop out of college and go to rehab. But her heart was closed, and she wasn't responding to any treatment. Both she and her therapist were losing hope.

Yet Nina voluntarily followed Ayasha out of the house. This coy-wolf had accomplished more in three minutes than professionals had been able to in weeks. Nina walked to the edge of the concrete patio and stopped just before the grass leading to where the other wolves and handlers were waiting and sipping water before the program started. There, suddenly, at that unfamiliar threshold, Nina's face tensed up. The impulse that had motivated her to come out of the house was subsiding and she was growing uncomfortable.

I moved closer to Nina and started our presentation, hoping to redirect her attention to the wolves. Looking straight at her, I addressed the whole group and gestured to Miko. "This is Miko, who weighs almost a hundred pounds. Despite being larger than many males, she is a female gray Arctic wolf mix."

Nina's brown eyes met Miko's amber ones, and Nina relaxed visibly as she listened to the wolf's story.

"Miko and her partner, Cloud, were surrendered to us by a couple who loved them," I continued, "but were unable to keep them.

The couple had three small children whose running and playing triggered the wolves' prey drive, so they felt it was time to find the wolves a new home."

I invited the residents to introduce themselves to the wolves.

"Please approach calmly, kneel to their level, and offer the palm of your hand in a friendly manner," I said, demonstrating the position I was describing.

As the other clients stepped forward, Nina hesitated for a few seconds and took what was probably the first step she had taken onto dirt, grass, and dry, crunchy oak leaves in a very long time. She walked straight to Miko.

Nina's fear was palpable. Her heart had a burning desire to *be* with Miko, so much so that, almost involuntarily, she was stepping over the boundaries of her phobias. At the same time, she was witnessing herself walking on dirt and crunchy leaves and getting more anxious. Her eyes widened and her breathing quickened.

Still, stepping across the lawn like this would have been impossible for Nina just minutes earlier. The house director could not believe his eyes. Meanwhile, Miko's gaze was fixed on Nina. The wolf was aware of her distress and yet remained calm, present, and open.

"Wolves are always okay with who they are," I said to Nina. "This is the first of our Wolf Principles." Nina took a deep breath and her body relaxed as surges of trust and strength rose within her. As Nina became more comfortable with Miko, she also became more comfortable with herself.

"We are going to go on a hike now, following the trail just behind the house," I said, strapping on my backpack. I started walking, signaling everyone to follow. When the group began hiking up the mountain trail, Nina, to everyone's surprise, came too, quietly walking next to Miko at the back of the group.

"Wolves give one hundred and fifty percent to everything they do," I said as the group trudged ahead. "This is the second Wolf Principle."

Miko and Renee Alfero hiking at Wolf Heart Ranch. *Photo by Christopher Xavier Lozano.*

Confidence swelled in Nina as she walked naturally with her wolf companion.

"Wolves let go of the past and make room for new things in their lives," I said. "This is the third Wolf Principle."

When we stopped for water, Nina slowly knelt and offered her hand to Miko. Miko began to lick her face, leaning on Nina until she was sitting in her lap, causing Nina to tumble backward onto the ground. Nina shrieked and laughed. For several minutes, Nina and Miko rolled in the dirt and played in complete freedom and joy—human and wolf as one.

I heard the word *miracle* whispered by the staff who stood nearby, their mouths open. *Miracle* is a beautiful word and it is not used often enough in my opinion. It comes from the Latin word for "wonder," and it is a reminder of the higher intelligence and energies that are part of the multidimensional world we live in. However, "miracle" can also be used to gloss over experiences without looking deeper into them, avoiding opportunities to discover and learn. Clearly, Nina's encounter with Miko was miraculous indeed. It connected her to a time before she'd been hurt, before she developed her protective phobic habits. Miko reopened Nina's heart and cracked a door to new possibilities, making room for her to connect to the wolf's ways and to herself. Her bond with

Miko awakened the memory of an ancestral wolf-human bond, which allowed Nina to return to her essential self.

Learning the first three Wolf Principles that day helped Nina begin to heal her past and present and to look forward to her future. Within a month after her first and only interaction with Ayasha and Miko, she was discharged from the rehab center, far earlier than expected. She applied for and was matched up with a therapy dog, and with the dog's help, she got a part-time job and went back to school.

THE NINE REALMS OF THE WOLF

Most people only see the wolf as an animal, as I once did. But the wolf has played a key role in human evolution, and we have lived in association with wolves for so long that if we look carefully there are many more ways to consider the being we call "wolf." Our observations and interactions at Wolf Heart Ranch allow us to grok wolves as multifaceted beings and also as interrelated ideas and archetypes in the human psyche. These experiences are validated by research in biology, genetics, ecology, behavioral sciences, anthropology, and mythology that demonstrates that wolves exist on numerous, subtle levels. The animals we see in the wild, hunting bison and deer, and those we care for at the ranch, who act as ambassadors in the human world, represent just two aspects, or realms of influence, of wolves. I see nine realms that can help us gain greater self-understanding and remind us of the primal, wild freedom we still carry, dormant, deep within ourselves.

Realm One: The Wolf Heart Awakens

Many people talk about the wild heart, or "rewilding" the heart. I prefer to talk aout *rewolfing* the heart. When was your *wolf* heart awake and alive?

We all have personal histories and experiences that influence the choices we have made and will make. But we humans often distort or repress our past experiences, which renders the truth of who we are and where we are in our lives elusive. This comes at great cost, because it keeps us from living a full, passionate life. Realm One is about clearing the lenses and uncovering the lessons contained in our life experiences, particularly those that have made a significant, lasting impact. In this chapter I offer mine. Experiencing a living wolf may not be possible for most people, but I believe that connecting with the real-life stories of wolves and humans can help us reawaken our wolf heart and reconnect with our life purpose.

Realm Two: The Ambassador Wolf

Many uninformed wolf detractors try to dismiss the importance of wolves by hiding behind this question: *What do wolves do for humanity?* The Ambassador Wolf embodies what can be learned from wolves in captivity and from the primal human-wolf connection in action, which you will see in the guiding principles behind the Wolf Therapy program. In this chapter I'll also share stories that will give you a glimpse of the power wolves carry as ambassadors for the natural world and as guides for humans.

Realm Three: The Ancestral Wolf

The First Nations in North America have a saying: "Wolves taught us how to be people." Referencing discoveries in anthropology and biology, we explore this question: *How did wolves make us human?* And we present the latest scientific evidence, including the theory of coevolution of humans and wolves.

Realm Four: The Wild Wolf

Validated by the findings of today's foremost wolf behaviorists and biologists, I offer observations that answer this question: *What can humans learn from wolves in the wild?*

Realm Five: The Human Wolf

There are many behavioral similarities between wolves and humans, both positive and negative. In this chapter I respond to *How is the wolf a mirror for humans?* and what happens when we ignore our wolf connection.

Realm Six: The Cosmic Wolf

In the summer of 2016, I had a dream vision that changed the course of my life. During that experience I received a wealth of detailed information from a higher, collective consciousness that presented itself to me as *Wolf*. In this chapter I present *Wolf*'s message for humanity the way I received and understood it.

Realm Seven: The Mythological Wolf

I am not the only one, or the first, to have received a *Wolf* message. Cultures around the world have been telling ancestral creation stories, inspired by *Wolf* guidance, for millennia. But modern humans have fallen into a state of isolation, forgetfulness, and disconnection. We believe ourselves separate from each other and the natural world around us; our more recent mythology, fairy tales, and folk stories—including Little Red Riding Hood, the Three Little Pigs, and others—reflect that. But the Mythological Wolf reclaims stories that reveal the nature of humanity's original relationship with wolves and the natural world, stories from a time when our wolf connection was intact.

Realm Eight: The Ritualistic Wolf

What did traditional wolf societies do with the Wolf *message they received?* They created practical applications and embodiments of myth in rituals, ceremonies, and rites of initiation, which I explore in this chapter.

Realm Nine: Your Own Wolf Practices

How can you integrate these nine realms into your everyday experience? Wolf's message of sustainability, evolution, and altruism is urgent—and carries significance for every human being walking this planet. We'll explore what you can do to maintain a connection with this vibration called *Wolf* and how to integrate the nine realms into everyday life.

According to the messages I received in my twilight encounters with *Wolf* consciousness, humans and wolves share a unique, ancestral bond that predates myth and legend, history and evolution. That bond has influenced all we've done and all that we are since the beginning of time. The way I understood it, the wolf is the only animal who truly cares what happens to humans, and its message reached out to all of us, from the most vulnerable people, those in need of healing and inclusion, to the privileged. We are united in the reality that we have all been prey to the darker sides of human nature.

True to *Wolf's* instructions, I have put forth my best effort to let this book be written not *by* me but *through* me. This is a book about wolves and humans conceived as a spiritual initiation not from a humancentric perspective, but from a wolfcentric one, both intellectually provocative and experientially enriching. The stories and findings are meant to be *felt* first and "linearly understood" second. One of the fundamental concepts I teach my advanced private students is that the intellect has a higher function as the conveyor and translator of energetic perception. *Wolf* showed me that the mind evolved as a very efficient tool for survival, but it was never meant to lead the way. It is meant to subordinate itself to our experience of life, nature, and consciousness as a whole.

If I have done my job, even partially, sections of the book will challenge some readers, while others will energize and inspire them, illuminating the path ahead. I hope that you will pay attention to the spirit of the message, and, more important, that you will drop

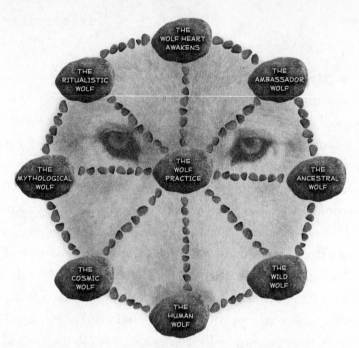

The Nine Realms of the Wolf. *Courtesy of Wolf Connection.*

in, and be present in your body. If you are able to direct your attention inward while exploring the content of these pages, you might experience a new perspective and expansion of consciousness.

This is a powerful pathway to claim your ancestral origins, your wild life force, and bring forth the totality of who you are. I encourage you to put the principles presented here to a practical test in your own life.

As a species, we have been on a journey through times of expansion, connection, and joy, as well as suffering, pain, and struggle. *Wolf* showed me that the cycles of the human journey are reaching their climax and about to get a lot more interesting. The message I was entrusted with is as vital to you, and to all of us, as anything can be. My wish is that by reading this book you will receive the *Wolf* message in the same way I did, as a direct transfer of consciousness.

Wolf Blessings,
Teo Alfero and the Wolf Connection Pack
Acton, California

REALM ONE

The Wolf Heart Awakens

taneda, and later had the great fortune of studying with his colleague Carol Tiggs, who trained me in the practice of *Tensegrity*, the modern version of the Warrior's Way, which they both learned from Don Juan Matus, a Yaqui seer and shaman. Tensegrity describes a combination of practices, including movements for the redeployment of energy and well-being, conscious dreaming, inner silence, and other self-awareness techniques. One of those techniques, Recapitulation, is a detailed energetic maneuver during which the practitioner relives her or his life experiences. It is a meticulous recollection that can reveal not only our personality and inclinations but also our deep energetic imprints. This kind of recollection has the power to transcend the personal level and tap into the essence of the human condition.

I'd like to share a few pivotal episodes I gathered during many years of recapitulating my own life in the hope that they will inspire you to discover the memorable events, as Dr. Castaneda called them, in your own life, and reclaim, in that fashion, the power hidden within them.

TALA, THE MESSENGER WOLF

One of the most powerful concepts of the Toltec tradition that Dr. Castaneda writes about is the *path with heart*. Castaneda's teacher Don Juan Matus said:

> Anything is one of a million paths. . . . Therefore, you must
> always keep in mind that a path is only a path. . . . Look
> at every path closely and deliberately. Then ask yourself,
> and yourself alone, one question. . . . Does this path have
> a heart? If it does, the path is good; if it doesn't, it is of no
> use. Both paths lead nowhere; but one has a heart, the other
> doesn't. One makes for a joyful journey; as long as you fol-
> low it, you are one with it. The other will make you curse
> your life. One makes you strong; the other weakens you.[1]

It is popular today to speak about the wild heart, and other authors reference the rewilding of our hearts—but my preference is to discuss the *rewolfing* of our hearts. *When was your wolf heart awake and alive in your life?*

Most of us experience life as an uninterrupted succession of circumstances and actions. We go from experience to experience with such momentum that we rarely slow down to pay real attention to what's in front of us. And we tend to tell ourselves the most convenient version of a story, one that makes excuses or justifies our behavior. It is not me who showed up late, over and over—other people are rigid and don't understand how busy I am. It wasn't me who overspent and lived beyond my means—other people have no vision or creativity. It wasn't me who didn't pay attention to my romantic partner—he or she was not supportive of me and my career.

You can't determine where you are going without first knowing where you come from. So at some point in our lives, it is wise to stop running away from ourselves and turn around to face reality. The good news is that once we do, we might be able to recognize that only a handful of experiences have actually made a real difference in our lives. By identifying those experiences and uncovering the lessons hidden within them, we can begin to ignite the radiance of the wolf heart. I don't know any better practice to accomplish that than *Recapitulation*.

I first encountered Recapitulation in the writings of Carlos Cas-

I feel that Dr. Castaneda was referring to various layers of experience when he wrote about the path with heart, speaking more of a mood, a certain aliveness within that comes from loving what one does and loving being alive, acknowledging the privilege of being able to walk this marvelous Earth.

The renowned scholar of comparative mythology Joseph Campbell wrote that we can embark on our initiatory path with heart, which he called the hero's journey, in two ways. One is by means of a conscious decision and deliberate action. The soon-to-be hero grows up in a culture that contemplates rites of initiation, so the hero is aware of the path ahead, is prepared, and makes a conscious decision to step into his or her destiny willingly. Examples include the vision quest of First Nations people or military boot camp. The other way to embark on the hero's journey is by surprise, when events "ambush" the hero and he or she becomes immersed deep in the journey without apparent choice.

I embarked onto my journey with the wolves through a combination of both types of initiations—I was both prepared and ambushed. On the one hand, I had made a deliberate choice to commit my life to the expansion of consciousness, and to be of service to future generations, many years earlier. But I had no clue as to what lay in store for me. One of the most unexpected and most beautiful events, which changed the course of my life, came in the form of a wolfdog pup named Tala.

Tala, which is Sioux for "wolf," was the four-legged love of my life. She and I met in December 2007 when she was six weeks old. I was a busy man, coaching and doing interventions for teens and their families in Los Angeles and also helping to lead Tensegrity workshops around the world. I was traveling and teaching in the Safe School Ambassadors program, a violence-prevention and antibullying curriculum for students at schools across the United States. I didn't have the time or desire to have a pet. Tala, on the other hand, had a different idea.

Tala, when I first met her. *Photo by David Kwak.*

Greg, a close friend who has been present at some of the most pivotal decisions in my life over the past fifteen years, called one evening. "I have three wolf puppies in my car," he said. "Would you like to see them?"

"Of course!" I replied.

Greg's girlfriend was breeding wolfdogs in her LA backyard, and he was trying to help her sell eleven puppies. Within twenty minutes I was playing with a lively female pup who wore a little pink collar. Even though I loved her instantly, I said, "Look, I have no time, room in my house, or intention of getting a pet right now. I'm super busy, but if I were to pick any of these pups, it would be this one for sure."

Tala, completely unaffected by my rejection, just continued to play with me and run around. She even jumped into a small pond I had in my front yard and then ran straight for me, soaking my slacks and shoes. Little did I know that she had picked me right then and there.

Over the next couple of weeks, all the other puppies were sold except for Tala. Greg asked again if I would take her. "Thank you, but no thank you," I said, so he decided to keep Tala himself. But Greg had two other dogs, one of which, for whatever reason, didn't like Tala and was aggressive toward her. The aggression kept escalating until one day Tala got hurt and Greg called me for help.

"I can keep her at my place for a couple of days if you want, until things calm down," I said.

At about midnight on the first night, Tala began howling outside my closed bedroom door, a sweet, high-pitched, endearing sound that pierced right through my heart. I didn't move to bring her in my bedroom, but something happened to me while I listened to her howl. The following day, pee, poop, and dog hair became acceptable in my home, even cute. I told Greg that I would consider keeping her, but he had also come to love Tala by then and, once his other dog seemed to calm down, he returned to pick her up and take her home. With great effort, I gave Tala back.

Two days later, Greg called to let me know another fight had taken place. "Come get her before I change my mind," he said.

And that was it. Tala and I became inseparable.

I'd grown up with a pack of German shepherds I loved, but up to that point in my life, I'd never felt for an animal—or another being, for that matter—what I felt for Tala.

Suddenly I was a single dad to a destructive chewing and peeing machine. She was eight weeks when I got her for good and, for many months, she would pee herself out of excitement every time I greeted her. She slept on a blanket on the floor right next to my bed, and as soon as she realized I was waking up, she would stand up on her back legs with her front paws against the side of the bed, her nose and ears appearing just above the edge of the mattress, and make puppy sounds while she waited for me to greet her. But if I did greet her, she would pee all over the carpet and the side of the bed. I had to ignore her, jump out of bed, and rush out of the bedroom and quickly walk through the house and out the front door into the yard. She would trot behind me, whining and excited to greet me while holding her pee. Only when we both reached the front yard would I turn around to acknowledge her, and she would lick my hand and my face while squatting. Once fully potty-trained, she graduated to sleeping on the bed with me every night.

Tala loved to chew—at wolf intensity. Within days, my entire inventory of furniture was riddled with teeth marks. Tala went through two couches before she was three months old. The second couch was demolished in about seven minutes while I was out of the house returning a video only two blocks away. By the time I came back, stuffing was everywhere except inside the couch.

Tala, pictured with the author at a few months old, was alive and awake. The embodiment of the wolf heart. *Photo by Yamin Chehin.*

Beautiful white-and-gray Tala rode in the passenger seat of the car and went with me everywhere. Everyone from the teller at the bank to the cashier at the grocery store knew her. She became a central part of my youth coaching work, and all my clients wanted to spend time with her.

WOLF CONNECTION: BEGINNINGS

In 2009, two years after Tala came into my life, I was looking for a new edge and direction to my youth coaching and empowerment program. I had been mentoring young men through outdoor activities such as camping, hiking, and rock climbing for years and now wanted a more powerful way to engage young people from all backgrounds, to get them to open up, find their own voice, and to trust and reconnect with who they truly are.

I was also looking for a playmate for Tala. I wanted to adopt a young male who would keep her company while I was traveling. Being a pack animal, I knew she would enjoy that. As a result of my search, not only did I find a partner for Tala, a handsome, one-year-old gray-and-brown wolfdog named Wyoh, but I also met fifteen other wolves and wolfdogs. The pack had been rescued by Tia Torres, star of the TV show *Pit Bulls and Parolees*, and she was caring for them at Villalobos Rescue Center, a pit bull refuge and adoption operation, which she had founded.

My heart opened fully when I met this pack. I immediately knew I could not leave them. I began visiting them twice a week to brush them, leash train them, walk them, and run with them. It was exhausting, but I was in complete heaven.

After about three months of volunteering at Villalobos, I was chatting with Tia when the words "You know, all my life I've wanted to start a wolf sanctuary" suddenly came out of my mouth.

No, I didn't!

To this day, I don't know where that came from . . . perhaps my inner seer, or perhaps the wolves or Tala were speaking through me.

The truth is, starting a wolf sanctuary was never remotely in my mind, but my heart was sincere, and those words felt absolutely true when I spoke them. I just realized that I would take care of these sixteen wolves for the rest of their lives. Tia heard my heart speak and she said, "Okay, I'll help you."

And she did. I was clueless, and Tia helped me understand dogs and wolves and taught me the ropes of the animal rescue business. She offered fund-raising ideas and, at her suggestion, I launched the first "Full Moon Hike with Wolves." The plan was that people would come to the rescue center during the evening, bringing food to enjoy and share potluck style. We would give a presentation followed by a hike with the animals under the moonlight.

The Reverend Michael Beckwith, founder and spiritual leader of Agape International Spiritual Center in Culver City, California, had unexpectedly signed up for the event on our Facebook listing. Although he didn't attend, his community became engaged, and seventy people showed up for that full-moon hike. We were able to raise our first few dollars and also to attract the original volunteers, who stepped up to help me take care of the pack. At the time, I didn't have a website, a team, a plan, or even a name for the group, but I was never alone walking and caring for the animals again. On Tala's terms, Wolf Connection was born.

A WOLF'S GIFT: RENEE, MAYA, AND ME

I had been working with the pack at Villalobos Rescue for about four or five months and it had become my routine to stop, at the end of long volunteer days, at the local café for a meal and a pitcher of lemonade, accompanied by Tala and Wyoh. As I arrived one evening, every table in the patio area was empty except for one occupied by a family of four. I sat down a couple of tables away from them with Tala and Wyoh at my feet, waiting expectantly for their customary bowl of delicious, fresh well water, which the servers always brought them. They had become local celebrities by then.

As I ate, Tala and Wyoh watched my every move, eyes fixed on my hands, salivating, hoping to get a piece of the action (which they did . . . "Okay, here!"). I was almost finished with my meal when I heard a voice ask, "Are those wolfdogs?"

"Yes, they are," I responded, looking over at the other table, where a young woman had addressed me.

"Can I say hi?" she asked.

"Sure. This is Tala, and this is Wyoh."

Confidently, she walked over and knelt down next to the table. Tala and Wyoh immediately stood and greeted her, licking her face.

"I'm Renee," she said, offering me her hand. Her demeanor and energy were bright, a blend of vigor and gentleness, and her interest in the wolves had a purity about it that touched my heart.

"I'm Teo. Nice to meet you."

Her parents and brother were watching the interaction attentively, asking an occasional question. Renee commented on how balanced and well behaved Tala and Wyoh were, mentioning that she was a student at a local college in its Exotic Animal Training and Management program. I told them about Wolf Connection, the other members of the pack I was working with, and that we made school visits. Renee asked if I accepted volunteers.

"I sure do," I said. "In fact, we are having a Halloween hike with the pack this coming week. Why don't you all come and check it out?" Her face lit up and she said that she and her family would be there.

Renee quickly became an integral part of the young Wolf Connection organization. She was energetic, driven, and eager to learn and assist with animal care and school presentations. I soon noticed that the wolves treated her differently than they did most of my volunteers. She had a natural confidence and nurturance when working with them, as if she were made to work with these specific animals, and spoke "animal-to-animal" language, not human-to-animal. They respected her, and perhaps cut her some slack due to her fresh, innocent energy.

Renee developed a beautiful, loving relationship with all of our wolves, but she particularly connected with Maya, a majestic high-content, cream-colored Arctic wolfdog who was part of the original pack of sixteen. Maya had been rescued when she was three years old, when Tia Torres brought her from a hoarding facility after the owner had died. Maya's father had been shot and her mother poisoned when Maya was young; she was skittish about and fearful of people when she first came to Wolf Connection.

But when Renee showed up at our small compound, Maya energetically picked her and never let her go. About a month after Renee joined us, the handlers and I were preparing to go on a hike. No one else present that day was experienced enough to walk Maya, so, rather than leave Maya behind, Renee grabbed a leash and took her along. They were instantly like two old friends. Renee said that magic was born that day and kept their hearts connected. They developed an unbreakable bond that only got stronger over the years. Their relationship comforted Maya and allowed her to learn to be more confident around people—for the rest of her life.

Renee believes that destiny drew Maya's and her souls to one another. They gave education presentations together, traveled together, and shared hotel rooms. One Thanksgiving, they gave a presentation for a group of twenty terminally ill children between the ages of three and nine who were stable enough to walk out to the hospital lawn. The parents and hospital staff had specifically requested Renee and Maya for the visit.

As Renee tells the story, "The children's eyes lit up the moment they saw Maya. After I gave a short talk, we had all the kids line up so they could meet her. Maya was an amazing ambassador for her kind. She licked faces, and the kids absolutely loved her.

Renee and her wolf counterpart, Maya.
Photo by Miranda Culme-Seymour.

"One girl in particular stood out—Lia, a sweet three-year-old girl battling leukemia. When it was her turn to meet Maya, she was so excited that she started to run toward Maya, but she was a bit wobbly from being so ill. I was shocked to see Maya moving forward to the little girl, to meet her halfway. Lia caught herself on Maya's thick-furred neck as she stumbled, then stood herself back up to look this powerful animal in the eyes. Maya licked her face gently. Lia giggled and hugged Maya, and I watched in amazement as Maya put her head down softly around Lia and closed her bright yellow eyes, as if to squeeze her and return the hug. They stayed like that for a few seconds and then, once they released, Lia gave Maya a kiss on her nose and went back to her parents.

"This is what Wolf Connection is all about: rekindling the ancient bond between wolf and human. This connection is not confined to age, gender, health, creed, faith, skin color, language, or social status. It is our birthright, for each and every one of us."

With time, Maya grew to her full potential and became the alpha female of the pack. Most captive wolves and wolfdogs are taken away from their mothers when they are very young, and they often come to us confused about who they are. Some of them only learn to howl for the first time with our pack. But because, for the first few years of her life, Maya had lived with her mother, a full

Arctic wolf, she had been taught to be a wolf by a wolf. That imprinted Maya with understanding and a gentle but powerful presence that the rest of the pack respected and followed. She was the epitome of what a true alpha should be—confident, gentle, present, compassionate—one of our top ambassadors to the human world, spreading the power of the *Wolf*'s message anywhere she went.

Maya and Renee worked together to teach our new rescues and members of the pack the way of the wolf and the law of the land, including how to play, eat, interact with people and other wolfdogs, and how to truly become who they were meant to be. After almost two years of working side by side with the wolves, I began to look at Renee differently. An undeniably deep connection was emerging in a powerful way, almost outside of my cognition or control.

The *Wolf* spirit, acting as an unseen orchestra conductor, and the members of the Wolf Connection pack, playing the musicians, executed a masterful piece that brought Renee and me together, for each other and for the wolves. The pack had to be formed for this project to flourish, the mission to be accomplished, and the *Wolf* message to be delivered—another manifestation of the path with heart acting as a golden thread weaving through the fabric of my life.

Three years after meeting, we got married at the ranch among our friends and families. Renee walked down the aisle with Maya, I walked down the aisle with Tala, and we met at the foot of a teepee and spoke exquisite vows to each other. When we said our "I dos," the entire wolf pack celebrated with a powerful howl.

Nine months into our marriage, one cold morning late in February 2014, Renee started her daily routine with the pack. Some of the animals seemed to be extra excited as she went enclosure by enclosure saying hi and performing the morning assessments, but when she came to Maya, the wolf approached her tenderly, put her head on Renee's belly for a few moments, pulled back, lifted her gaze to the sky, and let out a long and beautiful howl.

"Wait a minute," Renee said out loud. "What are you saying?" Renee went looking for me right away.

"I think I'm pregnant," she said. "Maya just told me, and if it's not that, there is something else going on."

Renee was indeed about a week pregnant, and nine months later our beautiful and healthy baby girl was born. Renee had a great pregnancy and the wolves responded beautifully to that energy. Chance—a majestic brown wolf who had lived his entire life chained at a roadside attraction in Alaska but dubbed "the linebacker of love" by the Wolf Connection team because of his build and loving disposition—would get really excited when he saw Renee and rest his head on her belly at every opportunity.

Our precious Miko, who had helped Nina and so many others, spent her last moments of life peacefully, resting her head on Renee's nine-months-pregnant belly. Her passing was one of the most painful moments of my life. When Nina was born a week later, we could see Miko's gentle strength, graceful confidence, and her loving, open heart in her. We like to believe that part of Miko's wolf spirit transferred into our daughter.

I choose to view my relationship with Renee, as well as the events leading to the founding and development of Wolf Connection, through the lens of the spiritual axiom that we are all connected and we are all one. The truth is, one only has to slow down and pay attention to experience this direct connection, just as our ancestors did at the time their wolf connection was a central part of their lives.

FROM CRADLE TO DEN

Early fall is the perfect time of the year at Wolf Heart Ranch, not too cool, not too warm, with a pleasant breeze that makes you want to be outside. The sun still sets all the way at the end of the valley, but soon will climb the mountain range, shortening the days in the winter.

Chance was beside himself with excitement every time he saw Renee, and would put his head on her lap at every opportunity. *Photo by Johanna Siegmann.*

Hiking with Tala, I was admiring the few clouds in the sky to the west, watching as they turned from an intense pink, to orange, then red, and finally to purple. Something about the entire scene made my body feel expansive, almost ethereal. I closed my eyes to savor the feeling of the gentle breeze on my face, and suddenly a distant memory from my childhood enveloped me. I'm five years old and on a family picnic outing. I can see the forest around me, and my sisters running up ahead. I remained there for an instant, however. That awakened dream, or vision, established an inner connection branching to other key moments during my upbringing that allowed me to access a clear view of another time in my life.

A descendant of Italian immigrants, I was born in Argentina in the 1970s, a time of terrorism, military dictatorship, and hyperinflation—a decade that hurtled a once-great nation into the depths of corruption and instability. My parents did a commendable job sheltering my sisters and me from that reality. My early childhood, in particular, was obliviously happy and optimistic despite the political and economic upheavals around us.

In my family, the kids are a priority. Our parents, grandparents, aunts, and uncles made sure the kids had every opportunity: music lessons, language classes, and sports. In my inner life, I inhabited a world of magic, where trees and animals were beings you could talk to and where dreams shared the same continuum with everyday reality. My mother took me to the pediatrician for scheduled checkups and to take care of colds and fevers, but for the complicated ailments, we went to the *bruja curandera*, or witch doctor.

Until I was about ten, my father ran the family textile-manufacturing business his father started. My father was a great designer and a much-in-demand consultant, and our family lived well. When the government of Argentina adopted a group of disastrous economic policies in 1975, economic collapse was swift, and within a few years, the ruin of the industrial sector took my family's business with it. Widespread unemployment, almost 800 percent hyperinflation, and social despair made life difficult for the entire population. My mother would send me to buy bread in the morning because its price would be doubled by the afternoon.

This was the period of Argentina's most infamous political unrest, including a military dictatorship and *Los Desaparecidos*, or the Disappeared. Between 1976 and 1983, any left- or liberal-thinking person, or anyone suspected of being so, such as artists, musicians, or liberal-arts professors, was at risk of being abducted by the government, never to be seen again. Many fled the country.

When I was ten years old, and without much explanation, we

moved to a humble, two-bedroom house next door to the family's factory building, which was no longer in use. I stood disoriented, surrounded by boxes in the living room as my mother told me, "Everything is fine," "There is nothing to worry about," and "It's all going to be okay." My body felt tense and compressed in the chest and head. My breath was shallow. I nervously nodded, pretending to be strong for the sake of my parents, or perhaps simply trying to be a good boy and look good.

"It is just temporary," my father said, and he refused to ever do any repairs on this house. My parents shared one room, and my sisters and I the other. Some weeks, we didn't have much to eat, and our happy family environment became poisoned by uncertainty and anxiety. My parents felt impotent and angry, and blamed each other, silently by day, and out loud in the evening, in fights I didn't fully understand. To help financially, my mother became a schoolteacher. She would prepare her classes at night at home, surrounded by books, making collages and posters, driven to encourage her students to learn. I admired her passion and dedication.

Argentina's military dictatorship finally collapsed with its defeat in the Falklands War—La Guerra de las Malvinas—and some twenty years after we had moved to the temporary house, and after we children had moved out and our father had died, my mother finally left that place.

I never realized how this period of my childhood affected me until a friend of mine said recently, "You dedicate your life to finding the disappeared, those vanished from their own hearts and lives, those who have forgotten their true potential, those who have been denied their birthright as free and plentiful human beings on this planet."

He was right!

. . . .

I joined the army in my senior year in high school. It was the last year of a mandatory draft and I wanted to get it over with, so I decided to do my senior year while in the army officer's school, the equivalent of West Point in the United States. My number didn't come up in the draft, so I could have avoided the whole thing, but I liked it and stayed two additional years as an infantry officer student, specializing in military engineering.

At the end of my second year in the army, my infantry company drove out by "blind transport," meaning we could not see nor were we told where we were headed, on maneuvers, heading to the northern part of the country for two weeks. It was exciting for me and my buddies. After being paired up, we dug a two-man foxhole and spent an entire day there, in hundred-degree heat, preparing for that night's gunfight.

As the sun went down, I felt both a pull and a push inside me, and the glowing orange, pink, and purple horizon swallowed me. Time stopped, nothing moved around me, and there was no sound from nature or the people close by. My attention expanded, as if I had just entered an augmented, multisensorial environment—like a 5-D movie, if there were such a thing. I had no thoughts. I felt no gravity. My sweaty, tired body felt suddenly light and rested and, for an instant, I was both a witness to the infinite and one with the infinite itself. Boundless space became the state of being, and I had my first glimpse of cosmic vastness.

It was one of the milestone moments that pulled me forward toward the life I have now, a moment that tugged at my consciousness with whispers of something bigger than myself.

Although I had an exemplary record, I eventually left the army, which created issues with my parents. I took some sales jobs and tried to complete my engineering degree, but sitting for long periods wasn't for me. I felt rejection and disapproval from my parents for the first time in my life and was ashamed. I became aggressive and violent around the house, and confrontational with my father. I even began playing with an unloaded handgun, pointing it at my head and pulling the trigger. With no idea of how to be a man, or what to do with my life, I felt lost.

On a random Sunday morning I saw an ad in the newspaper asking for seasonal employees for a prestigious ski resort in the Argentine Andes, offering room and board. This was the escape route I needed, and a chance to grasp my longtime dream of living in the mountains. Within a few days, I got the job and left without telling my boss at work or my girlfriend of five years. I pretended to feel bad about it, even tried to convince myself that I should. But the truth was that I didn't want anyone to try to stop me from taking this way out of the suffocating stagnation I was mired in, and I didn't care about my job or my relationship enough to consider my impact on them.

When I got off the bus in the Andes, the entire valley was covered in pristine snow from a storm the night before. The sky was bright turquoise, the air was fresh and crisp. I said out loud, "Nobody will ever get me out of here."

I became a skier and mountain climber and, with my high school friend Rodrigo, started an adventure company. During the winter, Rodrigo and I worked in the resort's guest service department, and in the summer we took families and children to do basic-level rock climbing, mountain biking, and caving outings. I noticed that I connected with kids and youth.

On our days off, Rodrigo and I climbed bigger rock walls together, just to find a ledge to sit on and stare into the distance, watching the sun go down. We had a special spot on a cliff, where, if we went there at the right time after dusk, we could see in the last light majestic Andean condors, with their ten-to-eleven-foot wingspans, floating past without moving a feather. Riding the air and heat currents, from the highest peaks down the canyon cliffs, they would glide to their nests, where they would feed their young and sleep. They would coast by at eye level, no more than fifty feet from where Rodrigo and I sat, silent and still, captivated by the breathtaking view.

One day, Rodrigo and I decided to climb a rock route that had never been climbed before. Two years prior, we had been featured in a television commercial climbing an easier route on that same wall and we had left behind some climbing equipment that we now wanted to recover. We geared up and checked our two-way radio headsets, which we used often because the high Andean winds made hearing each other almost impossible. I went up the wall first, going up a wide chimney formation. I found the hanging end of an old nylon rope we had used to lift some flags during the shoot, so I knew I was getting closer to where we had left the gear. I had forty or fifty feet of wall ahead without any cracks or holes to place safety gear, so I decided to free-climb it and attached a 3 mm cord with a running knot to the old nylon rope for minimal safety.

I radioed Rodrigo at the other end of the climbing rope to let him know.

"Copy that. I got you," he responded.

I continued climbing until there was no placement for safety gear, and no foot or finger holds of any kind either. The granite wall was as smooth as a countertop. The only possible move was a short four-to-five-foot hop to the other side of the chimney, where there was a large hold for both hands and where the porous rock would provide good friction for my feet when I landed. I radioed Rodrigo again to let him know that it was getting even trickier and to give me some rope slack, so I could make the jump.

"Slack," he radioed back.

As soon as I got confirmation, I went for it. But what I had thought was a large hold was the edge of a huge boulder, about six feet tall by three feet wide, resting on a ledge.

The author found his passion for working with kids while climbing in the Andes. *Photo by Diego Lopez.*

As soon as I landed on it with both hands and feet, the entire boulder, with me on it, tilted onto me until we were both airborne. I quickly kicked myself away from it as I kept falling head down, watching the boulder crashing and bouncing off the wall beneath me. Suddenly my fall stopped with a strong yanking at my waist . . . a lot sooner than it should have, considering I had not placed any protective gear on a long stretch of the wall. As I flipped myself upward, I realized I was not hurt. I reached for the climbing rope attached to my harness. only to see that it was cut clean about fifteen or twenty feet below me. It took me a few seconds to realize that I was hanging in midair, more than a hundred feet from certain death, thanks to only a thread of cord loosely wrapped around the two-year-old cracked, sun-damaged nylon rope.

In that moment I recognized that I am in this world to do something meaningful and that I had not yet accomplished it.

"Teo, are you okay?!" I heard Rodrigo shouting through the radio.

"I'm fine," I said. "I'm having a hard time moving my left leg and I have no rope."

"Repeat that," Rodrigo said.

"The boulder crushed the rope against a sharp edge. I have no safety rope," I repeated. "I'm gonna free-climb down until I can reach the other end of the rope so I can tie it back together and come down."

"Got it. Be careful," Rodrigo responded.

Later I heard Rodrigo's side of the story.

When the boulder hit me, Rodrigo could hear me yelling and falling above him, although he couldn't see me from his position. To try to get a glimpse of me, he took a quick few steps to his left and, just as he stepped to the side, the boulder crashed exactly where he had been standing a second earlier, barely missing him. The rock landed on and destroyed our backpacks and their contents, including stainless-steel thermoses—which were smashed into flakes—and continued to roll all the way to the bottom of the ravine. Yet Rodrigo was unhurt, and I came down the mountain with nothing more than a pulled muscle in my lower back. We silently picked up our remaining gear, walked back to the truck, and drove home. In some way, both Rodrigo and I were born again that day, our lives and destinies linked forever.

While living in the Andes, I read my first book by Carlos Castaneda: *The Fire from Within*. A coworker saw me reading that book and loaned me my first Tensegrity video demonstrating the movements that are part of the legacy of the shamans of ancient Mexico that Dr. Castaneda presents. Tensegrity practices have the goal of freeing our perception from the habitual interpretations of everyday life so we can move our body and act in the world with more awareness and clear intention. The word "tensegrity" is borrowed from architect, engineer, and visionary R. Buckminster Fuller, and refers to an architectural principle adapted from structures in nature such as atoms, cells, our bodies, trees, the solar system, and galaxies that are held together by their flexible or tension elements, giving these structures a highly adaptable integrity. For Dr. Castaneda, Tensegrity was a perfect description of the integrating and energizing quality of the movements, self-awareness, dreaming, and silence practices that Don Juan Matus taught him—a way to integrate with oneself, as a physical and energetic being, with others, and with nature.

When I first practiced the movements, it was as if a part of my being that had been longing to wake up was finally being liberated. I felt a jolt through my body, with energy moving around and through me. It was like nothing I had experienced before.

In *The Eagle's Gift*, Dr. Castaneda conveys Don Juan Matus's description of the Eagle as the cosmic source of all consciousness from which all life forms come and to which all life forms must return.

> *I am already given to the power that rules my fate.*
> *And I cling to nothing, so I will have nothing to defend.*
> *I have no thoughts, so I will see.*
> *I fear nothing, so I will remember myself.*
> *Detached and at ease,*
> *I will dart past the Eagle to be free.*[2]

These words became my daily prayer, a statement of intent for each day and for my life. Later I would realize that this level of surrender was not about attaining something in my future but about a state of being, a process of becoming, of remembering, of reclaiming a cosmic connection that is our birthright. In my understanding, he is speaking about the way energetic beings experience the cosmic journey. So, more than a prayer or statement of intent, it is an invocation of integration and acceptance.

Fourteen months after reading my first book by Dr. Castaneda, I had read all the books written by him, including *The Teachings of Don Juan* and eleven others on his apprenticeship with Don Juan Matus. I was so moved that I decided the time had come for me to act.

I remember the moment distinctly. It was late night and I stepped outside my house, which was at the top of a cliff overlooking Lake Lacar in northern Patagonia. I called to the wind. The wind became alive, it swirled around me and got into my nostrils, suffocating me and lifting me up.

A few months after that, I ended my climbing business, sold or gave away everything I owned, and bought a ticket to Los Angeles to seek out Dr. Castaneda, who, it was said, kept his location and movements private. I arrived at Los Angeles International Airport with only a few hundred dollars in my pocket, in a country I had never been to before, and with no idea of where to start looking for this elusive man. Soon I discovered that Dr. Castaneda had passed away, making his transition into spirit almost a year prior to my arrival in Los Angeles.

This might have seemed unfortunate, but my father had always praised me for my good luck. He believed the stars were aligned when I was born and often used a common Argentine expression about me: *Sos como los gatos, siempre caes parado.* In English this translates to "Like a cat, you always land on your feet." As if proving my father correct, among the first people I met in Los Angeles were two of Dr. Castaneda's students. I attended every Tensegrity workshop and class available. Every day from 8:00 a.m. to 5:00 p.m. I worked at a car repair shop washing cars for eight dollars an hour, getting home by 6:00 p.m. to practice Tensegrity movements and principles into the wee hours of the morning. This left a couple of hours to rest before going back to work. My dedication and devotion were absolute.

I was invited to join the team of Tensegrity instructors in 2003, which was a great privilege. Since then, I've co-led events all around the world, and this work has become the single most powerful influence in my life.

After I attended and assisted with several Tensegrity workshops and classes centered around family relationships, I realized that I had negatively judged my family, particularly my parents, and had been acting arrogantly all my life. I wasn't the nice guy I thought I was, even though I had always considered myself to be the son that any parent would want to have. I admitted now that as the firstborn in a fairly large Italian immigrant family, I carried a misguided belief that everything was supposed to be given to me. I had not stopped to consider how fortunate I was for the family I was born into and for the parents I had. I had never asked my parents what they gave up to support me so fully over the years. I had harshly judged my father's emotional distance and personal reserve, which he adopted whenever he was feeling hurt, frustrated, and lost. He was very loyal in relationships and business, and he was proud of that, which I had not acknowledged. For instance, when the Argentine economy had collapsed, he had tried to keep open the textile factory far past the point when it was financially viable, not just for our family but also for the workers, whom he cared about and considered to be like family. Realizing all this, I knew that I needed to review my link with my father more deeply but didn't know where to start.

Guided by Carlos Castaneda's colleague Carol Tiggs, I began a deeper Recapitulation, a more meaningful review of my life, to help liberate me from outdated habits and beliefs; to recognize my part in interactions and endeavors that worked and those that did not; and to see the line of *intent,* the touch of the Spirit that has moved through my life—and through my family and lineage. I could see that my father had never meant to cause any harm or tension in my family, but rather had sought to spare us from the burden he carried. He had felt pressed and very lonely in his fight, but he felt that, as men of his time were taught, he must dig in and protect his family at all costs without showing weakness. He worried that he couldn't financially support us and was fearful his wife and children would be disappointed in him, afraid of losing our respect and our love.

The time had come to call my father, to tell him how sorry I was for any grief or trouble I had caused him. He was very happy to hear from me. We talked about my education and work for a moment, and then I asked him how his business was going. "Good. Things are going a lot better," he said.

This time, instead of judging him, I appreciated his reserve, realizing that he didn't want to unload his problems on me. I said that I was calling to apologize for the times in my life when I had caused him grief and anxiety. I mentioned specifically the time when he disapproved of my decision to drop out of the military. I was ashamed that I'd reacted to his concern defiantly and aggressively. My father simply told me not to worry about it, that children are to be supported no matter what, to be put up with in any situation. It was a pretty emotional moment. I felt an old weight of guilt lifted from my shoulders.

Next was my mother, who cried on the phone as I expressed my regret. "Did I ever hurt you?" I asked her. "The saddest time for me was when you left for the United States and never came back," she said between sobs. I felt her broken heart and her resentment of the path I chose. How could I explain that the force of my destiny, one that I myself didn't understand, took hold of me and was guiding me? I listened to my mother, though, and told her how much I loved her and that I never intended to cause her any sadness.

One afternoon months later, I was sitting at home, remembering the feeling of having apologized to my parents. I called Carol Tiggs to share my thoughts.

"Your parents dreamed you forward," she said. "They've given you their very best. Now is YOUR time to give back, to at least say thank you."

I picked up the phone to call my father again. This time I thanked him for taking care of me for so many years. He did so when I was vulnerable as a child and as a teenager, and he supported me in every sense and in all my interests, beyond his duty as a father. I thanked him and my mother for staying on top of my education and health and for all the things they taught me. I told him that I could see, every day, how their influence manifests, in a positive way, in the way I do business, the way I relate to people. I told him that I have only beautiful memories of my childhood and that he and my mother were great parents and that I was very lucky to have them.

When I stopped talking for a moment, there was a tender silence between us.

Then my father spoke, his voice cracking, filled with emotion and affection. "I never thought I would hear these words from you," he said, "but to hear them is the best reward any father could ever get."

From then on, we truly connected. I grew proud of my father and my relationship with him. Often we would have long phone conversations about business, cars, politics, and the economy. He gave me wise business advice and we brainstormed new projects. He asked me about school. I asked him about his sailboat. Whenever I returned to my hometown, we spent time together. When his health deteriorated and he required surgery, I called him.

"I'd like to have you around for many more years," I said, "and it would be nice if you could take care of your health a little better." I paused and said, "I love you, Dad."

I could feel his breath get shallow in his excitement on the other end of the phone, nine thousand miles away, and him wanting to say, "I love you too, son." Instead, he managed to ask me how things were going with me and told me that he was happy that I was doing well and enjoying my life.

"We will talk tomorrow after surgery," I said. "Everything will be fine."

His heart didn't hold up under the anesthesia and he died the following day. My sister called me to give me the news.

My teacher says that the awareness of those who die remains around for a while after they are gone. She told me that if there was anything I wanted to say to my father, I could do that. I went to the ocean and told my dad that I wished he could have stuck around a little longer, that I loved him, and that I enjoyed our moments together very much. I said I would keep him in my heart forever, but if he had to go, he could go and be free. There was nothing unsaid, nothing unexpressed, nothing pending between us.

I told him that it had been an honor for me to be his son and to know him the way I did. I also said, "What a shame, Dad, that I judged you for so many years, and it took me so long to SEE you." As I spoke, I could feel him next to me, smiling, acknowledging my words, and walking with me.

After my father died, his cousin and best friend, Ricardo, told me that my father had told him about my call to say thank you and that they had cried together. My father lamented not being able to do the same with his own father. My father had taken care of his father, my grandfather, for years when he was bedridden and unable to eat, speak, or go to the bathroom by himself. Ricardo told me it had been difficult for him. I was twenty-two when my grandfather died but have no clear memories of his last years. I loved my grandfather very much and I didn't want to see him so ill. I have the feeling that my father didn't encourage us to see him like that either. Whenever I did see my grandfather, he didn't recognize me, and I was living in the mountains when he died.

Ricardo told me that the day my grandfather died, the paramedics came to collect his body, but their trolley didn't fit into the elevator of the apartment building. So my father carried his father's dead body to the elevator and, hugging him under the armpits, held him as the very slow elevator descended five floors.

When I focus on that moment of my father's life, I can feel how that five-story trip became an eternity for him, an event that marked his life. He swore to himself that his children would never have to take care of him as an invalid and that they would never have to carry his dead body. My father and Ricardo even made a secret pact that if one of the two became bedridden or handicapped, the other would hand him a gun. My father lived and died his way, and I will always respect him for that.

THE END OF THE BEGINNING

When I encountered Carlos Castaneda's work, I could have not anticipated how the events that were about to unfold would re-shape my life and alter my trajectory. The undercurrents that drove those events led me to refocus my purpose and to embark on my path with heart, toward the journey that the wolves had in store for me: Wolf Connection.

Wolf Connection was only a few months old when we began opening our doors to hold small events, such as movie nights with the wolves, to raise funds. In the early evening, we would guide visitors on a hike with the pack, interact with the animals, share a potluck meal, and show a documentary or wolf-related movie right next to the wolf enclosures. Adults sat in chairs or beach recliners, and the kids would lie comfortably on a blanket on the ground between the projector and the screen as the film was projected above their heads.

One night, Tala proceeded to walk onto a blanket and cuddle up with one of the kids, who was autistic. Tala did this without seeking permission, as was her style, and it was clear that her presence gave the little girl an anchor, someone to relate to. Tala made the gathering safer and more comfortable for the child.

They were both in bliss. What a picture they were—this charming eight-year-old girl with sparkling brown eyes and an infectious giggle, petting gentle gray-and-white Tala as she snuggled next to her. The scene was so heartwarming and moving that the girl and the wolfdog, rather than the film, became the highlight of the evening. I never saw the child again, but people who knew the family told me that the moment with Tala was very meaningful for their daughter and a milestone in her ability to bond and connect.

At eight years old, in 2015, Tala was diagnosed with an aggressive lung cancer, and within six months it was clear that she was getting ready to leave us. By February 2016 the veterinarian said there was nothing else to be done and gave her only a couple of weeks to live. But being who she was, Tala maintained her signature high spirit and continued spreading her love for another six weeks, until the day before making her transition. During her last week, I would give her fluids during the day and keep her company through the nights when it was more difficult for her to breathe. We would sleep for short periods; I reduced her fever with cold cloths; and we took gentle strolls under the stars. She had already begun saying good-bye to me and to the desert, the wind, the moon, and the land she dreamed as the home for Wolf Connection. On the day before her last, she went around to greet the volunteers working at the ranch in her usual animated, playful, and loving way. It was heartbreaking for me because I knew she was saying good-bye to them, too.

On Tala's last night, I cooked her a top sirloin steak, medium rare, and in the wee hours we went for our last walk on this Earth together. The air was cold and crisp, and the moon was full, illuminating the entire valley and the mountains around us. I could feel her spirit already leaving. At one point she stopped and stared intently into the canyon that went up into the mountain. She was listening to the call of her ancestors, considering for a moment whether to disappear into the darkness of the forest to die on her own terms, the way wild alphas do, at the end of a life well lived.

Although Tala had only a low percentage of wolf in her genetic makeup, she carried within her the heart, the passion, and the wisdom of an archetypal wolf. She had silently guided me to find the original Wolf Connection pack, and she was next to me every step of the way as the pack and Wolf Connection's mission grew.

Tala affected countless lives in her nine years; mine was only the first. Without her, I would never have started Wolf Connection and none of us would be here. The many wolves we've rescued and helped to live good lives would have had different destinies, even premature deaths, long ago without ever reaching their potential. Without her, the numerous people whose lives we have changed would have had different journeys as well. Without Tala I wouldn't have met my wife, and our daughter would not be running around playing and laughing as I write these lines.

Tala now rests at Wolf Heart Ranch, overlooking the wolf compound she helped create. In a different way she is still welcoming visitors who are about to have their lives transformed. Tala's consciousness quietly and wisely continues to mirror and guide me, the wolves who have chosen a life of higher service as members of the Wolf Connection pack, and the program participants who trust our four- and two-legged guides while making conscious choices to turn their lives around. Wolf Connection has made available entirely new levels of understanding and connection that propel me forward each and every day.

I feel deep gratitude for the honor and privilege to speak for the wolves. And to be completely honest, they didn't really give me a choice.

REALM TWO
The Ambassador Wolf

more than their fair share of emotional and psychological baggage from their family and environment. When I work with a young person like Andrea, I approach her healing as if it carries the potential to extend to her adoptive family, her birth family, and every member of her community.

As a toddler, Andrea had been placed in foster care. When she was three years old, she had been bitten in the face by a dog and, as a result, was terrified of dogs. As she grew older, she struggled with anger and had even considered suicide. Yet things were now improving for her. She was living with a wonderful foster mother who loved her and was in the process of permanently adopting her, but Andrea was finding it challenging to resolve the anger and fear inside her. My psychologist friend felt that Andrea was ready to face her fear of dogs—and there is no better way than to be exposed to the friendlier wolves at the ranch. Some are even gentler than most dogs.

Introducing Andrea to the pack slowly would be the best for her, so we began by just walking in front of the enclosures.

"This is Moonshadow," I said, stopping in front of an enclosure where a black-and-brown, large wolf–German shepherd mix sat. "He is a true lover with people, but he has not been treated very nicely in the past so he can be reactive to the other wolves. Do you know anyone reactive like that?" I asked. Andrea looked at me and nodded.

"Rezzie came to us recently, at seventeen years old," I said, pointing to the brown-and-cream female next to Moonshadow. "Rezzie's owner got really sick and couldn't care for her any longer, but before she entered hospice care she brought Rezzie here to have a loving place to live. We call her "The Bulldozer" because at every opportunity, she pushes on the gate of her enclosure to try to hobble her sweet old self to freedom!" Andrea smiled for the first time.

CHOSEN: LOGAN AND ANDREA

It was sometime in the first year of Wolf Connection's operation when one day I crested the hill leading to the small wolf compound and heard it: a mixture of howls and goofy exclamations of excitement. The pack has always had a way of knowing when I'm coming. And then I see them and they see me; the elation is mutual.

The sun's rays were already blazing above the desert. It would be a scorching day and I wanted to finish the morning routine—ensuring the wolves were safely in their enclosures, picking up food bowls from the previous day, cleaning up poop, and topping off water bowls—before it got too hot.

A small dust cloud let me know that a vehicle was pulling into the parking lot, and a few minutes later two people came up the trail toward the compound. A friend of mine, a psychologist who worked with children in foster care, was accompanying one of her clients, Andrea, whom I'd invited to meet the pack.

My friend introduced us, and the shy young woman with soft Latina features shook my hand without meeting my gaze, her eyes downcast. She was frowning and her nostrils were slightly flared. I wondered if she was afraid or intimidated because of the proximity of the pack. I could sense that she had been through a lot, like many other young people I work with. Energetically sensitive people like Andrea, who have lived in challenging environments, often take on

Logan's heartwarming eyes. *Photo by Mark Uehlein.*

Andrea's face had softened as she listened to the wolves' stories. She was no longer frowning, and her lips had relaxed. Her breath was expanding and deepening, her shoulders had dropped, and her steps were lighter as she walked. She was beginning to identify and bond with the wolves through their stories.

We passed in front of the enclosure of Logan and Lucas, two of the original sixteen Wolf Connection pack members. They were rescued from an apartment in San Francisco. It must have been a big apartment, because they were two of the biggest animals we ever had. Logan was a beautiful gray wolf–malamute mix, one of our gentle giants. Lucas looked the way I imagine the prehistoric direwolf would have looked. He was 140 pounds of full-blooded wolf, gray with black and brown markings. He was massive, dominant, and intimidating, with an unpredictable personality.

I felt that it was time for Andrea to have a direct interaction, but the moment I started to explain that she could meet the wolves, Andrea's eyes widened, her shoulders tensed, and her breathing became shallow, all her apprehension flooding back in. I stopped and explained that all she had to do was to kneel down and wait for the wolf to approach her.

After a moment, when Andrea seemed reassured, I led her to Logan's enclosure.

Logan's sheer size could have been off-putting, but his extreme gentleness and deep healing energy made him a welcoming, benevolent presence. His main gift, which he demonstrated on many occasions, was his ability to identify the most fearful and apprehensive person in the crowd and go to that person to put him or her completely at ease. Even Andrea in her anxious state felt this, and she walked in silence toward Logan and knelt down at the fence. Logan approached her with his head down, wagging his tail, and licked her hand through the fence. Then he walked away to the far end of the enclosure, as if to create space for Andrea to take in the contact and get more comfortable.

Seizing the opportunity, I opened the gate and let Andrea know that she could safely walk inside, which she did. Logan was still sitting at the back of the enclosure, ears up, panting slightly, majestic and at the same time curious to see and sense the new visitor. Kneeling, Andrea timidly held her hand out toward Logan. Logan sat still, waiting for the girl to come closer before he approached her, as if encouraging her to find the power within herself to meet him as an equal. The energy shifted, and Andrea's curiosity and growing desire for connection with Logan overcame her fear. She inched closer.

Logan waited and watched patiently, keeping the girl in his warm gaze. As he slowly rose and gracefully moved toward Andrea, his amber eyes connected with hers, as if to tell her that it was perfectly okay to be who she is and stay in that place of just being and feeling—that there was no hurry to be or do anything else.

Finally Logan came to sit by her side. They stayed in peaceful stillness and silence—the massive gray wolfdog and the crouching girl—for a long time.

Tears began to fall down Andrea's face. Between sobs she managed to say, "No one has ever picked me or loved me this way before." Overcome by the profound sensation of being chosen and loved by this beautiful creature, she cried and laughed and cried again. Her body released emotions that she had been suppressing for most of her life.

That one-day visit to the pack was a turning point for Andrea, and she ended up volunteering at Wolf Connection, helping me name some of the new rescues, and completely letting go of her former burden. Over time she acted on the hope she had carried within her for her future; she worked on her weight and body image, finished her education, and became a nurse.

That day was a turning point for me as well. It was the day when I began to see that I could translate wolf behavior into teaching and life-coaching tools. I had been shown that interactions with wolves could give troubled young people a safe space to access painful feelings, heal trauma, and find hope and a better sense of themselves.

Logan taught me a wolf lesson: *Wolves let go of the past and make room for new things in their lives.*

Logan lived in the present moment, and through his bond with Andrea, he gently supported her to be in the here and now, too, to let go of her pain and fear long enough to make room for this new experience. Logan also demonstrated another wolf lesson: *Wolves are into being, not into doing.*

Logan had sat patiently in deep silence with Andrea for a long time. His presence had helped her to drop down into herself and just be. That's when her healing began, which allowed her to face and release her sadness and trauma.

PRINCIPLES FROM THE PACK

My experience with Logan and Andrea gave me insight into an entire youth program format. I went to work in earnest.

I organized the wolves' lessons, called them "Wolf Principles," and they are now central pillars of the Wolf Connection programs. They are attempts to convey, in human language, something beyond our human reach. As such, they are alive and fluid, evolving as we continue learning from the wolves and the humans we serve.

The wolves embody these character and behavioral traits and teach them nonverbally, through their actions. And that is the first step toward learning from the wolves. Be present and observe. Before we explain even the first Wolf Principle to a visitor to Wolf Connection, we invite him or her to simply be present with the wolves and pay attention to every detail. In this way we try to facilitate a nonverbal knowingness, a process I have come to call *lupine humanness-ation*, referring to when people awaken to their true humanity through the ways of the wolf.

I wrote the Wolf Principles with the Wolf Connection students in mind. These young people, whom I hoped to serve, often carry such complex trauma that it impairs their attention and focus. They benefit from simple, accessible language they can connect with, easily remember, and apply in their lives.

When I translated the wolves' behavioral lessons into language, I realized they had been demonstrating another principle that would help me to help our young visitors:

Wolves communicate effectively. They keep it honest and real.

You never have to guess what a wolf is trying to communicate. If they are seeking interaction and play, they come up to you or another wolf, then jump or nuzzle and then run away; that is an invitation to play chase. When correcting a yearling, they bare their teeth and growl. When hunting, wolves vigorously chase their prey. When defending their territory, they lift their tails and raise their hackles—making themselves big—and show their teeth in warning; if the intruder does not respond, they run him off. In every one of these situations there is no doubt about what is being communicated.

AM I OKAY? ROCKY, ZIMBA, AND JACK

With each young person who visited Wolf Heart Ranch, I recognized more Wolf Principles. Jack was a bright seventeen-year-old who struggled with his self-worth. He was confused about what he should do with his life, as many other teens are. A talented guitar player and singer, he was trying to decide what to do once he graduated from high school. In an effort to be a "responsible" young man and make his parents proud, he was thinking he should get a job and go to college. But in his heart, he wanted to put off college for a year or two and tour with a band he had put together.

Rocky (right) and Zimba (left) were the life of many community presentations with their open and welcoming dispositions. *Photo by Yamin Chehin*.

Jack started coming to work with me at the ranch once a week, helping clean up the wolf enclosures, replenish water bowls, and prepare food. He was creative and smart, a capable problem solver, and he didn't mind hard work. On his third visit, it was raining heavily, and the high desert wind was driving the rain at a forty-five-degree angle. Rocky and Zimba, two gray wolfdog brothers, were having a great time playing around in the muddy acre-wide turnout on the hillside. But Jack seemed troubled, and I couldn't help but notice the contrast between the stressed-out young man by my side and the joyful, unfazed wolf brothers playing in the rain. I spoke to him about the wolves and what they can teach us. Then I decided to challenge Jack a little.

"I want you to do something I've done with the wolves in the past, something that really helped me."

He looked at me curiously.

"I want you to go into the enclosure with Rocky and Zimba," I said, "and by yourself, find a spot that feels right to you. Carlos Castaneda would call it your power spot. Sit down, and wait there."

"What am I waiting for?" he asked.

"You'll sit there in the rain, for as long as you need to . . . and you will wait for a clear question to come to you. The question can come in the form of a word or a phrase written in the air or seen in your mind's eye. It can come to you as words you hear, or as a *feeling* or physical sensation. So don't judge or qualify what comes; just pay attention," I said.

He looked at me apprehensively, as if silently asking, "And then what?"

"The wolves have ways in which they speak to us," I said, answering the unspoken question. "So hold the question in your mind and wait for the wolves to answer it. Pay attention and stay open. The answer may come to you through one of their actions, or their inaction, or in the form of a *feeling*, or as a word or phrase in your mind that seems to be yours, but is not, or simply as a change in your emotional state. You may be sad and all of a sudden you feel joyful, or your body may feel contracted and suddenly it relaxes."

He trusted me and followed my recommendation. He walked to the turnout gate, opened it without hesitation, and went in. He climbed the hillside a little ways and sat down in the mud, in the open, in the pouring rain.

He sat there, cross-legged, eyes closed, for about five or ten minutes. Suddenly, both Rocky and Zimba came down the hill, heading in Jack's direction. They stopped by his side, flanking him, Rocky on the left and Zimba on the right. Then they both moved closer to him and pressed their soaking wet bodies against Jack's, in the same way wolves use to show affection with one another.

They remained that way, almost motionless, for a couple of minutes, until Jack scratched their fur. Then they both pulled away from him in an almost synchronized way and went back to their muddy play. Jack spent an extra minute or two by himself, deep in thought. Then he got up and made his way down the hill and out through the turnout gate to where I was standing.

"What happened?" I asked. Jack's face was radiant. He was smiling widely and standing taller. He had the eyes of someone who had just received a revelation, a taste of enlightenment.

"It was amazing," he finally said.

"It felt that way," I responded. "Rocky and Zimba were supporting you powerfully. What was your question?"

He paused for a couple of seconds to gather his thoughts and he said, "Am I okay?"

"What a wonderful question!" I said. "And what was the answer from the wolves?"

"I *am* okay!" he said, smiling broadly, his eyes moist.

"Yes, you are!" I responded, smiling back at him. "And do you know who you are?" I pushed him further.

"I am a good person?" he answered hesitantly.

"Yes, you are," I said reassuringly. "What else?" I pressed further.

He turned to look at Rocky and Zimba still playing in the rain and took a deep breath.

"I love playing music," he said. "And I would love to tour with the band for a while after I graduate from high school."

A calm confidence and resolve now emerged in his deep, clear voice.

Jack's experience is a beautiful affirmation of these Wolf Principles: *Wolves are okay with who they are,* and *In order to be okay, wolves first know who they are.*

As I watched Jack leave, I reflected on this young man's courage. So many people, even well into their adult years, are not okay with themselves and lack the vulnerability, honesty, or bravery to even ask the question. Knowing their true nature and being okay with who and what they are are not things wolves work at. It is their natural state. It was humanity's natural state as well at one time, and it is time that we reclaim that for ourselves.

After a few months, Jack graduated from high school and went touring with his band. We stayed in touch for a while, and his confidence and happiness continued to grow.

SETTING THE INTENTION

At Wolf Connection we reclaim the strength and power of this ancestral relationship with wolves and apply it to everything we do, from our organizational message, philosophy, and employee code of conduct, to our donor relations, community development, and, of course, our programs. We strive to foster emotional and psychological maturity, starting with ourselves, so we can model the wolf ways for all humans, empowering them to become authentic leaders and conscious stewards of the Earth. This means that we put forth our clear intent and best efforts to awaken our wiser, ancestral senses and deepen a practical conversation that considers humans, and all life on Earth, to be sacred and precious.

I don't propose that we attempt to go back to the old ways. I want to be clear. This must be a time of collaboration and integration. Imagine the world we could create of the sublime practices and wisdom of our ancestors and our current life experiences, scientific expertise, and technological capabilities. Like the wolf, we can work together for the benefit of all. I believe that the wolf is the nonhuman animal who can walk that path of integration with us. As both tradition and scientific research show, wolves have walked next to us in other key stages of our evolution on this planet.

Wolf culture is more cooperative than that of humans, and its impact on the ecosystem more constructive. Unlike wolves, humans are collectively plagued by a sense of insecurity leading to greediness, self-doubt, and obsession. But these principles can help us remember ourselves, our origin and purpose, and our ancestral role of steward, rather than consumer, of earthly life and abundance.

Countless lives, both two- and four-legged, have been changed by these teachings. I encourage you to incorporate them into your life and not just consider them intellectually. The Twelve Wolf Principles are:

1. Wolves are okay with who they are.
2. In order to be okay with who they are, wolves first know *who* they are.
3. Wolves let go of the past and make room for new things in their lives.
4. Wolves are open to learning new things.
5. Wolves give 150 percent to everything they do, so they choose carefully what they agree to do.

6. Wolves live by the power of their bond. They care deeply for each other without giving in to drama and pity.
7. Wolves use their individual gifts and talents for the benefit of all.
8. Wolves communicate effectively. They keep it honest and real.
9. Wolves know how to lead and how to follow. You can't lead if you don't know how to follow.
10. Wolves collaborate and work together. They know that together they will succeed.
11. Wolves understand they are part of everything around them.
12. Wolves are into being, not into doing.

HEALING TRAUMA: WILLOW AND THE WAR HERO

War veterans come to Wolf Connection through various PTSD rehabilitation programs. Being former military myself, I personally love working with veterans. I was never deployed, but those who have been often come back physically, emotionally, and psychologically scarred. Listening to their stories of sacrifice and valor, and witnessing their struggles to adapt to civilian life and later their healing, are absolute privileges.

One Saturday morning, the Wolf Connection team drove to Malibu. We arrived a bit early at the program site, went in to set up, and greeted the veterans already assembled there, who were from various branches of the military, some of them from special units.

After we had gathered everyone together in a semicircle, we introduced ourselves and the wolves, allowing time for the veterans and the animals to get used to each other from a safe distance. Then we had our standard safety talk, when one of the program team reminds people to follow the wolf handler's directions. We repeat the instructions for greeting the wolves: participants can offer their hands, outstretched with palms up. We remind them to avoid patting the wolves on the head, or crowding them, and we suggest that they scratch the animals on the neck and chest. Once the wolves and the vets feel comfortable, the vets can kneel and greet the wolves at their eye level. "Just let the wolves come to you on their terms" is our consistent message to new groups. We also explain that in groups where more men than women are present, wolves are typically drawn to female energies more than to male, and we try to lighten the mood by saying something like, "Don't take it personally, guys, it happens to all of us!"

Willow embodies a calm strength and power that has affected many people's lives. *Photo by Chris Perry's Wildside Galleries.*

That day, this seemed even funnier because there were some very strong male veterans in the group. We had barely finished the safety talk when Willow, a typically shy and skittish gray she-wolf, standing with my wife, Renee—Wolf Connection's animal behavior expert—began pulling on her leash, leading Renee across the semicircle and straight to one of the group participants. Renee is quite capable of resisting Willow if need be, but Willow had rarely before wanted Renee to follow her toward people, so Renee allowed it.

The man Willow had singled out had been part of a bomb disposal unit. He had lost an arm and a leg, and a significant portion of his face was severely scarred, over which he had grown a beard.

Willow playfully jumped on this man, claiming him with all of her eighty-five pounds. She licked his face nonstop while leaning into him and standing in his lap. Here was this man with a large wolf rubbing her face on him and pawing at him and loving on him. The vet's laughter was so infectious that the entire group joined in.

I was reminded of another Wolf Principle: *Wolves live by the power of their bond.*

Later, the group shared their war and postwar experiences, and Willow's veteran said that the greatest pain for him had not been losing parts of his body, or the physical impacts and legacy of his time in service, but rather his sense of rejection by society. He went to war and came back a hero. He was proud of his service. He had never expected to be rejected. He described how kids were afraid of him because of how he looked. He struggled to face the alienation and isolation that resulted when he was not met with gratitude, acceptance, and a sense of being part of the community.

He began to sob, his body releasing pain and sorrow that had been bottled up for a long time. I felt he was crying on behalf of his family and his fallen comrades and their families, releasing the horrors of war and the pain that was created by it. His cry echoed back through history.

Once he composed himself, he said that being chosen by Willow, so affectionately and so fully, made him feel hopeful once again. Willow's profound love and acceptance inspired deep transformation and communicated at a primal level, beyond language; it was a way of telling him, *I see you past the outward appearance. I feel your pain and your strength. You are loved, and you are worthy.*

TAKING CARE OF THE PACK: WOLF 21

Wolf Principles are often observable to scientific researchers just as they are to us at Wolf Connection. Doug Smith, director of the Yellowstone Wolf Project, found the principles very engaging, remarking that he could see the impact they can make in the life of those seeking healing and direction. He did note, however, that the more esoteric principles imply, in his view, a consciousness or self-awareness he doesn't necessarily believe wolves have. Dan Stahler, a widely published researcher who also works at Yellowstone, enjoyed them and added that, in his opinion, the principles did not fully reflect the violence in the world of the wolf.

Rick McIntyre, one of the most experienced wolf observers in the world, who is well known because of his work at Yellowstone, recounted a story to me that represents one of the Wolf Principles he saw in the wild.

Wolf 21 of Yellowstone's Druid pack was known as the Super Wolf. He appears in numerous books and articles, as well as in the documentary *In the Valley of the Wolves* by Bob Landis, which features 21 in his prime.

Rick contends that 21 might very well have been the greatest male wolf who ever lived. Wolf 21's father was illegally shot and killed before he was born, and 21 was raised by a new male—Wolf 8—who adopted him and his seven siblings when they were six months old. When 21 was a yearling, he witnessed his adoptive father protecting his family and fighting a much bigger and stronger alpha male. With the opponent pinned, defenseless, in a position where Wolf 8 could have killed him, instead 8 beat up the intruder for a bit, and then let him go, choosing to defeat his opponent and leave him alive.

McIntyre believes that 21 assimilated this merciful act into his character, which, among other traits, made him an admirable alpha, warrior, and leader. Rick followed 21 for the rest of his life and, as far as Rick is aware, 21 never lost a fight, nor did he ever kill a defeated opponent. Wolf 21 used the minimum amount of force to establish dominance, and although he was invincible in battle, he did not demand a lethal-force outcome to be tactically successful.

Wolf 21 used his unrivaled status to protect his family and provide for them, and in so doing he maintained balance in the territory and among neighboring packs. He was willing and capable of demonstrating to the alpha males of rival packs who was the most powerful, and then he let those rival alphas return to their families and their duties. Wolf 21 exemplified the Wolf Principle *Wolves use their individual gifts and talents for the benefit of all.*

When 21 was still with his original family, including his mother and adoptive father 8, and he was still a young adult, he was clearly going to grow up to be a physically superior wolf. He was going out on hunts, making kills, and bringing food back to the pack. One day 21 came back with food to share with his mother and the other members of the pack. After he had delivered the goods, he really needed to rest for the next hunt, but he was pacing back and forth, in an unsettled way of a wolf that senses a predator is near or that something is wrong.

Then 21 spotted one of the pups from the spring litter and suddenly stopped pacing. All the tension and stress immediately drained out of him. He started wagging his tail and very playfully romped in the pup's direction. Something was wrong with this little pup, and he wasn't doing too well. He would try to walk along and would fall over all the time. He would walk toward a rock or a log, and then seem not to see it and walk right into it and fall over. Because his behavior was abnormal, the other pups wouldn't play with him and he was alone pretty much all the time. In a social species such as wolves, that could be a good decision because the one behaving strangely might have a contagious disease, although apparently that wasn't the case here. But 21 was looking for him. He romped over specifically to that little pup, sat beside him, and hung out with him for about an hour, big brother and little brother.

This is a beautiful demonstration of the Wolf Principle that states, [*Wolves*] *care deeply for each other without giving in to drama and pity.*

Rick McIntyre often tells that story to young children because it helps them relate to the wolves personally. He asks, "How many of you have ever had a day where you're sad, when things really aren't going well, and you come home from school, and your dog sees you and instantly knows that you're having a tough time and wants to come over and be with you?"

Wolf Connection was built on questions like that one. We aim to help people connect with their own life experiences and true nature. I like to imagine Wolf 21 using the opportunity to be observed by scientists and the public in the park to teach high-level leadership and altruism to any humans that care to pay attention.

PRISON DIVERSION: MIKO AND TOM

Tom was a charming sixteen-year-old who came to Wolf Connection after being expelled from school and arrested for selling drugs. He'd been given a second chance by his school and probation officer, which included enrollment in the eight-week Wolf Connection program.

Tom was well dressed and well coiffed, and he took pride in the way he looked and behaved, enjoying the status that his slick appearance earned him among his peers. He dreamed of becoming an actor. But Tom was unpredictable and moody, which reminded me a little of Miko in her early days at Wolf Connection. She could shift from being friendly to suddenly snapping at anyone nearby. Now, however, Miko was a calm, well-adjusted wolf. When she and Tom met, Miko instantly saw through his cool attitude to the real guy inside, and she loved him on sight. Tom himself was taken by Miko's beauty and poise, her authentic cool.

Despite his inner turmoil, Tom made a commitment to show up, and he gave his best effort. A lot of that commitment came from his deepening friendship with Miko. After a day at Wolf Heart Ranch, Tom would say things such as "This is the best day of my life" and "I wouldn't have missed this for anything." One day when he arrived he said, "I know Miko is waiting for me, so I have to come, no matter what."

During the eight-week program, students are asked to create a project that conveys their authentic self-expression—their unique *howl*, if you will—using visual arts, spoken word, carpentry, or film. They express what they have discovered about themselves, their emotional responses, and their behavior after spending time with the wolves. The project is to be about both the individual student and about their membership in the pack, since the howl of wolves expresses the individual voice raised in service to the pack. Tom worked with teammates on a video project about wolf conservation. They wrote the script and decided who would fill the roles of director, cameraman, and sound/microphone operator. Tom wanted to be the talent. Those kids were pumped! Before coming to Wolf Connection, these teenagers' default behavior was to be defiant and play it cool, a self-protection mechanism, and they were really difficult to motivate to do anything. But at Wolf Connection they interacted with and related to the wolves, which made the video project real for them. They realized their video could actually make a real difference in how people view wolves. This was a cause they could get behind, and they went to work.

Miko and Tom in the middle of filming. *Photo by Wolf Connection staff.*

At one moment during filming, Miko was standing next to Tom, who was speaking on camera about how wolves are misunderstood and that people should take the time to understand them. "They're not vicious," Tom said. "All they want to do is love and be loved." As Tom spoke, Miko began licking his face to the point that he was unable to continue speaking. Tom broke into a broad smile, love and happiness shining through his eyes.

Miko didn't care where Tom was coming from, what he had done, or what had happened to him. She only cared about who Tom was in his heart, in that very moment. The wolf became the doorway to the healing of Tom's heart. As Tom opened up more and let go of his need to lash out, he said, "Miko has taught me to shake it off, let go of the past, and make room for new things in my life!"

Miko was loving Tom to say, "Thank you for speaking for us, thank you for saying those words, thank you for understanding us, thank you for making a stand." For Tom, this moment marked the achievement of a new sense of pride, purpose, and belonging in him. Tom had gone from being a lost and confused kid to a strong, deliberate young man who ran with wolves—and with the people around him! This moment between Tom and Miko is available for viewing on the Wolf Connection website, www.wolfconnection .org, and is featured in the award-winning documentary *Medicine of the Wolf.*

THE RELUCTANT LEADER: KENAI, AYASHA, SUSAN, AND MATT

The Wolf's message is not only for "at risk" segments of the population. What does "at risk" mean, anyway? Every person walking this Earth is at risk of not living a full life, at risk of getting distracted and dying with regrets, incomplete, with could haves and should haves in their minds. That's why private and semiprivate visits are quite special at Wolf Connection. We get to serve people who would not typically come to one of our programs. Susan, a young writer with a lively personality and a keen intellect, and her younger brother Matt, a fit and attentive twentysomething aspiring firefighter, arrived at Wolf Connection on a balmy summer afternoon for a ranch tour, habitat visits, and a sunset hike with the pack.

Two of our program leaders, Sofia and Kimberly, were leading the tour that day, and Sofia began the presentation by discussing the lesson each member of the wolf pack has to teach, and the different roles each wolf might play in the pack at different times of their lives.

Kenai is one of the shyest members of the pack, but he has a heart-opening way of approaching the most closed-up youth. *Photo by Chris Perry's Wildside Galleries.*

Susan was deeply affected by Kenai, a large and strikingly beautiful black-and-brown wolf with intense yellow eyes. Sofia took the opportunity to initiate a conversation on leadership. She explained that there are two ways to talk about wolf roles in a pack. In the wild, a pack is typically a wolf family, so the leaders are simply called the mother and father, or breeding pair. But at Wolf Connection, the wolves come from different backgrounds, they are at different stages of their lives, and they are not blood-related, as they would be in the wild. Nonetheless, they are still social animals and organize themselves into roles that are better described as alpha, beta, omega, etc.

"How does an alpha behave in the world? What is the role of a true alpha male or female in human form?" Sofia asked after a pause.

Matt said, "A true alpha is a good leader, one who cares for the pack and watches out for everyone's best interests."

"How do all the roles work together as a team?" Sofia asked.

Susan responded that a team of writers comes together sharing ideas and allows a story to unfold, each bringing his best to the group in a collaboration and team effort. This is actually one of the main Wolf Principles: *Wolves use their individual gifts and talents for the benefit of all.*

"Kenai might be the up-and-coming alpha of the pack," Sofia said. "What do you say we pay him and his enclosure mate Ayasha a visit?"

His former owners had loved Kenai, but he had suffered from insecurities because his owners didn't communicate with him clearly. They spoke more of a dog language than a wolf language to him, which was confusing to him. It took a few years at Wolf Connection for him to get grounded and to find his role in the pack. Kenai was now six years old, a budding alpha who had only recently been finding his confidence when interacting with strangers.

Ayasha was a feisty eight-year-old white-and-gray wolfdog-coyote mix with burgeoning beta behaviors that commanded a lot of attention. She had been Wolf Connection's very first rescue. She had jumped out of a moving vehicle and roamed the forest for a couple of weeks before Animal Control could finally trap her, luring her with a slice of pizza.

Susan and Matt walked slowly to the center of the habitat and sat near each other on a large log. Ayasha, who was lying on top of her house, jumped down to welcome them while Kenai stood near the house, partially hidden by a low-hanging tree branch, peering at them from behind its leaves.

As Matt and Susan ran their fingers through Ayasha's coarse fur, Kenai emerged from behind the tree and walked confidently toward the front of the habitat closer to the end of the log where Matt was seated. He stopped to sniff a rock, and approached Matt from the side, sniffing his arm and leg, and looking into the young man's eyes. This was an unusual approach for Kenai to make to a stranger, so Sofia and Kimberly concluded that he had a message for Matt. Kenai was almost demanding that the young man make eye contact. Kenai eventually brought his face so close to Matt's face that they were almost touching noses and remained eye to eye for what seemed like a long time. A big smile appeared across Matt's face.

Meanwhile, Susan was following the interaction intensely as her right hand stroked Ayasha's chest.

Surprised by Kenai's insistent behavior with Matt, Kimberly asked, "Where are you in your life with respect to leadership?" Matt seemed troubled by the question. He looked away for a few moments, as if trying to decide if he should open up. Turning back, he finally said, "I am a volunteer with the Los Angeles County Fire Department, but I really hope to be able to train formally to become a real firefighter." Sofia and Kimberly could hear that some lack of confidence was holding Matt back.

"I've been recently asked to assume a leadership role with my peers but I don't feel ready for it," he added.

"What's stopping you?" Kimberly asked.

"I'm afraid to have the responsibility, because my mistakes would have severe consequences for others," he said. "I'd rather let someone else take the lead."

Kenai continued pushing Matt to look at him, and so Kimberly followed Kenai's lead and pressed him a bit further, too.

"Have you been recognized as a potential leader by your peers and supervisor?"

Matt nodded.

Now addressing both brother and sister, Kimberly asked, "What qualities do you see in Kenai?"

"Shy yet confident. Curious, strong, calm . . . a bit scared and yet bold," they said.

Kimberly walked up to Matt and knelt near him, making herself smaller next to Kenai so that he could remain comfortable and confident.

"You are the one seen as a rising leader because you have the qualities they are seeking, and you don't allow yourself to rise to the occasion because you are afraid you will make mistakes and put others at risk. . . . Is that what you are saying?" she asked.

"A Wolf Principle says, *Wolves know how to lead and how to follow. You can't lead if you don't know how to follow.* I commend you for your hesitation to lead," she said. "The best leaders are aware of the burden of responsibility ahead of them, and it is healthy to be reluctant at first. It also shows that you're aware that there is still a lot to learn."

Kimberly paused for a few moments to let those words sink in for Matt and then said, "Being someone who cares so much for the well-being of the team, couldn't the team be compromised if someone who is not meant to lead tries to take that position because you won't?"

Matt was pensive.

Susan looked at her brother, shifting her position on the log so she faced him directly, waiting to hear what he would say.

Kenai walked past the siblings, glanced at them both, then continued to the house with the low-hanging branch, lay down, and fixed his gaze on the entire scene. He seemed to acknowledge that his job there was done.

Meanwhile, Ayasha, belly up at Susan's feet, was shamelessly enjoying neck scratches. Matt's eyes rested on Ayasha. Then he glanced briefly at his sister, then at Kenai right behind her, and then he turned to face Kimberly. Clearing his throat, he finally said, "If I take that position and make a mistake, people could get hurt."

Without saying a word, Kimberly shifted her body from kneeling to sitting, inviting Kenai back into the scene.

Kenai stood up and walked behind the log where the siblings were seated and approached Matt from behind. He sniffed Matt and circled back to lick the young man's elbow, repeating this connect-and-retreat behavior a few times.

"What are Kenai and Ayasha showing you right now with their body language?" Kimberly asked.

"Ayasha is being sweet and vulnerable even though Kenai could step on her at any time lying in that position with her belly exposed!" Susan answered with a smile.

Matt noted that Ayasha seemed okay with that risk and that Kenai moved back and forth between maybe being comfortable while at the same time his curiosity pushed him perhaps into discomfort by getting so close and making contact.

"I love that you see that!" exclaimed Kimberly. "How is this working for them right now? Is Kenai making any progress?"

Matt thought Kenai was making progress because he was pacing himself, pushing himself to get closer in measured increments. Matt then shifted to sitting on the ground near the end of the log and Kenai approached again, leaned in, and lightly licked Matt's ear. Matt had a momentary expression of awe that melted into a smile.

Kenai walked away and Matt exhaled, his shoulders relaxing as he leaned back against the log with a big smile.

"Tell me more about what you see in Kenai," Kimberly asked.

"Maybe he's feeling more confident?" Matt said. After the twenty minutes they had spent with Kenai, the wolf had put himself in an elevated position on the house.

"Yes," Kimberly responded. "Is Kenai a full alpha leader now?"

Matt looked down at his hands in his lap, reached out to pick up a twig, and holding it, began making circles in the dirt. "Not yet," he offered. "But he is getting there."

"Yes," said Kimberly with a smile. Then she took a breath. "He is getting there with his own timing and through his own continued efforts."

Matt looked up and met Kimberly's eyes, nodding.

The following year Susan and Matt returned for a community hike and Matt reported that he did take the initiative to be on a leadership track at the fire station and that he was pacing himself. Every role has its learning curve.

Both Kimberly's and Sofia's leadership in this story, in being willing to both follow the demands of the moment and step into new areas of trust, learning, and growth lead us to another layer of the principle demonstrated in this story: *Wolves know how to lead and how to follow. You can't lead if you don't know how to follow.*

At Wolf Heart Ranch, we have been privileged to witness this immersion of visitors into a more conscious, effective, loving, and supportive way of being. We have experienced our own heart-opening healing, and the healing of thousands of people from all walks of life. As you will see in the next chapter, wolf lessons about how to hunt and live as a pack or tribe and character lessons like those presented here helped us to adapt at a time in our history when we might have otherwise become extinct. One can argue that we may very well owe our human existence to wolves.

REALM THREE

The Ancestral Wolf

We howl
With the wolf pack
To bring us back into balance
Beyond the broken places
Realigning all ages and races
To what's real
To what we can feel
In that stillness
Between breath and beauty

We howl
With words summoned
From under concrete streets
Like the earth's heartbeat bass-line
Keeping time with eternity
We rhyme to remind modernity
Of ancient roots
That run deeper
Than all the fears
That once kept us up at night
The lefts and rights of yesterday's reasons why

We cry
To create anew
To break through
To what's true
In that dead sea of lies
Where narrow minds try to capitalize

We howl
To heal the earth
To give birth to abundance
And possibilities beyond the block
And stock market
As the morning dew settles
On the surface of our souls

We howl together
To become whole
To become one
To greet the rising sun
With full hearts open to it all
The sweet wild call of creation.

CHRISTOPHER HENRIKSON

This poem speaks of the deep, ancestral wolf connection humans carry to this day. The wolves howl so that we can remember who we are, and we "howl" to answer the calling; reclaim our primal selves; and heal at the individual, community, and species levels. It was written by Christopher Henrikson, a dear friend and brother-in-purpose.

ANCESTRAL MEMORY

Our ancestral relationship with the wolf is the foundation of the Wolf Connection program. Directly and indirectly, we acknowledge our coevolutionary relationship with wolves, and aspire to connect with the ancestral memory of that bond every time we engage program participants in activities or discussions.

The author and Wyoh hiking and playing at Wolf Heart Ranch. *Photo by Chris Perry's Wildside Galleries.*

The wolf is the first animal humans ever associated with, and is revered by many indigenous cultures around the world. The Celts, the people of the Siberian plains, India, Tibet, northern China, Mongolia, the people of central and northern Mexico, and the wolf clans among North American tribes regard the wolf as a teacher, a symbol for courage, loyalty, strength, healing, transcendence, family, and teamwork.

Our common history with wolves dates back to at least the Middle Pleistocene epoch. Wolf and human bones appear near each other at Eartham Quarry, England, a site dating to approximately 500,000 years BP,[1] which tells us that—by this time, at least—we were living

near enough to wolves to end up leaving our remains in close proximity to each other. In southern France, an excavated cave at Lazaret
near Nice revealed that it was occupied by proto-Neanderthals from
about 186,000 to 127,000 years BP, and also that wolves were present,
though it is not clear whether they shared the space or lived there
alternately.[2] It is evident, though, that by this date wolves had special meaning to humans. When the cave was first excavated in 1969,
French archaeologist Henry de Lumley and his colleagues found
signs that the humans living there had built small tent-like enclosures
within the cave, near the entrance, possibly constructed of skins and
supported by wooden sticks. Each of these shelters shared a feature: a
wolf skull intentionally placed at the entrance.[3]

This early evidence of meaningful interaction supports the theory of human-wolf coevolution proposed by Austrian ethologists
Wolfgang Schleidt and Michael Shalter in 2003. They suggested
that humans and wolves have not only been collaborating but also
coevolving for much of their shared history.[4] Coevolution is the
process by which complementary evolutionary changes take place as
a result of two species interacting, leading to adaptations that benefit
both. Schleidt and Shalter proposed that we have learned some of
the behaviors that make us human, not from our chimpanzee-like,
primate ancestors, but from wolves. In their view, humans owe the
use of permanent dwellings, the ability to herd and hunt collaboratively, and our sense of loyalty and care of family, to observations
our ancestors made of wolves.

Archaeologist Robert McGhee also has suggested that we may
not have developed into the successful, dominant species we are
without the opportunity to learn from and imitate the abilities of
the wolves with whom we lived. This interaction with wolves developed over millennia and contributed to the veneration of the
wolf as a spiritual animal and teacher.

Yellowstone wolf biologist Kira Cassidy told me that studying wolves and their behavior helps her understand herself and other humans better. "I think it's remarkable," Kira said, "how wolves and humans ended up living on the planet in the same blip of time, preferring the same types of prey, the same types of places to live. And in the end, we got dogs out of it." She concluded, "I think there are no two closer species on the whole planet."[5] The wolf stands apart from all other animals in human consciousness, and perhaps in this we may detect a deeply felt knowledge of our ancient kinship. This ancestral memory, whether we are conscious of it or not, lives on in us.

Thousands of years ago, there was a long period of contact between wolves and early humans in Europe and Asia, beginning with proto-Neanderthals and continuing with anatomically modern humans (AMHs).[6,7] The extreme conditions of the last glacial period, from about 15,000 to 11,700 years BP, challenged many life forms. Some animals became extinct while others adapted and evolved. Evolution is not voluntary; rather it is a response to conditions that demand change. Coevolution is also a response to the need to change, but in this case the interacting species assist each other. As early humans and wolves endured increased pressure from the hostile environment, they leveraged the synergy between them to adapt and survive.

ANCIENT HUMANS LIVED ALONGSIDE WOLVES

By the beginning of the last glacial period, the population of Neanderthals living in Europe and Asia was declining.[8] The surviving Neanderthals lived in small, isolated groups,[9] often suffering from poor physical health,[10] partially due to poor nutrition. Neanderthals hunted using stalking and ambush techniques,[11] but the cooling climate eliminated the vegetation they used as cover.[12]

Additionally, as their numbers declined, they resorted to inbreeding, which compromised their immunity.[13]

But Neanderthals were not the only ones struggling. In Africa between ninety thousand and seventy-eight thousand years ago, the AMHs were also enduring "cold spells" lasting up to four thousand years. Winding back the molecular clock in our genome, researchers have found a genetic "bottleneck" at about seventy thousand years ago, when the total number of AMHs fell to between five thousand and ten thousand individuals—perhaps as few as one thousand breeding pairs.[14] In today's terms, we became an endangered species.

Some surviving AMHs migrated into Europe and Asia, where they encountered Neanderthals. The AMHs and the Neanderthals chose to live and mate right up to the time when Neanderthals became extinct as a separate species, about forty thousand years ago.[15,16] In other words, Neanderthals didn't really become extinct—the last of their people joined with the AMHs in Europe and Asia to form an amalgam genome that provided stronger immunity and integrated shared knowledge, skills, and practices in specific environments. In essence, the experience Neanderthals gained from hundreds of thousands of years' coexisting with wolves was passed on genetically *and* culturally. Presumably, wolves could have retained a similar genetic memory of their connection with us.

The AMHs brought an essential physical trait that allowed the offspring of the two peoples to literally "run with the wolves." A lighter frame evolved to chase down game over long distances. Additionally, they had developed long-distance projectile weapons, a technology the Neanderthals lacked. The two peoples combined their strengths, and what emerged were humans capable of long-winded running who could kill at a distance, were genetically adapted to northern-latitude living, and carried in their genes the ancestral memory of the shared history with wolves.

This merging happened just when the cold spells came deeper and faster, until the point of glacial maximum, between 27,000 and 22,000 years BP.[17] Some indigenous peoples still maintain oral histories that can help us understand the conditions our ancestors faced.

For instance, the elders of the Dene people of northern Canada—who call themselves "The Wolf"—have stories that trace back to the time when their ancestors left Siberia. They followed the wolves and the caribou walking north, then east, crossing the Bering land bridge, and eventually coming to Alaska. They describe the glacier-bound landscape they passed through as the body of a giant made of ice. "When the giant died, his lungs collapsed and became a great body of water," elder Patrick Robillard tells. Cut off from the continent they had come from, the Dene continued to the east and south into new lands, taking with them the memory of the journey the wolves led them on.[18]

During the glacial maximum, the wolves suffered as well, and, like humans, nearly became extinct. We needed each other to survive. Wolves offered tangible survival knowledge to humans, who were forced to adapt or die. In turn, wolves drew close to humans with the comfort of their settlements. Humans replicated survival strategies they observed in wolves; they adopted wolf social behavior, organizing in small tribes of extended family.[19]

A thorough review of anthropological research and the oral histories of Northern Hemisphere indigenous peoples reveals that many hunter-gatherer cultures acknowledge the wolf pack as their social template, with wolf clans being a feature of at least 60 percent of North American First Nations peoples.[20] Two important parallels persist today between wolf-pack structure and the internal organization of wolf clans: both consist of an extended family that is matrilineal, and clan members must marry outside their clan.

The specialized hunting techniques that put humans at the top of the food chain are based on those of wolves: hunting in groups, sharing risk, and coordinating efforts; following herds, living on their margins, and hunting young or weak individuals. As social animals, wolves also care for pack members if they are injured. Together, a pack of wolves can achieve what a single wolf cannot: pulling down a bison, for example. Wolves communicate to each other which individual in a herd to take down through gazing. The ability to follow the direction of a fellow hunter's gaze would "seem to be a social skill with immediate adaptive benefits."[21] Both humans and wolves hunt using this communication technique, because they have realized that "if someone is looking firmly in a particular direction, there is something worthy of attention in that direction."[22] Like humans, gray wolves have gaze-signaling eyes.[23] The color patterning around the eyes of canids relates directly to their gaze-signaling ability. For animals where the coloring around the eye is lighter than the rest of the face, the duration of gazing behavior between fellow species members is longest. Compared to fennec foxes and bush dogs, the gray wolf has the longest gaze duration.

Our ability to herd domesticated animals arose from following herds of deer-like wild game the way wolves do, which they have done for more than one million years. The earliest cave-painting evidence for humans following herds is found in Chauvet Cave, France, dated 30,000 years BP.[24] However, other archaeological evidence from Europe and Asia indicates that early humans were following herds since at least 400,000 years BP. It is indeed possible that they learned to do this by watching wolves.

When modern humans arrived in the cooler climate regions of Europe and Asia, they met Neanderthals, who were living in caves across Europe and Asia for hundreds of thousands of years. This form of shelter had not been as necessary in Africa prior to migration, where the climate did not warrant long-term cover. Caves provide a level of protection from predators and the weather that temporary structures cannot. Of course, many Northern Hemisphere animals besides wolves lived in caves or dens, but our AMH ancestors were strongly influenced by the unique hunting and denning behavior of gray wolves. It is quite possible, given our close relationship with them, that we learned cave or den dwelling from wolves.

THE SOCIAL WOLF

Wolves within a pack, in relationships with their blood relatives and adopted pack members, tend to be socially attentive, tolerant, and cooperative—critical survival tools considering the wide range of terrains and climate regions wolves inhabit. Our human ancestors who were hunting the same game and trying to survive in the same regions and climates would not have missed this. Early humans were keen observers of all aspects of the natural world—a key trait for survival as a hunter-gatherer—and they were witnessing one of the most successful predators on Earth. Adopting the social structure of wolves would have increased our odds of survival, including greater success at hunting, shared responsibility for raising children (increased chances that offspring will survive), distributing food among all group members (supporting all members equally optimizes a group's physical and mental state), and caring for the wounded or sick (contributing to optimal function of the group as a whole).

Over millennia, humans moved from the self-motivated, opportunistic behavior common in primates to the collaborative, benevolent ways practiced by wolves. The way that wolves care for each other, showing loyalty to fellow packmates, and their willingness to perform acts at great risk to themselves on behalf of the pack are essential features of the wolf's ethical makeup. When wolves gave the gift of their social structure to humans, they also passed on these ways to other humans. To this day, people who are members of a wolf clan must maintain a specific code of conduct based on behavior demonstrated within wolf packs. In those cultures where wolf clans are present, members play the role of protectors, teachers, or healers, as well as caretakers, hunters, defenders, nursemaids, and social directors.

Within the Gitxsan First Nation of northwestern British Columbia, Canada, wolf clan members base every aspect of their social interactions on direct observation of wolf behavior. The wolf shows great humility and self-control, keeping aggression in the pack within strict boundaries, and sharing food resources among all members. Therefore, humility and self-control are fundamental parts of the code of conduct to which everyone in the wolf clan adheres. If they do not, members risk being cast out—the worst possible fate for wolf and human alike. Feasting rituals accompany every aspect of life and all major decisions the wolf clan makes, for both the offering and the sharing of food are fundamental acts by which wolves acknowledge their bonds to each other.[25]

What indigenous people have known for thousands of years, scientists are just now confirming. In 2015, a research team at the Wolf Science Center in Vienna, Austria, published a study investigating social traits in wolves and dogs raised in identical conditions.[26] They assumed that dogs would prove to be more socially attentive, tolerant, and cooperative than wolves, because that is what humans would have selected for. Instead, they were forced to conclude the opposite: wolves paid closer attention to their pack members than dogs did. This work supported the outcomes of a 2017 study[27] that found that wolves outperformed dogs in cooperative activities.[28] Our ancestors observed and adopted these traits as part of our coevolutionary path.

Rick McIntyre telling the author that the alpha females lead the wolf pack and pointing at the author's wife behind the camera. *Photo by Chris Perry's Wildside Galleries.*

OBSERVING WOLF BEHAVIOR

Rick McIntyre worked as a Yellowstone Wolf Project biological technician for more than twenty years. Spending time with Rick in the field is a treat. He knows every wolf individually, including their genealogies, behavioral tendencies, and their pack dynamics. One morning during my 2018 research trip to Yellowstone, it was snowing heavily, and we took a break from wolf observation. I then asked Rick how witnessing wolves for so long had impacted his life. His response revealed the gift of a master storyteller as he shared an iconic Yellowstone story that illustrates how cooperation and altruism improve the likelihood of survival for a pack. I couldn't help imagining the impact observing wolves would have had on our ancestors, what they would have learned or interpreted to be beneficial to their human families.

In the early years of the wolf reintroduction program, Wolf 21 was the alpha male of the Druid Peak pack. When he joined the pack, there were four adult females, a mother wolf (30) and her three daughters, numbers 40, 41, and 42. Wolf 40 just happened to be born with a very aggressive personality and decided that she wanted to be the alpha female while very young, or so it seemed.

Rick said that 40 drove her own mother, and one of her sisters, 41, out of the pack. Then she went after her other sister, 42, who tolerated the dominance and chose to become subordinate to her aggressive sister. This situation made 21's life very difficult because, according to Rick, wolf packs are matriarchal—the females run the show—and 40 was the top wolf. The alpha male, 21, would witness her aggression to the other females, particularly toward 42, but he could do nothing about it.

In the spring of 2000, three of the females were pregnant, having mated with 21: 40, 42, and a younger one, 106. Because 42 and 106 were so concerned about 40's aggression, they chose to den away from her, leaving the main den for 40. Wolf 106 denned five miles to the east, and 42 had her den five miles to the west. This made it very difficult for 21 and the other adult wolves because, when they hunted, they had to bring food to three different litters that were ten miles apart.

The den that belonged to 42 had the most adult females because she had a friendly, benign personality, and she shared food and supported them. She had a lot of assistance with her pups. One particular day, late in the afternoon, she and her female friends came down from the den to hunt to feed the pups. But as they were leaving the area, 21 and 40 came in from the main den. And as always, as soon as 40 saw her sister, she ran over, beat her up, bit her, and pinned her down. And then 40 did that with all the other adult females.

Later, 42 had to go back to check on her pups. Her sister 40 was following her, and Rick worried about 40's intentions. He said he wouldn't "put it past" 40 to kill her sister's pups to ensure more food for her own pups. They went into the trees and, because it was getting dark, Rick couldn't observe them further.

The next morning Rick and some colleagues found a dying wolf, drenched in blood, near the road. They expected that it was

42, the gentler sister, thinking that when 40 and 42 got to the den the evening before, 42's pups emerged and 40 went after them. In that situation, 42 would have had to stand up to her more dominant sister, but in a straight-out fight, 42 could not have won; she lacked the killer instinct her sister had. But when the researchers took a closer look, they saw that the bloody wolf was 40, and she died within the hour from loss of blood.

Her whole body was covered with wolf bites, including one in the back of her neck so deep that her spine showed through. That was most likely the bite that killed her, although there were too many bites to be made by one wolf. Yellowstone staff think that when the two sisters fought, all the other females 42 had befriended over the years jumped in and helped her. The females let 40 go without actually killing her, but they had injured her so severely that she died of her wounds.

The following day, 40's mate, 21, was frantic about their pups, who would die for lack of milk, and went to 42's den and took the risk of leading 42 back to the main den. About an hour later 42 came back to her own den site alone, and over the next day and a half she carried each of her six pups in her mouth, one by one, to the main den. She had to swim a river, which was in a flood stage, and hold her mouth up as high as she could to keep the pup out of the water. With her pups transferred to the main den, 42 went to assist 106 to bring her pups there, too, effectively reorganizing the pack.

It was a month before the researchers could see what was going on with the pack, but one day 42 came out of the thick forest and stepped into a clearing, followed by 106, and right behind them, a lineup of pups. The average litter in Yellowstone is four or five, so just their two litters would have nine or ten pups. But twenty-one pups crossed that meadow, which meant that, rather than killing them, 42 had adopted and raised her sister's pups.

While the average survival rate for wolf pups during a year in the wild is no better than 50 percent, that year, of the twenty-one pups, twenty survived. Wolf 42 had exceptional organizational abilities and earned the admiration of Rick and other Yellowstone scientists.

I have incorporated this story into the Wolf Connection leadership retreats because it illustrates the difference between a repressive leader, one who bullies his or her followers into submission, and a compassionate, inclusive one, who puts the good of the group first. The story of Wolf 40 is the only documented case of a wolf pack killing their alpha—if in fact that is what happened, since the events that led to her death were not actually witnessed. Still, some of the veteran Yellowstone wolf people, who have been following the packs for years and collaborating with other park biologists to gather behavioral data, referred to Wolf 40 as a "bully" who got—rightfully—killed by her own pack. But Linda Thurston, a park guide who was part of the wolf project in 1995 at the start of the reintroduction program herself, shared another view of 40, based on her personal experience.[29] Linda had witnessed many instances in which 40 showed great tenderness and loyalty toward other members of the pack, which provides a more complete picture of 40's personality.

A less popular theory about what happened to 40 was developed based on reports by the park's coyote biologists. That night, they had been following some subjects and saw the Mollies wolf pack in the area where 40 was found near death. The Mollies were, and are to this day, the most physically powerful pack in the valley, and they had a fearsome reputation as both bison hunters and wolf killers. Considering this, there is a chance that Wolf 40 was killed by the Mollies and not by her own pack. Wolf biologist Kira Cassidy entertained this possibility and told me that it would better fit the pattern of behavior that was consistently observed. Also, Cassidy re-iterated that wolves hardly ever injure other members of their pack, let alone kill them, and the leading cause of mortality in wolves is being killed by a rival pack.[30]

It is true that each wolf has observable personal tendencies: some are shy, some are bold and curious, some are very timid, and some have a great way of handling stressful situations. But Kira Cassidy pointed out the risk of assigning personalities to the individual wolves, which can cloud the objective scientific process of data gathering, and she believes that there was probably a good biological explanation for 40's interactions with her sisters, daughters, and nieces.

The traits that made Wolf 40 a powerful matriarch left an important legacy of strong animals—ensured by her sister's choices—and some of her pups went on to become the alphas of other packs.

HOW HYPERSOCIAL WOLVES BECAME DOGS

Our coevolution with wolves led to one of their genetic lines evolving to become dogs. The starting point for this process was about forty thousand years ago, during an Ice Age when the environmental conditions in Europe and Asia were extremely difficult and challenged the survival of both humans and wolves.[31] Our Neanderthal relatives disappear from the fossil record at about this time, and the rates of extinction increased for species of large mammals of more than forty-four kilograms or one hundred pounds.[32] From this point until about twenty-seven thousand years ago, survival hung in the balance for humans and wolves, and the conditions were right for intensive coevolution. By twenty thousand years ago, the lineage of wolves from which all dogs were domesticated had become extinct.[33] It may be that, living alongside humans, and faced with starvation and killing winters, the wolves that are our dogs chose to get even closer to us. Perhaps rather than humans domesticating the wolf, something mutually beneficial took place.

Glenn Schiffman, an Iroquois wolf clan elder, shared this story with me one afternoon under the willow trees of Wolf Heart Ranch.[34] The People of the Longhouse say that the wolf sent the dog to befriend humans to steal their fire and bring it back to the wolves. The dogs agreed to the task, but once they gained the trust of humans, they decided to stay with them and never went back, leaving the wolves without fire.

The mystery surrounding how wolves became dogs, and the search for the genetic process that explains the domestication, has been a holy grail for molecular biologists for decades, and many contributions to the quest have been made to date.[35] *How to Tame a Fox (and Build a Dog)* authors Lee Alan Dugatkin and Lyudmila Trut[36] propose that an intense selection program took place over multiple generations, crossing only those animals that exhibited the desired traits of lower fear and aggression responses to humans. But this study had the advantage of restraint and containment systems that would not have been available to ancient peoples. We cannot underestimate the challenge of not having chains, cages, and unbreakable restraints, and they would have been dealing with wild wolves in full physical strength. In *The Animal Connection*, Pat Shipman[37] describes the process of domestication as one in which humans shaped the dog to become a living tool, a utilitarian view that gives no credit to the wolves' willing contribution, as I believe we should.

More recently, Pierotti and Fogg, who coauthored *The First Domestication*, suggest that humans and wolves were preadapted to cooperate with each other.[38] They propose a scenario where a lower-ranking pregnant female excavates a den near some bipeds and watches their camp. At some point a human female offers the wolf food and they learn to cooperate while living near one another. But how likely is this to happen, and would it lead to the development of dogs? Wolves may have been willing to live near a group of humans, but that does not mean they would have allowed humans to restrain them, or to choose for them whom they would mate with; and these two things would have been required for humans to breed wolfdogs.

Humancentric assumptions such as "WE subdued and domesticated the beast" are built into the modern concept of domestication. We tell stories in our own elevated image; we can't help it. These stories require some level of human domination and control. The oral histories of indigenous peoples, on the other hand, view the wolf as an equal, a sister/brother to be revered and respected, and tell us that the dog came freely to us, walking in from the wilderness to lie by our fire and be fed by us as one of the family. The People of the Longhouse say that there was a time when all nations were friends, spoke together, and that the human and wolf young played collectively.

This may in fact be exactly what happened, as new genetic research reveals. Legends from traditions all over the world tell of young children wandering away and getting lost in the forest, only to be adopted by a she-wolf or pack that raises the human as their own. It is noteworthy that the frequency of rescues and rearing by wolves in these traditional tales is far greater than for any other animal.

In July 2017, Bridgett vonHoldt, chief molecular biologist at Princeton University's canine genomics research lab, published a study that revealed a groundbreaking discovery—the key genetic ingredient necessary to transform the wolf into a dog is a behavioral trait called "hypersociability."[39] VonHoldt shared that hypersocial behavior is defined as taking an extreme interest in others, and it is accompanied by an inability to regulate the desire to connect socially: hypersocial animals have no control over their friendliness.

All the dogs that vonHoldt and her colleagues tested possessed the hypersociability trait, which no wolves did. Looking at the genome of the animals, vonHoldt found a region on chromosome 6 where the dogs were significantly and consistently different from the wolves. Previous research on hypersociability in humans had pointed to the genetic cause for this trait in humans being on chromosome 7, which is the equivalent to the gene region of dog chromosome 6. Humans who are missing genes or even the smallest parts of genes in this region have the behavioral trait of hypersociability. They are also of short physical stature with a short nose, broad forehead, and small teeth,[40] the same physical traits that are found in protodog skeletons dating back to the beginning of dog domestication,[41] an important clue that vonHoldt and her colleagues were on the right track. All the dogs vonHoldt genotyped had significant mutations in the chromosome 6 region, while all the wolves had only small variations there. In behavior testing, the dogs were uniformly hypersocial and the wolves were not. In fact, the dogs were so hypersocial that, as long as a human was present, they were too distracted to be able to complete a task that the wolves solved easily.

What is of great significance to the domestication of dogs is that this region of chromosome 6 in wolves is (like the equivalent region on chromosome 7 in humans) relatively unstable, meaning it is prone to newly arising mutations. That means it is possible for a wolf with a significant hypersociability mutation to be born to normal wild parents who lack the mutation. In humans this occurs about one in every ten thousand births.[42] Biologists do not yet know how frequently this happens in wolves.

Picture a super-friendly wolf, born to wolf parents, who behaves "like a dog." A mutation that causes hypersocial behavior could lead to that wolf being rejected or killed by its packmates. If it survives, it's forced to live alone. In *A Wolf Called Romeo*, Nick Jans[43] narrates how in 2003, Romeo appeared on the outskirts of a suburb of Juneau, Alaska. Over a six-year period, he became well known to locals. Romeo would approach people who were out walking in the woods and even play with their dogs. Romeo never appeared in the company of other wolves. Instead, he sought out human and dog company almost daily, a behavior pattern that eventually led to his death when he was shot by a hunter in a parking lot.

Bridgett vonHoldt told me that Romeo may well have been an example of a wolf who was born with the hypersociability genotype.[44] These wolves will occur naturally in the wild wolf population. In their 2017 study she and her colleagues found several wolves with minor variations in their chromosome 6 regions; these were the only wolves that displayed above-normal levels of social behavior toward humans. She believed that hypersociability probably exists on a continuum, with extremely hypersocial dogs at one end, and very human-avoidant wolves at the other end.

Why would wolves drive away a hypersocial pack member? From the pack's perspective, this is a wolf that cannot control its behavior the way that wolves must—and self-control is a big part of wolf social dynamics. According to vonHoldt, dogs, wolfdogs, and wolves with significant hypersocial mutations have a driving need for social connection with others, so powerful that they constantly seek it. A hypersocial wolf continues to behave like an insecure puppy even into adulthood, not respecting boundaries and not responding immediately to the social cues that its packmates are sending. We have only to look at how wolves behave when they encounter dogs to be able to picture the consequences for a hypersocial wolf. Wolves commonly hunt and kill dogs—perhaps not only because they see them as rival canines but also because dogs cannot behave in the way that wolves must behave to be accepted by the members of the pack.

We see this all the time at the Wolf Heart Ranch. The wolves with the highest wolf content don't have any tolerance or patience for the more dog-like (nervous and needy) behavior displayed by the animals with less wolf content. For example, Willow, a wolf, came to us as a year-and-a-half-old pup. Malo is a wolf-Akita mix who loves people and is always ready for a neck rub, indications he's more hypersocial. Willow and Malo lived together for a couple of years, but as Willow matured, she became less tolerant of Malo's behavior until one day she jumped on him, grabbed him by the neck, and pinned him down. We determined then that for Malo's safety they needed to live in different accommodations.

The discovery of the hypersociability mutation supports the theory of coevolution of human and wolf. In addition, a 2016 genetic study revealed that one lineage of wolves in particular was living near humans during the past thirty thousand to forty thousand years and that this lineage is now extinct in the wild. The only living descendants of those wolves are living next to us in our homes.[45] Knowing this, we can picture how the first dogs came to us—just as the People of the Longhouse said they did.

Imagine that during that incredibly difficult time in the glacial age, a wolf with the hypersociability mutation was born in a den near a human dwelling or settlement. Someone from the human group finds the wolf litter outside the den and sees one pup that, unlike its littermates, romps up playfully to the human and follows him or her home, rather than staying with its wolf kin. This wolf is fundamentally different in its behavior and remains like a puppy even after it is mature—not avoiding people, and even trying to please the people and be close to them. If such a puppy were female, upon maturity it might wander off to breed with a male from a nearby wolf pack, but it may come back—rejected by wild wolves, but still alive, having managed to avoid being killed by them, and now pregnant.

Hypersociability is a dominant mutation—so this "protodog" female would pass on hypersociability to 50 percent of her offspring. Half the pups will leave and join wolf packs. The ones that are like their mother will stay with humans. In time, without the need of enclosures, a group of humans would be able to raise a number of these early dogs, and eventually, just breeding them with each other, permanently secure the hypersociability trait in their dogs by producing pups that have inherited the mutation from both parents. These will breed true, and now dogs as we know them are a reality. This is a scenario that vonHoldt's research supports directly. The dogs we are so attached to today may descend from wolves who wanted our friendship, food, and fireside more than living with their own kind, because of a genetic anomaly. With dogs at their side, humans had a new canine companion who, in return for helping with the hunt, was guaranteed a meal and attention, and perhaps the attention even more than the food. In hard times this meant survival for humans and for their transformed wolves-become-dogs.

I believe this to be a very possible scenario—that a hypersocial young wolf came to live with a group of humans. That the wolf's presence opened the primal hearts of our ancestors who were alert and in balance with the natural world and acted upon it. This is more plausible, in my view, than the long process of selective breeding to "make wolves into dogs."

CONSTANT ADAPTATION—COLOR, IMMUNITY, AND WOLF-COYOTE MIXES

The domestication of the dog was not the end of the coevolution of wolves and humans. Wolves have continued to evolve alongside us, thanks to the fact that dogs and wolves can interbreed, and recent genetic research shows that wolves in North America carry varying amounts of domestic dog DNA, as do most European and Asian wolves. In fact, there might very well be few "pure" wolves left on Earth. But for wolves, necessity is the mother of invention, and the genetic evidence reveals that wolves are constantly reinventing themselves.[46]

Genetic research shows that somewhere between 7,200 and 1,600 years ago, a black dog that belonged to a group of North American First Nations people mated with a female gray wolf. When her pups arrived later that spring, some had black coats, and the black mutation has been in the North American wolf ever since. Black

coat color is caused by a mutation in an immune system gene—
beta-defensin CBD103—but like other genes, it has more than one job.

Black coat color offers a significant survival advantage over
gray-colored wolves for bacterial infections such as distemper.[47] So
why aren't all North American wolves black, since mutations that
are helpful tend to become more plentiful in a population? Researchers at Yellowstone found that being gray (meaning having no
copies of the black mutation) is a reproductive advantage for female
wolves, who have more surviving pups than black females.[48] The
result is an evolutionary balance in the wolf population—selection
for black (protects against bacteria-caused disease) competes with
selection for gray (increases the number of surviving pups).

To keep this balance, Yellowstone biologists have noted, black
wolves mate with gray wolves more often than black wolves mate
with other black wolves, and more often than gray wolves mate with
gray. Thus the black version of the gene is kept at a steady rate.[49]

Additionally, there may be a relationship between black-coated
wolves and lower levels of aggression.[50] Interpack aggression depends on multiple factors, such as wolf density in the area and the
season of the year, but the black dogs who passed the gene to wolves
may have been less aggressive to begin with because they had been
successfully domesticated and passed the hormonal change that occurs with domestication on to wolves.

The case of the North American wolf-coyote mix is another
remarkable adaptation in a short time span, a species that rose out
of the necessity of population decline due to extensive hunting by
humans 287 to 430 years ago, despite the scientific presumption that
fertile offspring could not be produced.[51] Just like the wolf-coyote
mix, a new, more resilient, ecologically viable, and aware version
of humanity is not only possible but absolutely needed if we are to
survive in a sustainable way for the long term.

Wolves have proven themselves capable of adapting to a varied range of physical environments, and they continue to evolve and adapt, as evidenced by their wide distribution, immunity, and their breeding with dogs and coyotes. Like humans, the wolf's evolutionary story is one of success in the face of many obstacles, and our success is a by-product of theirs. Humans might very well owe their current existence to wolves, but it appears that, as a species, we have forgotten the lessons our ancestors learned from them.

LIFE REDIRECTION: KYRA AND MICHAEL

We see the practical expression and impact of our mutually beneficial partnership with wolves every day at Wolf Heart Ranch. Michael arrived at Wolf Connection with the first foster-care group we ever served. He was fourteen years old at the time, a tall and handsome young man, and his refined features were masked by the hardened look in his eyes. The tension in his shoulders made him look as if he were constantly shrugging.

Michael's group had only five other boys and girls, but he was always accompanied by his own chaperone—a security guard of sorts—because of his violent tendencies. Michael had been placed in this group home, which had stricter guidelines for supervision, because he had difficulty controlling his anger. He'd attacked the staff at the group home several times, kicking and punching them. He'd broken a desk and a door and thrown a computer out of a window. He reacted angrily to teasing and got into altercations with his peers. By the time he came to Wolf Connection, his placement at the group home was failing and he was about to be sent to a locked-down facility with higher level of care.

On the first day at Wolf Connection, Michael listened to the troubling back stories of the wolves, occasionally nodding without saying a word. By the end of the day his eyes had softened, and he even shared some of his thoughts and feelings. He said that, even though many of the stories spoke to him—being taken away and passed around from home to home—he particularly connected with a wolf named Kyra, a lanky, gray-and-black female who came to us infested with fleas and with half of her ears missing after being chewed up by flies and who knows what else. Kyra was mistrusting, and she had been taken away from her home by the local Department of Animal Care and Control for being severely neglected. Michael saw himself in Kyra.

On his second visit, Michael asked for Kyra as soon as he walked in. His demeanor had changed, and he was more inquisitive. I began giving him ways to channel his anger. We went for a hike with Kyra to a nearby low hill, where Michael experienced firsthand Kyra moving through her self-doubt, seeking connection with him, and exploring nature. She was showing Michael how to *let go of the past and make room for new things in his life*, a practical observation of one of the Wolf Principles.

I also started teaching Michael how to use a hammer and a screwdriver, and how to abate weeds and brush using a machete as a way to focus his attention and channel his pent-up energy in a healthy way. Soon he earned his access to power tools and learned how to use a drill, handsaw, and a power screwdriver. By week four he was walking around the wolf compound with the tool belt containing a hammer, a screwdriver, a pair of pliers, some screws, nails, a machete, and work gloves. His caretakers' eyes were wide when they saw this "violent young man" carrying a machete.

The group home staff told us that on Tuesdays, when the group was to be driven to Wolf Connection, Michael was up on time in the morning, his bed made and his teeth brushed. He could not wait to be driven to see his wolf friends at Wolf Connection. The staff reported a significant change in Michael's ability to manage his emotions. He now decided to go to his room and be alone rather than give in to teasing by his housemates. After he'd calmed down, he told the staff member that he'd chosen to walk away because "If Kyra can learn to control her energies and move on, so can I."

Kyra was a fighter, and she taught that every day at Wolf Heart Ranch. *Photo by Renee Alfero.*

I told Michael that I trusted him no matter what. That meant more to him than even I could have anticipated. He never abused that trust or used tools inappropriately. Instead he focused on learning and eventually began repairing things at the ranch, finding pride in being of service to others. He even built Kyra a new wolf house to replace her old one. Michael's bond with the wolves grew out of being present in their lives, building and repairing chain-link fencing, cleaning the enclosures, preparing food and medications. This bond with the pack grew so strong that he began asking to be brought to the ranch to volunteer during off-program days as well. "I have to go, they're waiting for me," he told one of his caretakers.

Shortly after, he asked the staff at the group home to buy him a tool belt and some tools of his own, and he began repairing some of the things he had broken. He also fixed a leaking faucet and squeaky door hinges. One day one of his caretakers came to the ranch very excited to tell me that Michael was beginning to lead his peers on some positive behaviors around the house. He was seen telling another boy not to throw papers on the floor and to put trash in the trash can, where it belonged. His caretaker asked jokingly, "Who is this kid, and what have you done with the real Michael?!"

A week before finishing the program, Michael approached me and asked me if I would adopt him. I had grown to love this young man and appreciate him greatly. With genuine sadness, I told him that I would certainly consider it under the right circumstances, but that I was living in a small trailer in the mountains with no electricity or running water, taking care of a pack of wolves, and that the DCFS (Department of Children and Family Services) would never approve a placement or an adoption under those circumstances.

To this day that was one of the most difficult decisions I've ever made and one of the most difficult conversations I've ever had with a young person.

Michael graduated from the Wolf Connection program, and he was able to successfully stay in the group home. He and I remained in touch. Every now and then I would pick him up and we would see a movie, eat pizza, or go to In-N-Out Burger, his favorite. I'd watch his baseball games, and afterward we'd pick up burgers for all the other boys in the group home. He became the president of the student council in his senior year in high school. He's had a few girlfriends, and he was loving, faithful, and a gentleman to them. At the time of this writing, he is a representative for a company that delivers premade organic meals to homes.

Wolves reflect back to us the essence of who we are, minus the story we have of ourselves. What we've learned from them influences our individual and community existence to such depth that we don't even notice it. Schleidt and Shalter were able to pierce through the thick veil of humancentric narrative that permeates modern civilization when they wrote in 2003 that "the impact of wolves' ethics on our own may well equal or even exceed that of our effect on wolves' changes in their becoming dogs."[52] We see this ethical influence of wolves on people every day at Wolf Heart Ranch, in the way we communicate, contribute, and experience emotion. At a fundamental level, I would go as far as to say that what we call *humanness* (our vernacular for the adjective "humanity" at Wolf Connection) might have been, in fact, invented by wolves.

REALM FOUR
The Wild Wolf

*NOW this is the law of the jungle, as old
and as true as the sky,
And the wolf that shall keep it may prosper,
but the wolf that shall break it must die.
As the creeper that girdles the tree trunk, the
law runneth forward and back;
For the strength of the Pack is the Wolf, and the
strength of the Wolf is the Pack.*[1]

Wolves are members of a collaboration, a family united by a single shared purpose: to give their all for the well-being of the pack. The wolf, *Canis lupus*, once inhabited every corner of the Northern Hemisphere. In this chapter I invite you into the world of the wild wolf— through the lens of the clarifying and enlightened research that dispels the fiction of violence and aggression that has been unjustifiably attributed to the wolf for centuries. The willingness of wolves to risk everything whenever necessary and without hesitation, fueled by their innate drive to protect their family, is a critical lesson for humanity.

In February 2018, when my wife, Renee, and I took my book team to Yellowstone National Park, we worked with guides Linda Thurston and her husband, Nathan Varley, who own Wolf Trackers. The temperature hovered at zero degrees Fahrenheit at six in the morning on the first day, and the sun was nowhere to be seen when we drove through the historic archway at the Gardiner—North—entrance.

As soon as we were inside the park, I asked Linda to pull over. I got out of the van and took a moment to connect with the land and the life in it. I took a short stroll, breathed in the cold air, and gazed up the valley and into the dark mountains. I walked up to a tree and some bushes close by, took out my pouch of sacred tobacco, and with a prayer of humility and thanks, I asked for forgiveness on behalf of the human race and permission from the guardians of the land to come in. I sprinkled a pinch of tobacco at the base of the tree as an offering to pay my respects and closed my eyes, and a powerful wave of emotion enveloped me, a mixture of sadness and deep love. Despite the cold, my body felt warm and my heart open. Tears rolled down my face.

The next day, we were driving through the park on the icy main road. Just as some light was beginning to shine through the thick cloud cover, we spotted wolf expert Rick McIntyre walking up a snowy trail by himself. His radio-collar telemetry tracking equipment indicated that the Junction Butte pack was nearby, and he was hiking up and around the mountain to a perch overlooking the next valley to see if he could spot them. We quickly jumped out of the van and grabbed our gear to join him.

As I walked on the snow-covered trail, memories from my time in the Andes flooded in. The softness of the fresh powder pushing against my legs and knees, the distinctive "crunch!" of the snow under my feet, the cold wind on my face, and the silence of the mountains welcomed me. I immediately loved this wilderness, with its gently falling snow that quieted my mind and nourished my soul.

Once we caught up with Rick, he asked me to carry his telemetry antenna and take the lead, packing down the snow to make it easier for him to trudge upward. I saw the essence of Rick at that moment in his life: an elder, a wise man, no longer carried by his body so much as by his love and passion for the wolves and his work. A celebrity in the wolf world, Rick has spent tens of thousands of hours observing packs, including in Denali in the 1970s, and he has not missed a day tracking in many years. Tracking wolf packs and studying their behavior are not what Rick McIntyre does; they're who he *is*. Yet Rick had decided to retire from the Yellowstone Wolf Project two weeks after our trip, so I felt fortunate to be able to spend time with him.

The snow was getting steadily deeper by the time we reached the spot Rick had in mind. He assembled his telemetry equipment and we set up our tripods and spotting scopes. After a little while other wolf-tracking veterans joined us, and soon we were a pack ourselves, brought together by our shared passion.

What a beautiful way to live, I thought. I felt a deep, wordless bond with all these strangers as we quietly waited, side by side, for the wolves to appear in the valley below us. Even though we couldn't see them, we knew they were there, somewhere behind the low ceiling of cloud cover.

Peering intently through the spotting scopes, the shooting training once drilled into me during my time in the military more than twenty-five years before poured into my mind. The unwavering focus, the silence, the thumping of my heart, the sound of my breath resonating inside my head. It all became a meditation at that moment.

My joy was increased because I was sharing this experience with my wife. The wolves had brought us together in the most beautiful and unexpected way, and our relationship was being renewed and deepened as we searched for the Junction Butte pack through the scopes, in the cold, side by side.

Getting to the wolf observation sites was as exciting as the observation itself.
Photo by Teo Alfero.

On the following day, the snow stopped, the sky cleared, and we set out into the park before sunrise in search of wolves. At about 9:00 a.m. we were headed back from Lamar Valley with Linda Thurston when the radio alerted us that all eight members of the Junction Butte pack were visible from a rest stop on the road that was just minutes from where we were. We headed immediately up the road, jumped out of the vehicle, and rushed to set up our spotting scopes. Sure enough, there they were in the distance, taking turns eating from a carcass.

As we got settled with our scopes, Rick recounted the genealogy of each Junction Butte pack member, describing their behaviors in detail. A generous educator and mentor for many others who observe the wolves, Rick McIntyre is the wolves' keeper of stories.

"What you are seeing now are the beginnings of the courtship ritual. They won't be mating for another few days, but you can see the black males 1047 and 1048 testing the females, 969 and 907, respectively. There is an uncollared male that can also be dominant and try to compete for 907. They are rehearsing the mounting, the females moving away, the male appealing to the female again, mounting, thrusting, coming off again. This will go on for a day or two."

As I watched the wolves through a Swarovski spotting scope, another long-recessed aspect of my shooter training revisited me, and I calculated the approximate distance to them using the time between the moment I saw them howling through the scope, and the time I heard the howl. Sound travels at a speed of about 1,100 feet per second, or 343 meters per second, which we can round up to 350 meters per second. So when I saw the wolves howling with no sound at first, I began counting 1,001, 1,002 . . . and after four or five seconds the sound of the faint howling arrived, and I estimated the pack to be 4,400 to 5,500 feet (1,400 to 1,700 meters) away.

Renee, Teo, and Linda at the snowy perch. *Photo by Chris Perry's Wildside Galleries.*

As we left after that first day of observing the wolves, I wondered if the pack's behavior had been affected by our presence. Psychologists have demonstrated that an "observer effect" occurs when people know that they are being watched, and they alter their behavior in response. In other words, the observer alters the behavior of the individual or phenomenon observed. The wolves had seemed unaffected, even unaware of us standing about a mile away. Wolves generally avoid interaction with humans, but we don't know the effect that even minimally intrusive field observation may have on them. Would the Yellowstone wolves behave differently if they lived in an environment free of any human presence?

At an energetic level, perhaps the wolves were aware of us watching them and of our feelings toward them. I see the influence that wolves and humans have on one another not as a hindrance or "pollution" of their natural behavior, but as something that improves both species. This belief fueled my interest in speaking to the Yellowstone researchers about more than the biology, ecology, and wolf behaviors that are the focuses of their work. I wanted to get a real sense of the humans behind the scientists and even obtain a sense of what impact their work around wolves was having on their lives.

Over the next two days in Yellowstone, we followed the pack's activities and witnessed the ritualistic courtship dance between the alpha and beta breeding pairs, each with a gray female and a black male. It was exhilarating to spend hours in silence, completely focused, not missing anything, comparing notes with the other wolf watchers, the human pack brought together by the love of wolves and the unique experience of being part of their lives if only for a brief moment.

Dan Stahler is a jovial and welcoming man, who in addition to being a biologist with the wolf project is a professor and researcher in the Department of Ecology and Evolutionary Biology at UCLA. He is husband to a fellow wolf biologist he met at the park, and a father. Dan passionately believes in the national parks system and he believes that parks have spiritual, environmental, and economic meanings for people. He is personally gratified to be protecting wolves and being a spokesperson for a species that has no voice of its own. Dan explained that the Yellowstone research program is set up for distance monitoring precisely so that observers avoid affecting the animals' behavior. When the observations are done well, the wolves will not know the humans are there. Sometimes the wolves are closer and could be aware of people in areas such as the "front country"—for instance, near a road that intersects a pack's territory—but most of the research is done with the intention of minimizing impact on the wolves.

Nonetheless, the program has been criticized for darting and handling the wolves, extracting blood, and using radio collars. Critics argue that the Yellowstone wolves are no longer wild once subjected to these research interventions. Dan said that he and other biologists struggle with how much and how often to interfere with the wolves, but the research team continues to feel justified because wolves are a protected species residing in a protected area, and monitoring protocol is essential to ensuring that the species thrives. Further, researchers have confirmed that there are no long-term behavioral changes in wolves that wear collars compared with wolves that do not. Researchers have witnessed recently collared wolves back with their pack chasing elk the next day. They've seen them fighting off a grizzly bear from a kill and raising their pups, showing no physical or behavioral changes from contact with the research team.

Once in a while, an accidental encounter happens. "When you spend this much time in the field, you're gonna run into them," Dan said. "One time I was monitoring a den site with pups about a mile away through scopes, and I encountered a wolf that just happened to be traveling back to the den. I was hiking up to our observation spot and we just crested the hill at the same time, literally, and surprised each other. It was a yearling, so it was more curious. And we connected, our eyes locked, and that gaze is just super powerful—spiritual."[2]

Sheila Archer, the academic researcher who assisted me throughout the writing of the scientific chapters of this book, also describes the sense of wonder of field research:

What we know is very small, and what we don't know is enormous, and it will always be so. It is necessary to resist the temptation to become self-important, something that all scientists face and must learn to refuse. . . . Ideally, we remain humble, and keep our hearts focused on the joy of the chase, the fun of trying to find an answer to a question. For this, we are rewarded with moments in which we experience a state of awe, a sense of wonder that fires up our spirits.[3]

WHAT IS A WOLF?

While field scientists collect observations of wolf behavior, geneticists focus on what is happening inside the wolf at the molecular level, searching for connections between the inner wolf and the outer wolf or wolf behavior. Scientists from these two disciplines examine these questions: What is a wolf? How does it do what it does?

The gray wolf is one of the most successful carnivores in the world. Once the most ubiquitous mammals on Earth, they epitomize fluidity, adaptability, versatility, and efficiency. For hundreds of thousands of years, they have persisted through the Earth's most dramatic environmental upheavals. The indigenous Turkic–Mongol people of the Altai Mountains region of Eurasia describe wolves as "The owners of the spirit of the land,"[4] and science confirms that

where they live, their biology is a direct expression of the ecology of that landscape. Flexibility is written into the DNA of gray wolves, a feature that has allowed them to adapt to an array of ecosystems encircling the Northern Hemisphere.

Regardless of the geography or landscape features of the location they occupy, wolves thrive. The gray wolf's size, build, coat color, immune system, and hunting behavior evolved to work in its particular environment.[5] But no matter where they live, their superb physical structure is matched with behavior patterns that enable members of a gray wolf pack to perform together as a field of moving elements that collectively achieve what a single wolf cannot.

The author (right) with Dan Stahler. *Photo by Chris Perry's Wildside Galleries.*

NOTHING CAN STOP A WOLF

Founded in 1872, Yellowstone is America's first national park. Beginning in the 1940s, park managers, biologists, and conservationists initiated efforts aimed at reintroducing gray wolves into the park. The Yellowstone Wolf Project introduced thirty-one wolves into the park between 1995 and 1997, returning the most influential carnivore to the area's ecosystem. Doug Smith is the director of the project.

Possessing a commanding presence, Doug shakes your hand with a firm grip, looks at you in the eye, and speaks his mind confidently and with the authority that decades leading the Wolf Project have given him. I asked Doug to indulge my curiosity and tell me a bit about how he came to devote his career to studying wolves. I thought his story could inspire some of the young students at Wolf Heart Ranch who are searching for a career path.

The author with Doug Smith, director of the Yellowstone Wolf Project. *Photo by Chris Perry's Wildside Galleries.*

Doug's father had a passion for teaching kids about nature, so Doug grew up on a farm in rural Ohio that was converted into a summer camp for children. A book about wolves—a gift from his brother—was one of the early catalysts for his professional interest. When he was fifteen, Doug ambitiously wrote letters to wolf biologists all over North America, asking to work with them. They all kindly wrote back but declined to hire him. Unfazed, he tried again at eighteen—and this time one said "yes," a scientist named Erich Klinghammer, who worked with several captive packs in Indiana. He told Doug, "Okay, you can come and be a wolf mother." Doug learned how to wean and imprint captive wolf pups, an exhausting but deeply fulfilling entry into the world of wolf biology. After working for some time with Klinghammer, Doug was offered a job at Isle Royale working for Rolf Peterson. Following that, he worked for Dave Mech in Minnesota. Each job led into the next and came with the recommendation of his previous employer. As Doug describes it, "Within a period of twelve years, from about eighteen to thirty years of age, I worked for the top three wolf biologists in the country, possibly in the world. And I applied for this job (at Yellowstone) when I was thirty-four." Now he is one of the most prominent individuals in the wolf world.

According to Doug, "There is nothing that can stop a wolf." This is why, he explained, we cannot consider gray wolves in Canada and those in the United States to be different sub-species. He used mice to illustrate his point. "If you have a river and there's a mouse population on one side and a mouse population on the other, they can't get across the river, so through time they evolve into different species."[6] But since there are no geographic features in North America that can keep wolves apart, there is no significant genetic differentiation between populations in different regions. Even an ocean cannot limit wolf movement, as wolves have managed to swim to most of the islands off the Pacific Northwest coast. The border between

Canada and the United States is irrelevant to a wolf on the move. Many of the original wolves in the Yellowstone Wolf Project came from Canada, and although they carry the genetic signature of the wolves from the regions they previously lived in, it is a mistake to consider any of the wolves at Yellowstone to be drastically different from the previous inhabitants of the area, simply because they were transported from different locations on the continent.

Wolf detractors have tried to make the case that the Canadian wolves brought to Yellowstone in the nineties were larger than local wolves, and therefore might kill too many elk because they were "too big." The researchers refute this argument. The fact is, as soon as a wolf arrives in a new place, it begins to adjust to its environment, and the wolves in Yellowstone are already smaller than their Canadian predecessors.

"Wolves move at the scale of a continent," Doug Smith says. When a wolf leaves one area, it might travel hundreds of miles to another. The accepted record is about a thousand miles. Everything flows freely in the natural world, including wolf species genetics, so in Doug's view, it is bogus to call a wolf Canadian or American. I left my meeting with Doug energized, inspired, and wondering if, with slight differences between continents, the wolf's territory could be even described in global terms rather than continental. Today the wide span of the Bering Sea creates a significant barrier, but at one time their range was continuous, encircling the Northern Hemisphere.

A WOLF FOR EVERY NORTH AMERICAN ECOTYPE

In 2016, a group of leading scientists[7] studied the six gray wolf ecotypes that occur in North America: the British Columbia, Boreal Forest, Arctic, High Arctic, West Forest, and Atlantic Forest ecotypes. In each case, the wolves have adapted to the ecozone they inhabit. For example, the Boreal Forest gray wolves are larger and have longer legs than other gray wolf ecotypes. This is a helpful trait for wolves who may have to survive on bison, a prey that only the largest wolves can hunt successfully. In comparison, the Arctic wolf is relatively small and slightly built. This allows Arctic gray wolves to run faster and change directions more quickly than a Boreal Forest gray wolf, enabling them to catch smaller prey, such as Arctic hares. Additionally, Arctic and High Arctic wolves are white. Like many other animals they share the high latitudes with, being white is a distinct advantage, and both prey and predator alike have adapted to blend in with snowy surroundings. The darkening of coats appears in wolves living just south of the Arctic, in the Boreal Forest.

Research on wolf populations on islands off the Pacific coast[8] of British Columbia found an interesting differentiation: island-dwelling wolves are 20 percent smaller than the coastal mainland wolves. This is the result of something biologists refer to as "insular dwarfism," the "island effect," or "Foster's Rule,"[9] which states that when mainland animals colonize islands, small species tend to evolve larger bodies, and large species tend to evolve smaller bodies. Island wolves also differ in diet, deriving 85 percent of it from the ocean, whereas the coastal mainland wolves get only about 30 percent of their food from the sea.[10] There is also a difference in coat color. While coastal mainland gray wolves have black coat coloration about 50 percent of the time, only 20 percent of island wolves have black coats. Something about the island environment makes being gray in color more advantageous. Each wolf ecotype is a lesson in practicality, and adaptations are all examples of the fluidity and awareness of wild wolves.

THE CIRCUMPOLAR WOLVES

Biologist and wolf tracker Nathan Varley jokingly said to me while driving through Yellowstone together, "Wolves are like humans and feral dogs—they're everywhere." Meaning, they're adaptable.

They can live anywhere, just as humans do. Wolf populations have come to vary in physical appearance, depending on where they live, and just like humans, the genetic differences between their various ecotypes are minimal, the only changes being those necessary to optimize life in that particular landscape.

The wolf ecotypes in North America are similar to those in corresponding ecozones across Europe and Asia. For example, the Boreal Forest, Arctic, and High Arctic ecozones run across the Northern Hemisphere, and the wolves living at these latitudes, called Holarctic wolves, are physically and genetically similar.

Wolves of Africa, Saudi Arabia, India, and the Himalayas, on the other hand, overlap genetically a lot more with each other than with the Holarctic wolves. These gradients of relatedness show that wolf populations mix with each other over vast ranges, and a 2017 study shows that genetic diversity can be impacted by populations 530 miles—or 850 kilometers—apart![11] The wolves in the outer regions of the Arabian Peninsula, and those adapted to Turkey and India, are smaller and lighter than their European and Asian kin. They have short coats with no underfur, a demonstration of "Bergmann's Rule,"[12] which states that a mammal's body size varies according to the temperature of its environment.

Additionally, "Allen's Rule"[13] states that animals adapted to cold climates have shorter, smaller limbs and appendages than animals adapted to warm climates. For example, the Arabian wolf has ears that are proportionately larger in relation to its body size when compared to northern wolf ecotypes, an adaptation that developed to help disperse body heat. Generally speaking, small body size and large ears are common adaptations in desert environments.[14]

Yet in some ecotypes, looks can be deceiving. New research has added the desert-adapted African golden jackal to the list of wolf ecotypes, even though it has "jackal" in its name; this is a misnomer. A 2015 study[15] at the Smithsonian Conservation Biology Institute confirmed that African golden jackals and Eurasian golden jackals are distinct species and that their appearance is a result of adaptive convergence, not genetics. The African golden jackal (wolf) descended from a distant wolf ancestor that first entered Africa from the eastern end of the Mediterranean 1 million to 1.7 million years ago. Although the African golden wolf is closely related to the gray wolf, distinct behaviors set them apart. In many respects, their social behavior, diet, and hunting routines are more like those of the North American coyote.[16] African golden wolves keep smaller family units, consisting of the breeding pair, their current litter of pups, and occasionally one or more yearlings from the previous year's litter. They do not live or hunt in extended family-based packs, nor do yearlings stay on much after the next litter of pups is born. While African golden wolf family members do share tasks in pup care, the mother does most of the feeding; and when hunting or scavenging, they do so in mated pairs and not in packs. They seldom take on prey their own size, and prefer to hunt newborn gazelle fawns, hare, mice, and other small rodents.

The Himalayan wolf is a close relative of the African golden jackal (wolf).[17] The Himalayan ecotype has evolved with improved oxygen efficiency in high altitudes. DNA was collected from Himalayan wolves and compared to that of dogs from the same region. Evidence suggested that adaptive introgression, the transfer of genetic information from one species to another, from wolves to dogs provided a significant increase in oxygen absorption.[18] One theory is that hunters realized that wolves had adapted to tolerate exertion at high altitudes and bred their dogs with those wolves to "improve" them.

THE ROLE OF WOLVES IN NATURE

Where wolves live, the entire ecosystem thrives.[19] Wolves do far more than just regulate the herbivore population. The ways of the wolf in Yellowstone have a cascading effect in the ecosystem, influencing virtually every aspect of the Yellowstone basin environment. Most people have encountered mention of trophic cascades, if only through popular videos such as *How Wolves Change Rivers*,[20] seen by tens of millions on its originating site alone. Since the wolves' return to the park in the midnineties, the park forests have improved, populations of ungulates have stabilized, and small mammals have increased, as have their medium-size predators such as coyotes and foxes. Of course, many other environmental factors, including seasonal weather patterns, drought, and heavy precipitation have contributed to the Yellowstone ecology, but Yellowstone Wolf Project biologists, and other scientists, agree that the presence of this apex predator in the ecosystem has played a substantial part in what is being witnessed there. Trophic cascades are waves of regeneration, adjustment, and regulation that result from the top of the food chain down. Brenda Peterson, author of *Wolf Nation: The Life, Death and Return of Wild American Wolves*,[21] describes the cascades beautifully. Being chased into the forest cover by wolves affects the eating habits of elk so that they feed away from riverbank willows, allowing regeneration of previously eroding riverbanks. The willow regrowth slows the flow of creeks and rivers, inviting industrious beavers to build dams where they have not done so for decades. Insects, fish, birds, and other wildlife also return.

Linda Thurston said, about the impact of the wolves on the broader ecosystem, "I see the wolves scavenging, but not in the sense that a vulture would." While wolves will consume a carcass when they come across it, performing a "cleanup" role, they also maintain herds of herbivores by selectively taking down only the weak, the old, and the excess young, thereby choosing prey whose removal will not diminish the herd's overall wellness and longevity. Further, wolves cull only what they need, stopping when they are satiated.[22] Wolves hunt older members of elk herds. "When they can no longer keep up with the rest of the herd and have fallen behind, the older members of the elk herd will be picked off by the wolves. So, the wolves would come upon a herd that has an old animal, and they test it, and they see if there's a weakness, whether it's gum disease, not getting good nutrition, or it's bad arthritis, or liver flukes that are affecting the animal's strength; and they home in on that animal. They separate it from the others using collaborative hunting strategies, and they take it," Linda says. "Part of the wolf's strategy is to run their territory throughout, and I love to think the wolves know every elk, bison, and deer in their territory."

If this is true, of course, wolves are able to identify individuals and target them in advance, or as Linda Thurston quipped, the hunting wolf might be thinking, "Oh, yeah, there's that old bison I've been watching . . . for a long time, and today is the day."

Wolves must weigh risk against outcome daily, especially in hunting scenarios. Spending tens of thousands of hours in the field observing every aspect of the lives of wolves, biologists are often moved by what they witness.

One day while observing wolves hunting, Doug Smith saw a wolf take a kick from an elk. Over the following few months the wolf project team noticed this wolf slowing down somewhat, but in time, he looked okay. However, after four months, he began to limp and lose weight. Even so, he was still hunting for his pack, and was observed killing an elk by himself, a heroic feat for any wolf. Shortly after this, a rival wolf pack came into his pack's territory and killed him. The researchers went out to collect the corpse, and as is their practice, they sent the skull to a taxidermist. When the skull came back from the taxidermist, they discovered that the lower jaw was cracked in half. The amount of pain the wolf had been in for the previous four months of his life was unimaginable, and Doug was amazed that the project staff had not observed the extent of his injury prior to his death. Doug mused that a person with a similar wound would have been hospitalized, been put on intravenous fluids, treated with multiple surgeries, maintained on pain medication, and given months of physical therapy to resume a modicum of normal life. Yet this wolf was out there leading his pack, taking down an elk by himself, with a broken jaw.

The wolf had to go on. He could not allow his pain to stop him from functioning, wallowing in a sorrowful haze, as a human might. The wolf's example made Doug decide then and there that he was happy to be alive and he would avoid self-pity and self-indulgent thinking in the future.[23]

ALPHA, BETA, AND OMEGA . . . MOM, DAD, AND THE KIDS

The language and terminology that scientists use today to describe wolf pack structure and dynamics are quite different from those of even a few decades ago. In his sweeping and powerful book *Of Wolves and Men*, author Barry Lopez[24] described some of the first recorded wolf observations made by soldiers during the expansion of settler occupation, when American armies pushed across the continent in the 1800s. Soldiers observing wolves at that time used military terminology to refer to the roles and hierarchy of members of a wolf pack, including general, sergeant, and lieutenant. And then, of course, they believed that the pack leaders were all male.

By the late 1940s, wolf behavior was being observed using the scientific method, and in 1947, Rudolph Schenkel, a researcher at the University of Basel, Switzerland, published the terminology that became standard. Studying a group of captive gray wolves, he applied "alpha" to the breeding pair's male and female. Then he tagged the subordinates as "beta" and "omega" wolves. The term "beta" described helping wolves who, by assisting the efforts of the alpha, acted like second-in-command members of a military organization. Schenkel assigned the term "omega" to the pack's most submissive members, holding the lowest positions in the social order.[25] The male of the breeding pair was believed to be in charge.

Schenkel assumed that gray wolf packs were a collective of self-motivated individuals constantly competing for dominance, with the strongest and most aggressive maintaining leadership. His own historical and cultural perspective colored his understanding and interpretation of what he saw. Until this point, researchers had drawn conclusions based only on the observation of captive wolves, having not considered that wild wolves might present a different picture.

Biologist David Mech built upon Schenkel's work, but by 1999 he had disavowed the terminology he had previously upheld, explaining that the previous assumptions about wolves had been based too heavily on the captive packs of unrelated individuals.[26] Nathan Varley said to me at Yellowstone, "Describing wolf behavior by studying wolves in captivity is like publishing conclusions about human behavior based on studies done only within a prison population."[27]

Mech spent thirteen summers observing wild wolves on Ellesmere Island, Northwest Territories, in Canada. His work revealed that wolf packs usually consist of a breeding pair and their offspring from the previous one to three years. The wolf pack is a family, Mech concluded, "with the adult parents guiding the activities of the group in a division-of-labor system in which the female predominates primarily in such activities as pup care and defense, and the male primarily during foraging and food-provisioning and the travels associated with them."[28]

Observing wolves in a natural setting over a long time has continued to improve our understanding of their social behavior. Field observations in Yellowstone since the reintroduction of wolves have less gender bias and focus on the division of labor and pack-sustaining roles that male and female wolves play. Males and females perform equally valuable roles, even if they differ sometimes according to sex, and there is no need to label one as being dominant or having more significance over the other. What a powerful lesson for human societies to learn!

Laurie Lyman amassed more than 2,600 pages of wolf observation field notes, which became the foundation of Nate Blakeslee's 2017 book *American Wolf*. While we were watching wolves together in Yellowstone, Laurie told me that what she had learned of wolf interactions and social dynamics changed her pedagogical style and the design of her classroom during her years as a K–8 schoolteacher in San Diego, California. "My whole classroom was decorated with wolves," she said, "and I guided my student behavior based on wolf behavior. How they treat each other, how they work as a group, and all of that. And it worked really well. In fact, my whole school gathered around it." For Laurie, watching the wolves is like overlooking a playground with many differently aged playmates—little children, gathered in a safe space like wolf pups, in the sandbox; the kids in third to fifth grades playing together (the yearlings); and the older kids, hanging around at the tables, sitting and chatting, and those would be the young adults, the hunters, and the aspiring alphas.

This is also how we see older youth and adults at Wolf Heart Ranch, where we added "hunter," "tracker," and "nanny" to the alpha/beta/omega terminology we use for our wolf residents. The rescued wolves and wolfdogs we work with and care for are typically unrelated, often brought together as adults from around the country. They all have been spayed or neutered, so the roles of mother, father, and breeding pair do not apply.

Teo and Renee Alfero observing wolf behavior with Laurie Lyman (center).
Photo by Chris Perry's Wildside Galleries.

In contrast, the social dynamics of a wolf pack in a natural setting are determined by age and kinship, so the terms "alpha male"
and "alpha female" are often replaced with "breeding pair." Generally, the breeding pair is the oldest male and female, and they
maintain their primacy by suppressing other pack members from
breeding. Although other members are impregnated, scientists
speculate that pregnancies don't always come to full term because
of the mother's nutritional health and immunity differences. The
breeding pair provides stability to the pack by drawing upon their

combined knowledge and experience for the benefit of the other members, who are most often their offspring.

David Mech observed that all young wolves are potential breeders, and almost always leave their originating pack upon maturity, remaining only if an unrelated wolf of the opposite sex has filled one of the breeding pair positions. It is possible for a young wolf to stay and become a mate with a stepparent. The notion that nonbreeding pack members are bullied or inferior in some way is a false assumption based on outdated observations of captive groups of unrelated wolves. In the wild, dominance contests within a wolf pack are rare, a fact subsequent research supports.[29] "Any parent is dominant to its young offspring, so 'alpha' adds no information," and the terms "mother" and "father" are more meaningful. The only time the term "alpha" is useful is in the relatively rare situation where a large wolf pack contains multiple litters. For example, a pack might be made up of the original matriarch and her daughters, with the fathers being the patriarch and unrelated adoptee males that have joined the pack. In this situation, the older breeding wolves likely dominate the younger ones, and so "alpha" reflects that relational aspect.

COLLABORATION OVER COMPETITION

The Canyon pair came together to form the Canyon pack in 2008 in Yellowstone. They were the breeding pair until the spring of 2017. She was white and never got a number because she was never collared. He was silvery gray and his number was 712. This pair was together for nine years, and they both lived longer than average. He was eleven and she was twelve when they died. This was one of the very few times such a long life match has been recorded in North America.[30]

Today, biologists have a better awareness of how different but complementary sex-specific roles work in a pack.[31] In the case of the

Yellowstone packs, males were more likely than females to chase rival pack members, and "chasing behavior was influenced by the sex of lone intruders, with males more likely to chase male intruders."[32]

Male wolves, with their larger physical size, are better suited to pack defense. That said, it is advantageous for a breeding female to be large as well, as this improves the odds that her pups will survive to maturity.[33] The difference in behavior between sexes "suggests male and female wolves may have different strategies and motivations during inter-pack aggressive interactions related to gray wolf mating systems." Within wolf packs there is also "[a] division of labor between pack members concerning resource and territory defense,"[34] suggesting that the intense competition between rival wolf packs results in selection for specific traits related to aggression. Rather than defending against rivals, female members of a pack, who are often the swiftest runners, use this ability to chase game, thereby playing a critical role in hunting strategy. The oldest female, who is usually also the breeding female, is most likely to make the call on when and what to hunt, when to go to the den, and other pack movement decisions. Together, male and female wolves balance each other.[35]

Both sexes help to raise the pups. "Whether that be a mom and a dad or an older brother from a previous litter, having to run a grizzly bear out of the den area to protect pups, to swimming a flooded, high paced river with food in its belly to bring back food to regurgitate to pups, to defending against a neighboring pack. That dedication and commitment to their family, to their pack . . . is just extraordinary," says Dan Stahler, adding, "I try to be a good father and a good husband, and my parents really are a model for me, but wolves have reinforced that. You study them, and you are constantly mesmerized by what they deal with on a daily basis to survive and to raise their families."[36]

AGGRESSION . . . SOMETIMES RITUALIZED, SOMETIMES REAL

In the wolf pack, there is no competition for rank. Violence between packmates is uncommon.[37,38] Wolves within a pack do not turn on one another and provoke a battle to the death. These statements have been confirmed in Yellowstone observations,[39] and statements to the contrary are false.

Wolves make demonstrations of their "rank" with each other in a ritualistic posturing, not a battle. Wolves physically interact in a demonstration designed to maintain structure. It is the avoidance of violence in these interactions that is key to stabilizing relationships in the pack.[40] Rather than expressing dominance, wolves follow "a natural age-based order with the current breeders at the top and offspring or non-breeders subordinate, an order so natural and automatic that it is seldom contested."[41]

Social hierarchies in wolves are determined by sex and by age. The strongest expression of aggression is in same-sex interactions rather than between opposite sexes. This is particularly true between captive females. It is common knowledge in the wolf, wolfdog, and even dog rescue world that you can pair a male and a female in an enclosure, even put two males together, but never should two females be housed together. Similarly, aggression between wolves of similar age is more likely than between wolves of quite different ages.

According to biologist Kira Cassidy, the frequency of aggression incidents "track[s] exactly with testosterone rising and falling. It starts to rise in the fall, in the early winter, in prep for the breeding season. It's at its highest during the breeding season. And then it drops dramatically in late March and early April, right when the females have their pups. Because every wolf in the pack, even the big males, experiences a spike in prolactin, which basically kills testosterone molecules, and every wolf wants to now take care of the pups. That's the only time I see the females being very puppy-like and submissive as they're trying to get their mate and even their yearlings who've never done this before to regurgitate food for them. And so they'll be licking their faces and wagging their tails."

This evidently works as a coaching and teaching strategy, because the yearlings learn to regurgitate and help with the care of the pups.

Wolves do not waste energy struggling to dominate each other, but reinforce their position using a language of postures. The avoidance of violence with fellow packmates is a sustainability mechanism for the pack. Uncontrolled conflict escalation could "lead to social disruption and hence jeopardize cooperative activities."[42] Pack members in conflict with each other tend to engage in friendly postconflict interactions (the more closely related they are, the more likely they are to "make up"), and these friendly interactions reduce the chances of a second aggressive interaction by 50 percent. In other words, built into wolf social behavior is a mechanism for bringing two pack members who have been in conflict with each other back together, reaffirming their bonds of affection, so that the pack's ability to work as a team is not impaired.[43]

I have observed this personally with Luna, a yearling who came to Wolf Connection when she was just twelve weeks old. She lives in the house with my wife and me, our daughter, two cats, and two other wolfdogs: Wyoh, who is ten years old, and Nova, who is six. We often observe Luna going to Wyoh and especially to Nova, making herself as small as possible, tail tucked it, nibbling at the other wolf's muzzle, as if asking to be corrected and put in her place. Sure enough, Nova shows her teeth and gums, picks up her hackles and tail, and puffs her chest out, pins Luna down by the neck, and gives a deep, dominant growl. Luna then whines, lying belly up, and Nova lets her go with no more than some slobber on Luna's fur, and they then proceed to some ritualistic play and possibly start the sequence again a while later. Luna is asking Nova to reassert her dominance and leadership, which, in turn, reassures each of them. It is reassuring for a pup to be reminded of who is in charge and that things are being handled.

Rather than engaging in a struggle for dominance, wolves from the same pack check themselves and each other to avoid conflict escalation. But this applies only between packmates. The attitude toward wolves of rival packs is completely different. Strangers are usually considered to be dangerous, a fact that makes filling a vacant breeding pair position a real challenge. Wolves will avoid breeding with a close relative, which ensures the long-term genetic well-being of their pack. So when there is a need for a new breeding male, wolves will allow a nonmember male to approach—alone. Just imagine the level of vulnerability the new arrival assumes in doing this: a single wolf walking up to a new pack, asking for acceptance. This willingness to be fully vulnerable, in a position that clearly could cause his peril, surely illustrates how significant belonging is to a wolf.

Young females that disperse from their pack of origin at maturity can usually find males from rival packs to join with and form a new pack, but it is highly unlikely they would be accepted into an established pack. The Yellowstone Wolf Project team has never seen a female join an existing pack as a subordinate. Males, on the other hand, disperse more than females, and a young male more easily finds a pack in need of a new breeding male or he may entice a female away from her original pack to form a new one with him. The process takes days if not weeks, during which the adoptee will satellite the pack and interact with the alpha male, who will be intensely dominant until he eventually accepts the new member of the pack. During all these interactions with "strangers," wolves are literally risking their lives to find a mate and an adoptive family, perhaps because they recognize that the alternative is far worse. Wolves survive by being together. A lone wolf is a miserable wolf, and very likely a dead wolf.

When a wolf is rescued and brought to Wolf Heart Ranch, he or she goes through a period of quarantine in an enclosure of his or her own. This is because, first, we want to assess the new wolf's health and ensure it poses no risk of contagion to the pack. This seclusion also provides the wolf with a period of acclimation before introduction to the pack, and it allows us to assess his or her behavior. A new wolf is always on her best behavior in these early days. Her instinct is to be accepted by the pack and to do whatever it takes to fit in. The yearning to belong is even stronger in captivity, because the wolf does not have the option of leaving to pursue another pack. So we often see new pack members crouch and tuck to physically make themselves small, and imitate the behavior of wolves in neighboring enclosures, such as howling when the rest of the pack howls. This hopeful creature watches intently, paying careful attention to the actions of the rest of the pack, as if to pick up guidelines of behavior and cues for appropriate social interactions. It usually takes the new wolf two to four weeks to show us her true personality and temperament.

Captive wolves have no choice. If the pack dynamics do not work and one of them wants to leave, they are not able to. This is likely the main reason people see wolves as aggressive. Until a couple of decades ago, all we knew about wolves is how they acted in captivity, where confined space heightens tension and limits the animal's natural proclivity to satellite until the mood of a more dominant wolf is more agreeable. Even at about feeding time, which can be a time of aggression with captive wolves, it is not so with wild wolves, where the option of stepping back and waiting for a turn exists. One of the Yellowstone researchers told me that they have watched wolves make a kill and then the adults, who put in the most work, go off and sleep without breaking into the carcass at all. The pups or yearlings, the ones that did not do as much work during the hunt, will start the feeding.

Arctic wolves on Ellesmere Island are unafraid of people, so it is possible to be closer to them while observing them. Kira Cassidy said, "I definitely noticed the more subtle interactions and ways of communication. Some of them are dominant, some are subordinate, and they're constantly checking in with each other through body postures, physical contact, and even little noises to make sure that it stays the same. It's much easier to observe that in captive wolves, but you bring in that aspect that they don't have to cooperate with each other to hunt large prey." Captive wolves do not have the daily worry of feeding themselves or staying safe from rival packs, so their main preoccupation is the pack dynamics, rather than getting things done. This is a type of "neurosis" that develops in captivity that wild wolves simply do not have.

Within wild packs, aggression between members is controlled to maintain the pack in a state of optimal function. In a tussle with a packmate who is also a relative, a wolf must decide how far that fight will go. If one or both are injured and cannot hunt, the pack's survival is jeopardized. Rival packs, however, can detect each other at a distance and often have howling contests, which gives them the opportunity to assess the situation, perhaps to avoid conflict and move away. Older females are wiser, can assess a confrontation better, and choose to retreat if the situation in not advantageous.[44] Males, on the other hand, rarely know when to walk away. Male confrontations are more often fatal for one or more of the wolves. Though not every meeting leads to a battle, when it does, the level of aggression can be lethal. In fact, battles with rival packs are the leading cause of wolf mortality. Packs from neighboring territories test their rivals when they encounter each other. The choice to fight is a life-or-death decision. As Doug Smith put it, "Being the top predator, this is the way the wolf has to self-regulate and keep their population in check."[45]

TERRITORIALISM

The reason for sociality is typically not hunting. A single wolf can kill every prey species. It may not do it as efficiently on its own, but it has been done. The driving force behind sociality is probably territoriality. To hold and defend a territory, having many is better than having a few. The alternative to a territory is a home range, which is not vigorously defended. A home range is a loosely defined area of use that other animals overstep. If the other animals get too close in the range, there may be a confrontation. But territory will be vigorously defended every time. Territorial clashes are a method of self-regulation, because when there are clashes, the participants kill each other. However, there are many accounts of rival wolves not killing the other pack's pups and even sparing young females. Perhaps pups and young, healthy, breeding-age females are seen to be assets to the species and so are preserved regardless of which pack they belong to.

Because aggression must be tempered with wisdom, the elders of the pack play a pivotal role. The decision of whether to enter a conflict with a rival pack or to retreat appears to rest with the eldest members of wolf packs, who have the most experience with these potentially deadly situations. They weigh everything, taking into account the number of rivals that have appeared and the lay of the land, and then decide whether to fight or withdraw.[46] The elders of a wolf pack may also play a key part in selecting what game to hunt. Loss of an elder can potentially result in the remaining younger members choosing to hunt livestock rather than wild animals.

SHARING RISK AND REWARD

Wolves act as a unit; they are coordinated and relentless. They take turns during the pursuit, which can last for hours and cover many miles. Depending on their size and experience, they take on particular roles, each playing the part to which they are best suited and sharing the risk. A wolf accepts the risk of a crippling or fatal injury each time it engages—to hunt is to potentially face one's own death, and the selection of prey is never taken lightly.[47]

Gray wolves hunt a wide variety of animals. When available, their preferred meal is reindeer, moose, or elk, but they will hunt smaller or larger game if necessary. Bison are on the menu only in the coldest winter months. According to research in the park, elk are approximately three times easier for wolves to kill than are bison.[48] The Mollie pack in Yellowstone has adapted to this challenge by maintaining a significantly larger pack than their elk-hunting rivals in the rest of Yellowstone. It takes two to six wolves to pull down an elk, whereas successful bison capture requires nine to thirteen wolves (and more is better).

The Mollies are not just more numerous, but also tend to be physically larger than the members of the other Yellowstone packs, a direct result of their specialization. Similarly, the bison-hunting wolves in Wood Buffalo National Park in Canada are physically larger as well. Being larger makes wolves heavier, and therefore slower, so selection for larger size also has a downside, as specialization reduces the menu options.[49] However, size is not the only thing being selected for when the game gets bigger and more dangerous. The level of cooperation among pack members hunting large and dangerous prey increases as well. To be successful at hunting bison requires that more members of the pack be willing to come within range of the potentially deadly prey and share the risk.

People make the assumption that wolves are ferocious creatures and can kill at will, whatever they want, and as much as they desire, but investigation and observation have proven that wolves are successful only about 20 percent of the time while hunting elk, and they risk their lives every time they approach their prey. Dan Stahler commented, "I think it's gone underappreciated what wolves have to go through just to get a meal every couple of days."

Not every wolf takes part in every hunt; sometimes individuals fill other roles. In an average Yellowstone pack of ten wolves, there are only two or three "star players" who do almost all the successful hunting and killing, just as on a soccer, basketball, or baseball team, a few individuals are the high scorers. In other words, wolves need to field a full team, but of those, just two or three need to be hunting and defensive "stars." Legendary Wolf 21 was the epitome of what a good leader should be. While 21 was often the one who did most of the work to kill an elk, he was usually the very last one to eat, and that was fine with him.[50]

STICKING TOGETHER

The pack is a team whose members support each other, and at the same time, each wolf has a role, depending on his or her temperament and skills. "Sometimes a wolf that is not the best hunter—and even though he might be a large, tough-looking male—he chooses to run the day-care center," says Rick McIntyre. Rather than hunt, he is happy to help protect and take care of the pups. By doing this, the wolf is fulfilling an important role, where his size and strength in a defense situation will be essential to the well-being of the pack, and where his gentle nature makes him an excellent nanny.

Caring for others is a central aspect of wolf social behavior. Wolves act as caregivers not just for youngsters, but also for the sick and injured. A study looked at the energetic costs of sarcoptic mange, an infection caused by a parasitic mite that burrows under an animal's skin and causes itching and pain, on Yellowstone wolves.[51] This disease can be fatal, as wolves with mange lose body hair, which can cause them to lose weight because their bodies have to use more calories to try to stay warm. Researchers had assumed that the risk of infection increased with the size of the pack, and was a cost of group living. But they found that group size did not predict infection risk, and that, if the pack was large enough, there would be a sufficient number of healthy wolves that could hunt. When they killed, they shared food with all members of the pack, sick or healthy. Eventually the sick members recovered, thanks to the social support of group hunting and territory defense provided by their healthy packmates.

Wolves take care of their injured as well. When a wolf is badly hurt and cannot hunt, it is not left behind to starve. Wounded wolves can and do recover from broken limbs and other major injuries and return to active duty when they are healed. Dan Stahler told me a story of a wolf that the researchers darted for collaring. They had been watching this wolf cover long distances hunting with the pack, for a couple of years. When the tranquilizer took effect and they got up to him lying under a tree, they realized that this wolf had only three legs. Wolves have successfully recovered from seemingly catastrophic injury, often because of help from packmates.

Altruism is alive and well, and it is a fundamental trait of the gray wolf.[52] Wolves display altruistic behavior in saving a packmate while it is under attack. A wolf that could get away without injury instead puts itself in this dangerous position. "Perhaps they do this with the hope of reciprocation someday, but it may be that they simply care about each other," Kira Cassidy observed. "They have a spike in all of the feel-good hormones—dopamine and oxytocin—that make them feel connected to each other, and they probably have a spike of stress hormones when someone they know is in danger. Humans do the same thing, dogs definitely."[53]

CONSCIOUSNESS IN WOLVES

Wolves think, they problem solve and make decisions, but Doug Smith does not believe they have a consciousness. "Consciousness, if you can define it," he said, "would be like being aware of yourself, aware of your mortality, and I don't think wolves have that."[54]

Each day wolves face life-and-death decisions, and the bonds they share support and energize the pack as they engage in the ceaseless effort to find food and defend territory. They must strike a balance between caution and bold action, between passivity and aggression, and the wolf resolves each dilemma brilliantly. Every conflict or hunting decision engages the wolf's judgment. *Is this worth my life?* they ask every time. Death is the wolf's adviser at every turn.

Using death as one's adviser is a cornerstone of the ancestral wisdom taught to Carlos Castaneda by his teacher Don Juan Matus, and the wolf demonstrates this axiom powerfully. Using Doug's definition, that is a sign of consciousness. For humans, life-and-death decisions were at one time daily occurrences, just as they continue to be for the wolf. But we have changed, and we now behave more like prey animals, fearfully imagining danger at every turn, when, historically and statistically speaking, we have never been safer. Using the fear of death as a basis to judge our decisions, for modern humans, may also be a way to appreciate life and to focus efforts on savoring each precious moment. It is about staying awake and alert in the midst of a deluge of potential distractions, remaining joyful and completely engaged as you acknowledge that this may be your last day on Earth. Many of the researchers I interviewed for this book said that their approach to life was altered by the wolf's "lust for life," as Doug Smith called it, adding, "They aren't aware they are going to die tomorrow, so they face life full on," something he admires immensely. I would conclude exactly the opposite: I think that wolves live their lives boldly, and without looking back, precisely because they know this can be their last day on Earth.

At Wolf Connection we teach the Wolf Principle *Wolves give 150 percent to everything they do.* This is because they are in harmony with the cycles of life and death. Whatever the human interpretation of consciousness, wolves possess a virility, a sense of aliveness, and an approach to life that puts modern, civilized, and somnolent humans to shame.

FAMILY FIRST: TRIANGLE AND HIS SISTER, WOLF 571

Rick McIntyre shared a story with me he gathered thanks to observations of Laurie Lyman, who accompanied him that day.[55] Years ago, the Druid Peak pack's pups were in a rendezvous site in Lamar Valley, and most of the adults were away on a hunt. The only adults left were a middle-aged female, 571, and her little yearling brother, a black wolf known as Triangle because he had a white blaze on his chest in the form of a triangle. Suddenly they heard howling, and three big male wolves came into that area from outside the park. Whether they knew it or not, they were getting very close to the pack's pups.

The female, 571, was a low-ranking adult in the pack and had never had pups herself. Basically, she served the role of helping everyone else, and it was up to her now to figure out how to deal with this situation. Triangle had a really bad case of mange.

Rick said he looked like a drowned rat and had a lot of sores over his body. He was hurting so much that he could not actually lie down, and he tried to sleep standing up. So he was not only young, he was not only sick, he was really hurting. Triangle and 571 were outnumbered, so 571 decided on a risky strategy. She started to move toward the pups, which meant that that was also toward the three enemy wolves. Her little brother was used to being with her, so he followed. As they moved toward the enemy wolves, they were spotted, and the three big males charged directly at them.

She quickly turned around and ran back where she had come from. That also caused Triangle to run with her. In her mind maybe what she wanted was for those males to actually chase her, because that drew them away from the little pups, who were totally defenseless. Now, 571 was the fastest wolf in her family and usually led the hunt, so she was in front and very confident that she could lure them away and then outrun them.

And she did something else deliberate. As the three enemy wolves were running toward her, she suddenly cut off in a new direction. Triangle understood what she was doing, so he cut off in the opposite direction. And the three big males continued to run after her.

Now she had succeeded in luring them away, not only from the pups but also from her little brother. And all she had to do was just run as fast as she could—she would leave them in the dust and would save the day.

But one of the males, against all expectations, even though he was much, much bigger than she was, was faster than she was. So as fast as 571 could run, every time she looked over her shoulder, he was gaining. And he got closer and closer and she just could not go any faster. And then he lunged forward and bit her in the rear end and smashed her to the ground.

Now, she was the granddaughter of Yellowstone's greatest wolf, alpha male 21, who was the undisputed, undefeated heavyweight champion. She had his blood, his genetics flowing through her, and she was not about to put up with this guy, so she jumped up, turned around, and bit him on the face. He didn't expect that at all, and he didn't like it.

He hesitated for a moment, and she used that opportunity to run off. But a few moments later, he caught up with her again, slammed her to the ground, she bit him in the face again, got away a second time, and he went after her again.

When he caught her the third time, he held her down long enough to allow the other big males to join him. And now all three were attacking her, and she was on her back fighting for her life, but they were biting her at will.

One of the males stood right over her throat, and the way that one wolf kills another wolf is with a deep bite to the throat. It's pretty much instant death. He opened his jaws as wide as he could, and with all of his strength, he just crunched down on her throat.

But 571 was wearing a radio collar, so he actually did not do any damage because he bit into the battery component. The attacker was confused by what happened; it took him a few moments to figure it out. But now he could see that the collar only protected some of her throat, so if he bit a little higher or lower, he would be able to kill her.

And just as he was about to do that, Triangle, the sick little brother, ran back to rescue his sister. The skinny sick little hairless wolf had run all the way back, and he surprised and bit this big wolf, the second big wolf, the third big wolf, and they didn't know what was happening because it went so fast . . . it was a true surprise attack.

But after a few moments they realized, "Hey, it's just a little guy, this is nothing." Now, one of the big wolves chased Triangle, who got away, while the other two wolves went back after

571, who had jumped up and run off. By the time they caught up with her, she had jumped into the river and was trying to swim to the other side.

But they caught up with her and began attacking her again. Now they were holding her under the water as they were biting her. Either they were gonna kill her with the bites or drown her.

Meanwhile, Triangle had shown great heroic capabilities, but just one little wolf like him wasn't enough to save his sister, but once again, he came back. He jumped off the bank, dived into the water, dog-paddled out, and attacked the guys once again. This time they were so angry at him that they forgot all about the sister, so all three went after him.

She got to the other side of the river, ran right past the researcher observers, circled around, and headed back toward the den area, which is a really safe place for her to be.

The fast male caught up with Triangle and bit him on a hind leg. But Triangle took his other hind leg and kicked the guy in the face, which caused him to let go. He was able to run across the road to the den area and escape.

A day or two later the rest of the pack came back. The alpha male at that time was 480, who was the father of both Triangle and 571. Now, 480 was somewhat of an average alpha male, very capable. But he was not the same alpha male that 21 was. Wolf 21 was actually his father-in-law; 480 was paired off with 21's daughter. And he knew 21. It would be like in the human situation, the son-in-law and the wife's dad is just this unbelievably impressive guy that you just can't measure up to.

In any case, 480 figured out what was going on: there were enemy wolves in his territory. Wolf 21, in two particular incidents, by himself, to protect his family, fought and defeated six wolves. But 480 would not be able to fight these three wolves by himself.

A couple of days after 480 came back, he and all the Druid wolves were on the north side of the road, and the three enemy wolves were howling to the south.

Perhaps 480 wanted to organize his entire pack, run across the road, and charge at those guys to drive them out of the neighborhood, because they totally outnumbered the three. Maybe the younger wolves had seen the injuries on Triangle and 571 and were too afraid to confront them. Nonetheless, 480 was responsible for figuring out how to deal with this, but he couldn't fight them by himself, and the pack didn't seem to want to follow him to have a coordinated attack.

It seemed as if 480 had decided to go after those guys. He crossed the road and headed straight toward the trees where the other wolves were howling. He disappeared into the trees, and then a few moments later he came running out. His tail was tucked all the way under his rear end, he was running for his life, and right behind him were those three big males, all with vertical tails.

He ran across the road, he ran back toward the den area with the three wolves right behind him just about to grab him and kill him. They went behind a hill and into a forest.

About a minute later, the forest exploded with wolves, and they were all running back down to the road. The three wolves were out in front—they were the ones that had tucked tails now. Right behind them, only a few yards away, was 480 with his tail vertical, right behind 480 was little Triangle, and right behind them was the entire Druid pack. It was an ambush. Wolf 480 had taken the risk of going by himself; his intent was to trick them into chasing him back toward the forest, where his entire pack was hiding. He got them there, he survived that, and as soon as he got into the trees, he turned around and went after them, and his family helped him, including Triangle.

I believe that wolves have an awareness that they belong to a greater, natural collective. Their role as ecosystem balancers is not only a result of biological programing and instinctive drive. They experience the world beyond their physical, biological senses just as we humans do, and since they don't have the distracting inner chatter with which we are burdened, they may experience the world more deeply, cleanly, and clearly.

REALM FIVE

The Human Wolf

"Only the mountain has lived long enough to listen objectively to the howl of a wolf,"[1] wrote a young Aldo Leopold, hunter for hire during the early 1900s, when wildlife population control programs were established in the United States. Leopold became committed to writing about his conservation message for the general public in his fifties, drafting *A Sand County Almanac* just before his untimely death. In it, Leopold reflects on the moment his heart awakened and his eyes metaphorically opened for the first time:

> In those days, we had never heard of passing up the chance to kill a wolf. In a second, we were pumping lead into the pack, but with more excitement than accuracy. When our rifles were empty, the old wolf was down and a pup was dragging a leg into impassable slide rocks. . . . We reached the old wolf in time to watch a fierce green fire dying in her eyes. I realized then, and have known ever since, that there was something new to me in those eyes—something known only to her and to the mountain. I was young then, and full of trigger-itch; I thought that because fewer wolves meant more deer, that no wolves would mean hunters' paradise. But after seeing the green fire die, I sensed that neither the wolf nor the mountain agreed with such a view.[2]

The wolf has been humanity's evolutionary partner for perhaps hundreds of thousands of years, and yet for the past few centuries we have been on a relentless wolf hunt. Fear-based superstition and ill-intentioned folk stories surfacing in Europe at about the time of the Inquisition usurped ancestral knowledge and wisdom, replacing it with the confusion and ignorance that have led to us nearly extinguishing the species.

Fortunately, wolves are making a comeback both in the wild and in our hearts. Nevertheless, modern humans' strange view of nature and strained relationship with it make us the most peculiar creature. We often behave as if separated from nature; we praise ourselves for our intelligence and sophistication over "primitive" animals. However, wolves have a message of collaboration, altruism, and sustainability that can be the key to our alignment with all other life forms on Earth.

Humans are more similar to wolves than some people care to admit. Hunter-gatherer societies who see themselves as descendants of wolves have adopted wolf behaviors. For instance, self-control is a fundamental aspect of behavior for all First Nation wolf clan members. They say that the wolf has taught humans how to live in order to help them. Imitating wolf behavior, these cultures ritualize conflict. Trudy Spiller, keeper of stories for the wolf clan, Gitxsan First Nation,[3] told us that rather than entering into an intense physical battle that could result in injury to packmates, wolf clan members practice self-restraint. They gather and resolve conflict in a collective manner, with the full support of the rest of their clan, in a public meeting where everyone has a chance to speak, and to decide what should happen.

Like wolves sometimes do, early peoples employed ritualized methods to resolve conflict between social groups, minimizing harm to both sides. For example, the *Mabinogian*, a written account based on the oral history of the first people of Wales, includes a description of how groups in conflict might each name a champion, who would fight on behalf of their entire group, preventing widespread casualties. Today, one can argue, this behavior continues in the form of modern sports events where teams "do battle," competing as a form of ritualized aggression. The benefits are obvious: sports bring people together, and instead of killing each other, we have fun together. The playful or ritualistic expression of aggression is ultimately just as much a human thing as a wolf thing.

A popular story speaks of an elder teaching his grandson about life. "A fight is going on inside me," he said to the boy. "It is a terrible fight and it is between two wolves. One is evil—he is anger, envy, sorrow, regret, greed, arrogance, self-pity, guilt, resentment, inferiority, lies, false pride, superiority, and ego." He continued, "The other is good—he is joy, peace, love, hope, serenity, humility, kindness, benevolence, empathy, generosity, truth, compassion, and faith. The same fight is going on inside you—and inside every other person."

The grandson thought about it for a few moments and then asked his grandfather, "Which wolf will win?"

The grandfather simply replied, "The one you feed."[4]

While the wolf can bring us together, serving as guidance to our hearts, that fierce spirit can also bring havoc and open conflict without regard for the consequences when polluted with anger, resentment, and egomaniacal pursuits—things wolves do not have. The older, more experienced wolves are in charge of the pack in the wild, but that is not always the case with the human packs today, exposing us to the danger of following wrong leadership.

Humans and wolves share similarities but also have differences when it comes to territory, pack, and self.

TERRITORY

Glenn Schiffman, a wolf clan member and friend, shared a traditional Seneca story with me. "It is told . . . that human beings moved to an area and discovered it was the territory of a large wolf pack.

They knew that with great effort over a period of years, they could kill all the wolves, but this would make them a changed people, no longer members of Earth's natural order. So the human beings chose to move away and leave the land to the wolves. In later years, when faced with a critical decision, someone from the tribe would stand up and ask, 'Tell me my brothers, tell me my sisters! Who speaks for the Wolf?'"[5] I'd say that's what it means to be a human being.

Fortunately, there are well-informed, intelligent, and emotionally mature human beings who speak for the wolves today in science, conservation, policy, education, and First Nations cultures. At Wolf Connection we speak for the wolves to shed light on the wolf-human relationship, and to translate the message wolves have for all of humanity. We are passionately committed to embodying heart, and the balance that is possible among all living beings.

Few species are as territorial as wolves and humans. Humans have rationalized war and tried to justify genocide as a defense of territory. We have organized legal and social infrastructure for the management of property, and on a global scale we have destroyed life over territorial claims. In contrast, the Seneca story above speaks of cooperative ways that have been lost, ways from a time when humans and wolves regarded each other as peer predators with a mutual interest to preserve the natural balance of things.

During my 2018 trip to Yellowstone National Park I met with men and women who have dedicated their lives to the protection and scientific understanding of wolves, and in so doing, speak for them as well. Doug Smith, the Wolf Project's director, is certainly one of those scientists. He and I discussed the wolf-human relationship and the social tensions in northern Europe and North America where wolves had previously been eradicated and are now experiencing population recovery. We both agreed that a deeper understanding of how people live in the areas where wolves have returned, and awareness that humans have encroached into lands already occupied by wolves, could tell us a great deal about ourselves and our society.

Doug referred me to *Wolf Conflicts: A Sociological Study*,[6] the only book either of us is aware of that examines the motivations underlying opposition to wolves' presence on land occupied by humans. Even though the study was conducted in Norway, I feel strongly that many of the authors' conclusions, made after a decade of devoted study, can be extrapolated to the reality wolves face in North America. The central causes of conflict are power struggles between local residents and scientific and governmental organizations, which are blamed for forcing wolves into territories in which people live, work, or recreate.[7] Wolves are merely catalysts and unfortunate targets of the human social conflict.

The intimacy of the wolf-human bond. *Photo by Chris Perry's Wildside Galleries.*

In the Kettle Mountain Range of northeastern Washington, a large and healthy wolf pack known as the Profanity Peak pack lived in a 350-square-mile territory. Their range overlapped with public lands leased to ranchers for cattle grazing. In the summer of 2016, local ranchers released their cattle near the pack's den site, which pushed away the deer, the wolves' usual prey. In the absence of wild prey, the pack began killing cows. Ranchers put pressure on the state, and the state ordered the killing of the entire pack, which triggered an intense political, social, and financial battle. Government officials were threatened; universities conducting wolf research lost funding. Knowledge and dialogue could have reduced wolf blame and fear-tainted reports of wolf sightings and livestock killings. Instead, the research intended to show where wolf territories overlap with grazing land was terminated at the same time the Profanity Peak pack was terminated.[8]

Wolf conflicts are not between people and wolves but between people and people.[9] However, the anger caused by opposing political, religious, and ideological views, as well as deep-rooted issues of identity, social recognition, and pride, are unfairly directed at the wolves. In other words, wolves are just another excuse for conflict over self-validation. Ironically, "being right" is as important to humans as the hunting territory and den locations are to wolves, and we defend it with equal intensity.[10]

Groups engaged in traditional land use such as forestry and resource extraction have the most vehement antiwolf attitudes. The conflict is between people who view land as a resource to be used and abused, and those who contend that animals and nature should rightfully exist independent of humans. For the former, the land is there to be plowed, the forest cut for lumber, the river's purpose is for drinking and crop irrigation. And valid arguments can be made to defend that view, since these resources make our modern lives possible. From this perspective, the wolf is encroaching on "their" land and eating "their" deer. The opposing view instead contends that the land, the forest, the river, the deer, and the wolf have as much right to live and thrive as we humans do.

Wolf detractors who have utilitarian views of nature often ask, "What do wolves do for people?" At Wolf Connection we answer that question thoroughly. We showcase what wolves do for people and remind visitors and program participants to look at the old traditions as well as science. We propose that wolves and humans share a much deeper connection than most people realize and that the two can coexist.

But antiwolf groups consider the wolf an "intruder" on their land. They find validation in the argument that extensive pro- tection of nature is a romantic notion, and they mistrust envi- ronmentalists and wildlife biologists. These groups raise concerns about the safety of women, children, and the elderly in places where there are wild animals, and they are resentful of the gov- ernment and "city people," whom they see as forcing predators on hunters and rural communities.

Prowolf people believe that the wolf has an obvious place in the world, and it belongs in the forests around them. These humans are happy to share the forests with the wolf. There are anti- and prowolf people living in both urban and rural areas, so the conflict over wolves is a complex issue that cannot be simplified as "rural vs. urban."

Interestingly, the *Wolf Conflicts* researchers found that views of the wolf are expressed similarly by both sides. In their narrative, words such as "superior," "wild," "genuine," "pure," "unpolluted," "smart," "socially intelligent," "strategic," "dominating," "beautiful," and "magnificent" were repeatedly used by anti- and prowolf people alike.[11] There was also unity in the admiration for the wolf's pure and wild nature. This reminded me of the definition used by author and environmentalist Paul Hawken, who refers to "wild" as harmonious, balanced, abundant, deeply rooted, fearless, and of benefit to all.[12] Unfortunately, that is not the most common view of the wild, as some groups believe the wild is something that must be tamed—unreliable, out of control, and dangerous.

Additionally, people interviewed in the *Wolf Conflicts* study had accurate knowledge of wolf behavior and social structure. They mentioned the extraordinary social equality and loyalty seen within wolf packs. But when they were asked about details of wolf biology, their knowledge was less proficient. For example, people mistakenly believe that wolves are capable of incredible rates of reproduction and conclude that population control is essential.[13]

The Lost Wolves of Japan by Brett Walker describes the circumstances leading to the extinction of wolves in Japan, even from the mountain shrines where they were once worshipped as "the large-mouthed pure god." Until the late 1800s Japanese farmers considered the wolf a sacred animal and partner that kept nuisance animals away from crops. When American industrialized farming and cattle ranching arrived, sought by the Japanese government, American antiwolf beliefs also arrived. An aggressive antiwolf campaign was launched, in which embalmed wolves were photographed "eating" sheep, and only a decade later so many of the positive stories, legends, and traditions around wolves faded from public awareness; and in only thirty years wolves were completely eradicated from the country.

Prior to this time, Japanese grain (rice) farming was considered noble, and the raising of animals for meat consumption was disdained.[14] But to develop and expand beef ranching on Hokkaido, to modernize the industry, an American adviser recommended eliminating wolves from that island as an efficient method of increasing livestock production.[15] This required an attitudinal shift away from reverence for these creatures who assisted farmers to viewing them as pests to be eradicated. The Japanese did not have stories such as

"Little Red Riding Hood" or teachings about man's dominion over the Earth. But they desired modernity, and they adopted the anti-wolf attitudes and methods of the United States. Strychnine-laced carcasses were placed for wolves to find. An attractive bounty system was put into effect. Ainu hunters, who believed themselves to be descended from wolves, were employed to kill wolves.

Walker writes, "Wolf hunters saw wolves as our 'natural self,' meaning that the bounty was a temptation for people to corrupt themselves. I can only imagine what it did to those hunters' souls to kill wolves indiscriminately like that. They probably lived the rest of their lives in shame and died stripped of their wholeness and honor."[16] I wonder how many of those hunters saw the green fire fading away in the eyes of those wolves, as Aldo Leopold did in the opening quote of this chapter?

Humans believe they have the authority to make life-and-death decisions with respect to wildlife and natural ecosystems. Hunters practice what they think of as "predator control," as well as hunting for food, while farmers believe they must keep the land clear and "productive." Both groups see themselves as stewards of the land, playing an indispensable part in nature's balancing act. But so do scientists, conservationists, and government agencies, with their forest management and wildlife reintroduction programs.

I propose that we reconsider the meaning of "stewardship." At Wolf Connection, we attempt to empower future generations of leaders to become conscious stewards, but we certainly don't mean: *keep the land productive no matter what, cut the forest so you can plow, and cull the predators so we have more game to hunt.* We foster leaders who consider the good of all life forms, not just humans, for generations to come, in all their decisions.

Opposition to wolves is rooted in people's perception of themselves and the world, and until we truly understand the motivations and views of the people we disagree with, the path forward will remain unstable, and what happened in Japan could easily happen in America and Europe as well. Change is required, and however unlikely some presume it to be, change is possible.

PACK

Wolves remind us of our true social nature and the need every human has to bond with and relate to other living beings. Wolves' social structure and moral codes are based on compassion and benevolence, and their actions are heart-centered. This is true when raising their pups, caring for each other, and even when they protect their territory or hunt with deadly intensity. From an open heart we can make choices that are life-affirming, and we are conscious of how our actions affect all around us.

At Wolf Connection, some of the youth program participants come from challenging backgrounds, where they have learned that maintaining a tough attitude or at least the appearance of toughness is essential for survival. They posture, they make fun of the program leader, or keep their headphones on, projecting a lack of interest in what is being said. They feel too vulnerable to show their honest emotions, which in some cases could be dangerous for them.

Yet students do open up to and become part of the wolf pack. The wolf pack in turn consistently encourages these individuals to expand into vulnerability with other humans to potentially form two-legged packs of their own.

Sammy had been a tough kid who got expelled from school for selling drugs and getting into fights. On day two at the Wolf Connection program he said, "I don't want to fight anymore—I actually feel like crying most days."

Sonja revealed her struggle with a secret when she said, "I'm struggling with my identity, be it gender or sexual orientation."

Carlos dropped the posturing and shared, "I feel guilty about how I act with my family."

When we ask our students what it is like to open up to others or hear peer-pack members share authentically, their responses are moving and beautiful: "I can relate," "I am not the only one," "It feels like we're becoming a real pack," and "I feel closer to my pack-mates." Students learn not only that safe spaces exist, but also that by taking the risk to be open and true to self, they facilitate a safe space for others. They learn that true bravery lies in the courage to show up, discover their own voice, and deeply connect.

This also applies to the program leaders at Wolf Connection. We may teach the wolf message, but we deal with challenges just as any of our students. The difference is that our students *know* they need help, and most of them will grab any rope you throw to them. On the other hand, many of us adults believe that we function just fine in our everyday lives, and can be resistant about admitting that we have work to do. I guess we often teach what we need to learn.

Every time a group of people comes together to work on a task of any value that they genuinely care about and feel personally invested in, misunderstanding and miscommunication are inevitable. This can result in wounded feelings, overreactions, and friction in communication and behavior. In our modern society we are conditioned to strive for security. We appreciate predictability. We expect that our job will be there tomorrow, that our family will have a roof over its head next month, and that we will be able to retire at some point. Unfortunately (or fortunately), the only constant at Wolf Connection, and in life, is change. Constant change demands constant adaptation. How can we navigate constant change in a world that values security and predictability? We do it with the support from our pack or packs, of course, our close circles of family, friends, and coworkers. Tight bonds of friendship and respect have developed over the years among the Wolf Connection human pack, and we constantly support each other both personally and professionally. Especially when things seem

162 THE WOLF CONNECTION

hopeless and we don't see the path ahead, those close to us are the ones who will pull us through . . . just as wolves do.

The story that Doug Smith shared of male Wolf 755 illustrates psychological and emotional resilience, when the wolf put the pack's needs ahead of his own. When 755's mate was shot by a hunter, his daughter assumed the alpha female role, but because wolves will not inbreed, meaning mating with her father was not possible, she left. Wolf 755 paired with a female from another pack who became pregnant, but she was killed. He found another female and stayed with her for a few months, but left her. Doug thinks that this coupling was not "compatible," as the researchers cannot otherwise explain the split-up. Wolf 755 was with three females in a span of a just over a year. He then paired with a fourth female and they had two litters of pups together. Doug said that a story like this gives one hope for life, as it demonstrates the emotional resilience to recover from tragedies.

While 755 and his mate's second litter of pups were a couple of months old, three male wolves from another pack came in and took over his pack. They possessed the advantage of greater numbers, and 755 was forced to leave. These invading wolves stayed with his mate and his pups. Doug wondered if the female was thinking, "I've got no choice. If I'm going to survive, I have to succumb to this," and what 755 was thinking; perhaps, "If I don't go along with this, my pups die. I might die."

When these three males were away for a couple of months, 755 visited his pups. But finally he left. And that pack taken over by the three invading males is still going. The female, 926, stayed with her mate, 925, until he was killed by another pack. Rick McIntyre swears that the male diverted attention away from his mate and pups so he would get killed and they would remain safe.

The wolves who killed 925 did not kill his pups, and four of them moved in. Yet none picked up with the surviving female, 926, and they eventually left. Even a screenwriter for a Venezuelan soap opera would have trouble making up such an intricate story.

Humans, too, live in a multipack world. We live this rich life, and each of us has memberships in different packs, fulfilling different roles in each of them. For instance, we might be the alpha with our kids at home, but a beta or a middle-rank wolf at work. We are still the goofy omega with childhood or high school friends where others are the alpha and mid-ranking wolves. We are so used to belonging to multiple packs—a sports team, an affinity group, live or online course collective, online mentoring community—that we don't notice the great fluidity and adaptation skills we employ to navigate the intricacies of going from pack to pack in a healthy way. We figure out how to get along, collaborate, cooperate, and find consensus. We create better systems, using our abilities to assess risk and move forward.

As the leader of an organization that, since its inception, has been growing aggressively, with systems that need annual modification or they become obsolete, I needed to figure out a way to create a constant in the midst of change. That constant is a solid set of values to which everyone can relate and embrace personally. The Wolf Connection team developed our culture, communication, and code of conduct, which I ultimately simplified into five pillars: **Curiosity, Radical Ownership, Focus, Trust, and Heart.**

Curiosity: We don't take situations for granted, and we don't make assumptions about why other people do what they do. Instead we get curious. We ask Why? What? When? Where? and How? We seek clarification before, during, and after any situation or interaction. This prevents us from coming to conclusions, taking things personally, and being guided by faulty assumptions.

Action: Start your conversation with the words "I'm curious about _____," and fill in the rest.

Radical Ownership: We don't point fingers. Instead we ask ourselves in *all* situations (no matter how removed it might feel), *What is my part in this?* Imagine how different a world we would live in if people led with that.

Action: When we see the temptation of blame and complaint coming up, even if you don't know what your part is yet, say: "So here is my part _____."

Focus: We stay on task, focused on our area of responsibility and priorities. We avoid distractions and gossip. Focus overcomes resistance. If we are not clear on what our area of focus is, we get curious.

Action: Every Sunday night or Monday morning, plan your week and write down the top three things you need to accomplish. Nothing else can occupy your attention until you have those things in the bag.

Trust: We trust ourselves and each other implicitly, because we are working together for a cause we all believe in and care about. We trust that we have the best intention in our hearts and we offer support to each other from that place. We trust even when we do not want to. We trust when it hurts. We trust when we push each other's buttons. We first offer trust to receive trust. With trust present, it is more difficult to take offense; it is easier to take risks with each other. Trust is the first stage of development for a child; without it, there is no safety, no bonding, and no growth.

The main reason we do not trust is some version of "I don't want to be hurt again." Every one of us has been hurt in some way. And that should tell us something. Getting hurt—physically, emotionally, or psychologically—is part of life. If you walk out the door every morning (or don't) and risk interactions with other human beings face-to-face or virtually, chances are that sooner or later misunderstandings will happen, expectations will not be fulfilled, promises will be broken, and you are going to feel hurt. I'm not talking about people coming after you or trying to hurt you on purpose. It's simply that, to quote a famous bumper sticker, "Shit happens." The truth is we give "getting hurt" too much importance and use it as an excuse to hide. But getting hurt is overrated.

The only things that break trust for me are ill intentions.

Action: Respect yourself and others, and be willing to get hurt.

Heart: Wolves represent the healing of the human heart, and I define Heart as passion, courage, fire in the belly, the burning desire and willingness to stand for something and face life full on, without leaving anything on the table.

Action: Life is short. . . . Just go for it.

The Wolf Connection team loved these pillars from their inception. Then nobody practiced them. The pillars became another way to point fingers and come to me, complaining, "He/She/They are not being curious!" or "I don't feel trusted." Soon I realized that it wasn't them but my leadership that needed to level up; just putting forth a set of clever words was not going to magically get people to trust each other and work as a team. I had to demonstrate the principles myself, hold the container steady, and give it time. The five pillars are now practiced at every level of the organization, from the newest volunteer to the leadership team.

Frameworks like this one are not new. They have been formulated since humans evolved their discerning prefrontal cortex. Yet, these practices seem to be part of the human dysfunction. We know there is work to do, we know there are tools that can provide a path to a happier and more fulfilled life, and yet most of humanity prefers the easier, lower-level existence with all of its drama.

This is because, as some of our students say, "It's hard to look at yourself, to be vulnerable, and to do the work." My answer is always the same: *What is hardest is living a half-life and dying without ever discovering your purpose and what you are capable of.* Our relationship with wolves over the past few hundred years is a perfect example of human stubbornness and insistence to continue behaving in ways that can very well lead to our doom.

SELF

Psychologist Carl Jung wrote, "As far as we can discern, the sole purpose of human existence is to kindle a light of meaning in the darkness of mere being."[17] It's a great line, and Jung may have known something the rest of us do not. But what do those words actually mean? What is their practical, everyday life application?

Poets, artists, and teachers around the globe, the brilliant minds that brought us spiritual and mystical traditions, modern philosophy, psychology, theology, and science have looked at the human condition from every angle, and yet humanity's emotional intelligence remains in its infancy. The extraordinary capacity humans have for discernment, innovation, and creativity is matched only by our ability to burn down the place at the drop of a hat. When humans get lost, they are capable of terrible destruction and cruelty.

Have you ever seen a dog turn in circles a few times before lying down on your kitchen floor? Perhaps you have seen a dog relieve himself or herself, walk ten or twenty feet, and then kick dirt in random directions. Wolves walk in circles to flatten the high grass or snow and form a bedding pad to be more comfortable and insulated, and they kick dirt back to cover their feces to mitigate scent. When dogs do this, they're behaving according to "leftover" instincts. Many dogs live their lives confused about their nature, divorced from their wild origins. The vast majority of humans also live their lives confused about their nature and clueless about their origin. Our inner compass is rusty and doesn't always point north, so we depend on other people and institutions to figure out what we should think, feel, and do.

Wolves are a reminder of our natural origins, and a compass for our evolution and success on this planet. No other animal has had the influence wolves have, and can have again, on the human race. One can say that without wolves, humans have no future.

Veteran wolf watcher Laurie Lyman's life has been transformed by her wolf behavior observations. "I expanded beyond what I ever thought I could be. My whole mind-set about the world, and how everybody fits in together. Everything becomes heightened, especially in the winter, when it's quiet. I hear the call of the raven. I watch, and a lot of times that's where the wolves are, they're calling to each other."[18] Laurie redefined her state of being and adjusted her sense of her own importance in the world because of her experience of the wolves. She has a recalibrated sense of priorities, which she credits to the privilege of watching packs at Yellowstone. "I've learned and try to teach a lot of people, especially wolf watchers . . . don't concentrate on what you've missed. Just concentrate on what you've seen. Because we've all seen amazing things."

FEEL LIKE A WOLF

In *Wolf Conflicts*, the authors concluded, "To try to change perceptions of the wolf among opponents of the current management regime is hardly worth the effort. Opposition to wolves arises in a conflict between social representations of the wolf and the representation of the land as productive, usable land, and these fundamental interpretations remain impervious to information from the government, scientists, or others. They are rooted in people's perception of themselves and the world, and any assertions challenging this perception will be dismantled and made to tally with existing perceptions, that is, the core of the representation. And . . . this core is nonnegotiable."[19]

I can see how those beliefs may *appear* nonnegotiable from a sociological or government program perspective, but I disagree that they are inflexible from a human potential view. I firmly contend that people are capable of change, even those who appear entrenched and immovable in their opinions and thoughts. At our core, humans are designed for adaptability. Our entire history of evolution on this planet, including our association with wolves, is proof that humans can fundamentally alter their ways, identities, and beliefs to survive. At Wolf Heart Ranch we constantly witness people profoundly shifting their views of the world and of who they are in it as a result of their experiences with the wolves. "Hardened" individuals come seeking support after being incarcerated, or those who grew up in neighborhoods where they didn't know if they would be alive at the end of the day, whose parents, uncles, and older siblings were part of a gang and who became gang members themselves. After living in a constant state of hostility and hypervigilance, being marginalized, abused, and rejected for most of their lives, these men and women have become poets, artists, and ambassadors for trust and love. We see similar realities in other diverse groups, such as previously incarcerated people and even war veterans.

If members of opposing gangs are able to come to the table and find a dialogue after they have been fighting and even killing each other for decades, if victims of abuse are able to forgive the abusers and move on, and if gender and racial reconciliations are taking place during retreat and other programs at Wolf Heart Ranch, there must be a way for ranchers, farmers, scientists, government officials, and hunters to find common ground and build from there. Everyone in the conversation wants the best for their families. They all care about safety. They want to leave a better world for their kids and their kids' kids . . . correct? I believe that opening the conversation around such nonnegotiables is worth the effort, no matter how daunting the task may seem. This is the only viable way forward, not only to restore the natural balance for the wolves but for humans as well. If we are not willing to come out of the trenches of limiting and divisive beliefs, identities, and worldviews, I don't believe we have a bright future ahead of us. When both pro- and antiwolf groups stop trying to push their agendas, step away from old belief structures, and open their hearts, then perhaps a way will become clear.

The wolves are not the problem. We are.

Wolves' emotional processing is a lot cleaner and more direct that ours. Their perceptions are not fogged by ego. Consider how humans experience anger—as an expression of indignation and of taking offense. It is a human-generated construct: aggression plus judgment. Wolves experience aggression, an energetic surge that has a precise, calculated, and practical application. For example, wolves will aggressively correct a youngster for taking a dangerous risk, and they will respond aggressively to a threat to defend themselves. Aggression bolsters stamina and strength during a hunt; it is in service to the animal's survival. Anger is rooted in emotional imbalance and does not serve us. When humans get angry it is all ego—things are not going our way, we feel unrecognized, and our selfish desires are unmet.

When my first wolfdog, Tala—Wolf Connection's cofounder— was a pup of four or five months old, she and I went walking on the beach in Venice, California, at night. We were deeply bonded by then, a true pack of two. At one point I distinguished a soft coloration on the sand perhaps two hundred feet away that suggested that a flock of birds was either resting or picking oysters from the sand. I realized that Tala noticed them, too, because she lowered her head and picked up her pace. We took off running together and I gave Tala an instinctive command with a brisk forward motion with my arm: hunt!

It was the first time I'd done that, but Tala clearly understood because, without hesitation, she darted ahead of me and disappeared into the darkness. Her physical power was breathtaking. As I slowed I heard splashing and then the sound of casual trotting in the water. After a moment, Tala emerged from the twilight with a seagull in her mouth that was bigger than she was. The bird still flapping its wings with the last bit of energy it had. Tala dropped the majestic bird in front of me and, with two bites, crushed its entire body. Even though she was a pup, she had a powerfully calm expression on her face, and her intensity was intimidating.

I knew what I had to do. I felt a surge of adrenaline and my heart raced. I took a deep breath and pushed her mouth away from the dead bird, as if to claim the kill. I established, in that fashion, my dominance and leadership over her. As soon as we got home, I gave Tala a small piece of the bird's flesh, as her reward for the hunt, and I fully cleaned and cooked the bird to honor the kill in the way ancestral hunters would have done.

Tala taught me calm aggression without anger that night. She gave me the gift of her fierce, focused intention. She showed me how a wolf kills with an open heart—the way I have come to understand that the samurai do—and I glimpsed her primal sense of confidence and determination, something that has supported me in my personal and professional life since.

Fear is another emotion we humans experience in a peculiar way. Kira Cassidy says, "We are an interesting creature because we're the most destructive predator on the planet and yet as a species we are constantly afraid of everything. We think [we] are at the verge of doom at every turn of the corner. Wolves' decisions are based on their instincts and past experiences. They are risk-averse, of course, but I don't think wolves experience fear the way we do."[20] The human mind has the puzzling ability to create a dangerous story, believe it, project it into the world, and become fearful of it. Wolves respond to the facts of reality in their environment; we don't.

When I was a young child, about seven, I was convinced that at night someone was slowly creeping up the stairs leading to the second floor of the house. The old English-style house had two flights of wood steps with a landing in between, creating a 180-degree turn.

The solid wood steps would shift with humidity and temperature changes during the night, making creaking sounds that, to my young ears, meant someone was creeping up the stairs. I would call out to my parents in the other room in a whisper that never woke them, which meant I was on my own facing the imminent danger. Most nights I hid under the blankets, bracing myself. Some nights I was brave enough to tiptoe out of my bedroom and peek down the stairs. I never saw anyone, of course, but that never changed the perception that most nights "someone" was creeping up the stairs to murder us all.

Unfortunately, many humans remain imprinted with childhood fear such as this. Like any other prey animal, a fearful person often tends to "project" and "see" potential or even real danger everywhere. Any loud or unfamiliar sound, a fable or movie that portrays people or animals in a certain fashion, reinforces those fears.

Humans create fear-inducing scenarios. *Wolf Conflicts* notes that the group that expressed the least fear of wolves, in terms of physical-attack risk, were people living in rural neighborhoods where wolves were sighted from time to time. They had practical experience with encountering wolves and felt safe. In contrast, farmers and hunters were more likely to state that children or the elderly were at risk. This group was likely to express the feeling that they themselves were not afraid of wolves, but that "others" were and insisted that fear of wolves was potentially crippling and interfered with the "others'" quality of life.[21]

What we do not understand we fear. The rural people who had actually experienced an encounter with a wolf did not fear them, while those opposed to wolves who had never encountered a wolf expressed the greatest fear—though they did not own it.

Wolves have a rich spectrum of emotional expressions, which can help us recalibrate our emotional processing and experience. Wolves express deep sadness and loss, and grieve when a family member dies, but there is no self-pity—the loss is not about them. They also express pure affection that we can interpret as love, without any show of neediness or possessiveness. They act with complete commitment and "what's done is done," so there are no expressions or experiences of guilt or shame. They experience joy without making a display of self-centeredness.

At Wolf Connection we use the words "wolf" and "heart" interchangeably, as wolves are a constant reminder to bring our hearts to every situation, particularly interpersonal dynamics. Wolves also use heart to demonstrate psychological and emotional tenacity. Wolves often get injured, which can be a long-term challenge, but they don't self-sabotage or self-loathe, as humans do. Wolves don't feel sorry for themselves and go on living rich lives, in spite of the pain or struggle.

"That's what wolves are all about," Dan Stahler told me, when he was recounting stories of exceptional wolves in Yellowstone: perseverance. "I think a lesson to humans is a reminder of our natural instinct. Humans have come up with excuses to forget what the natural instinct is . . . in the face of adversity you don't quit, you push on."

That is true for wolves in the wild as well as for the captive animals we rescue and care for at the ranch, which is so appropriate for an organization working on the wolf-human connection, since most of us are captive humans, trapped in our conditioning, limiting beliefs, fears, and negative self-talk.

Humans and wolves carry the shared memories of our ancestral link and our joint history. Carl Jung theorized that we are born with the memories and experiences of our ancestors encoded in humanity's collective unconscious,[22] and there is a growing body of research indicating that we carry within our bodies a wealth of information from our ancestors encoded in our biological makeup, and that these records have a direct impact on how we perceive and respond to the world we live in.

Consciousness of our impact on the world, whether it is the natural environment, our local and global communities, or simply our immediate circles of coworkers, friends, and family, is no longer a luxury or a choice, but an absolute necessity. I believe we must face and consciously adapt to the complex reality of our times, both as individuals and as a species, or we very well may be on our way out, and the mighty human race, with all we know and all we've accomplished, will become another short blip in the history of this pale blue dot floating in the corner of the galaxy.

The wolf is the old friend we betrayed after he had been living alongside us for millennia. I contend that even after turning on wolves in the most ruthless way for the past few hundred years, they are still trying to rebuild our bond and continue with us on a long-lasting, sustainable journey.

REALM SIX
The Cosmic Wolf

Dreaming can only be experienced. Dreaming is not just having dreams; neither is it daydreaming or wishing or imagining. Through dreaming we can perceive other worlds, which we can certainly describe, but we can't describe what makes us perceive them. Yet we can feel how dreaming opens up those other realms. Dreaming seems to be a sensation—a process in our bodies, an awareness in our minds.[1]

THE WOLF DREAM

My body feels electrified during full moons. I can't help it. I've become increasingly aware of this in the past fifteen years, but I have probably experienced it my entire life and my parents simply blamed it on the extra ice cream after dinner.

The moon's position relative to the Earth and the sun affects the tides in large bodies of water, such as lakes and oceans. Some even claim it also affects plant life, animal behavior, and the human body. But in our modern, urban, indoor lives—overstimulated, overly distracted, overworked, and glued to our technology—we rarely look up at the moon anymore, let alone notice the effect it has on our biology and electromagnetic field.

During a full moon, my energy is as high as a high tide. A surge of fire-like energy starts at my feet and rises through my legs, up my spine, and into my neck and head. I get jittery, aggressive, and aroused. My hands are warm, my heart beats a bit faster than usual, and there is a subtle but palpable tension in my muscles, as if my entire body is ready to spring into action.

It is a very powerful and creative state, yet even though I experience it every month, it often catches me by surprise. Sometimes I'm unaware of what's happening until I reflect days later. In the meantime, it can be difficult for me to focus. If I'm not careful, I can end up misplacing that excess energy overworking, or watching TV with pizza and ice cream until 3:00 a.m.

On June 28, 2015, a Sunday, just a week after the summer solstice and a few days before the full moon, I was tired and my body ached. I fell asleep early, soon after my wife and I got our little eighteen-month-old girl to bed. The early summer night was pleasantly cool after a warm Southern California day. A soft breeze was coming through the wooden blinds at the bedroom window—a delicious night that reminded me why I had picked the high desert as the home for Wolf Heart Ranch.

At first I didn't know if I was still asleep or had woken up, but I didn't remember opening my eyes, or the shift in perception that takes place when you do. Then I realized that I wasn't experiencing the effects of gravity on my body, or any sense of *up* or *down*.

"Okay, I'm dreaming," I said, generating a dreaming sound, the kind that is not perceived with the ears.

I've had amazing, generous teachers over the past twenty years who trained me in, among other arts, the practice of dreaming the way Carlos Castaneda and Florinda Donner-Grau described it in their writings. The basic premise of it is extremely powerful in its simplicity: *become aware that you are in a dream and you can act.*

In this context, I dream quite often, both asleep and awake. However, there are only a handful of dreams that I can say have changed the direction of my life.

This dream in the summer of 2015 had that catalyst quality for me. As soon as I joined the awareness of the dream state, I felt the presence of a foreign yet strangely familiar vibration, like a different density in the "air," although there is no air in the dream world. This vibration was combined with a gentle but firm pressure in my energy field that was accentuated on my head, heart, down my spine, and the backs of my legs.

An awareness that was not my own came to the forefront of the dream experience then and introduced itself. It "said," or rather transmitted vibrationally, on a level that I could receive through images and kinesthetic sensations and translate to language, that "their" name is *Wolf*, and "they" are a collective consciousness fed by the life force of every wolf that ever existed and will ever exist—a force that is intimately woven into all physical or organic life on Earth. The way I understood it, this *Wolf* consciousness is a twin vibration to that of *Human*, one that has accompanied us since the beginning of time—humanity's connective link to physical life on Earth. *Wolf* is the key, so to speak, that unlocks the perception of physical life on Earth for humans.

Copious amounts of precise and direct information came through in the form of what *Wolf* called *Feeling*.

Wolf explained that I was able to understand their message because *Feeling* is the true universal language. We can use *Feeling* to communicate with any source of consciousness, whether it resides in biological life forms such as other human beings, animals, insects, or trees, or is emanating from elemental spirits such as those found in fire, water, wind, or minerals. We can also use *Feeling* to tap into nonphysical beings made of lighter or denser energies, as well as the consciousness of those who walked Earth before us, and the massive awareness of Earth itself, as well as other planets and celestial bodies.

The way I understood what *Wolf* said is that, at the beginning of time, or at the time of no-time, *Wolf* and *Human* were one—a united, cosmic light consciousness, omnipresent and free. In truth, we were far from being *Human* at that time, so I use the word in italics; a more energetically accurate word to describe us at that time of no-time would be to call us . . . *Wolf.*

Once I was able to assimilate that understanding into my being and my awareness, a breathtaking kaleidoscope of colors and physical sensations exploded in front of me—image after image that were *Felt* and perceived with my entire body, rather than seen with my eyes. I focused on the sensations and realized that these colors were in fact image sequences revealing a story from a time before time.

Wolf and prehumans traversed the universe together as a single frequency of consciousness. Then we dissociated and became a twin vibration—cosmic traveling partners. Our duality had the alchemical capacity to create physical life. And we manifested our consciousness corporeally in a multitude of planetary systems, and we arrived, here, together, to assume our respective physical forms.

The aspect of us that embodied on Earth found physical life on this planet fascinating, a playful experience of consciousness. Of course, we were not human yet, as humanness is an extremely recent phenomenon. And we were not even humanoid, at least not all the time, and not in the way we understand humanity today. Our physicality was fluid, so we could shift forms, not only back and forth between human-like and wolf, but also to other life forms and elements. We could regain no form and travel great distances instantaneously; time and space were not the rigid and defined continuum we experience today.

Wolf explained that, in that state of fluidity, we were able to access knowledge and consciousness directly from the cosmos. Life was not about learning information to be stored in the brain, but about experiencing and acting on the content of direct knowledge.

This connection with *Wolf* remained present on all our levels of consciousness for a very long time. How long is difficult to say, because this is not a linear description bound by the ordinary parameters of time and space, but a multidimensional tale of unity and boundless experience of consciousness that took place over aeons of time—and in a nanosecond.

Wolf went on to show me how we forged our perception of this temporal reality and conceived the self—self-reflection, self-importance, identity, or the ego, as an extraordinary, sophisticated tool for the perceptual specialization needed. As Carlos Castaneda's teacher Don Juan Matus said, "Self-importance is not something simple and naïve. On the one hand, it is the core of everything that is good in us, and on the other hand, the core of everything that is rotten. To get rid of the self-importance that is rotten requires a masterpiece of strategy. Seers, through the ages, have given the highest praise to those who have accomplished it."[2]

Wolf explained that the deleterious aspects of our self-importance rendered our perception murky as we submerged into a trance state of sorts and forgot about our cosmic origins. Our harmony with the natural world became flimsy and elusive. But our original fluid state of being and shape-shifting—that is, our cosmic traveling ability—remains dormant, a latent possibility for each of us.

Wolf revealed that the cosmic equivalent of the word "wolf" literally means "heart" and that this consciousness continues to be with us, quietly whispering messages of harmony, unity, and balance.

Wolf went on to explain that, at a few precise, strategic times, they have intervened more purposefully to help us grow and evolve. The last time this occurred was when we developed into *Homo sapiens*. *Wolf* intentionally applied extraordinary pressure on us, causing our DNA to change and evolve and, within a few generations, we began to look like modern humans.

Wolf explained that there is another period of influential imprinting coming that is of equal or greater magnitude, one that will also alter us at the DNA level. This time, however, we will not change our physical appearance as much as we did last time; rather, a cellular cleansing and optimization of regenerative capabilities will occur. The mutation will be more prominent at the consciousness level and will give way to an integration of our energetic capabilities throughout the span of our entire cosmic and Earth-bound evolution. The veil between the seen and the unseen will become our playground and the boundaries between space and time will regain their pliability.

According to *Wolf*, this process of integration of consciousness is governed by the stellar and planetary movement through the cosmos. Our solar system is entering an area of a galaxy that has a higher frequency, which in turn will raise the frequency of Earth and of all the life on it.

Humans will feel the shift the most because of how energetically handicapped we are. But this higher vibration will make it easier for most of us to do that, and almost impossible for those humans who are too invested in keeping things the way they are. And, just as it happened with our prehistoric ancestors, not everyone will make it through this evolutionary jump.

My dream vision lasted what seemed like an eternity in the sleeping-dream state, until an intense jolt of energy woke me abruptly at about one thirty in the morning. Yet the vision continued for two more hours while I was in the waking state, which was disorienting. I had been dreaming, and then I opened my eyes, and got up to sit on the floor of my studio, where I continued seeing and receiving the same sorts of images and messages I had been receiving while sleeping.

What was transmitted that night was what I understood as something that could be referred to as the original *Wolf Codex* or *Cosmic Wolf Records*: a comprehensive, integrated description of our cosmic

origins, our evolution and journey to this point, and the evolutionary success that is possible and available for all of mankind. *Wolf*
imparted to me that I could not keep the information transmitted
during this vision to myself and that it was my duty to share it
with whoever would listen. They instructed me to go find my wolf
brothers and sisters, those carrying, consciously or unconsciously,
the wolf message in their hearts and in their blood.

Once I regained my "normal" sense of self, I felt resistance to
sharing *Wolf*'s message. *Who will believe this stuff?* I thought. I knew
what I saw, and I knew to my core that it was real and true. But as
a serious man who has undergone austere training, and the founder
and director of a reputable charity rescuing animals and serving at-
risk populations, I thought, *What will happen when I tell people about
this transmission? Will I lose credibility or damage my reputation?*

Despite my resistance, I knew that this message was critical and
could bring some sense to the confused times we live in. It had to
be shared, and I had to share it—and in a way that made sense to
a broad audience of different social, religious, political, and scientific worldviews.

I sought validation of *Wolf*'s messages in different disciplines,
which led me to the research presented in this book, and confirms,
from different angles, the content in my vision. As it turns out, I am
not the only one, or the first one, to receive this conveyance. Many
cultures around the world have known aspects of *Wolf*'s message
for millennia, represented in their creation legends and ceremonies
of initiation.

Over the past four years since the "download" from *Wolf*, my
energy has increased. I feel younger and have more vigor and physical strength. My energy field had expanded, I have more power and
more clarity, and I feel less attached to both the power and the clarity.

Physical cosmology, which studies the composition of the universe and quantum theory, contains some theories that are similar

to this dream vision of our Wolf Connection.[3,4] Just prior to the Big Bang, all the matter in the multiverse was unified in a single unimaginably dense point—the singularity—which would eventually comprise the multiverse. As the singularity expanded outward, quantum theory says that all particles within it remained connected or "entangled." Because of their original interaction within the singularity, these particles continue to behave as though they are still engaged, even when separated by huge distances after the Big Bang. This means that no particle's state within the multiverse can be described independently of the state of others. Instead, we must describe a quantum state for the whole system—everything is connected to everything else.

In alternative views of time, everything occurs in an infinite present, so the explanation for entanglement is plain. If everything is now, current, and present, then the distance between particles is irrelevant. The confusion arises only because of our insistence on clinging to a mainstream conception of time.

Translating this to our cosmic relationship with wolves, I believe that since *Wolf* and *Human* were once one, before wolves were wolves and we were humans, our beings continue to behave as if we are interacting, and we continue to react to one another's energy.

Ceremonial leader Wolf Wahpepah shared with me a story that is told by the People of the Longhouse. Before humans had fire, humans and wolves shared a friendship deeper than what humans and dogs experience today. But there was a falling out. The details of the falling out have been lost, but it is known that it was the humans' fault. After that, the Creator of All Things decided that *Human* and *Wolf* would no longer be brothers, but their link could never be fully broken. From that day forward, the wolf nation and the two-legged nations would walk separate paths but would share a mutual destiny: "Whatever happens to one of our nations will happen to the other." As long as there are wolves there will be humans.[5]

We could also say that as long as there are real, compassionate, awakened humans, there will be wolves.

If the wolves lose, we all lose.

Quantum entanglement plays an important role in the biological processes of many of Earth's life forms. Some biophysicists have theorized that plants use quantum entanglement in photosynthesis, the process of using solar energy to make food out of carbon dioxide and water, but until recently there was no evidence. A UC Berkeley team of researchers, however, described how plants maximize the efficiency of photosynthesis by harnessing a feature of quantum entanglement called quantum tunneling.[6] Quantum tunneling may also be at work in the process of genetic mutation—changes in the genetic code. Cells may use quantum tunneling to selectively mutate certain genes in response to environmental signals. This mechanism allows our DNA to sit in a state of readiness, shiftable in a nanosecond to the most optimal configuration.[7] This theory runs contrary to the central dogma of biological evolution, because it implies that mutations do not occur randomly, that evolution is not blind, and that environmental conditions matter significantly in determining the speed and type of mutation that will occur.

Since the particles in our bodies are "in relationship" with all the other particles distributed through the multiverse, and since observation shifts matter from the realm of the possible into the actual, our DNA may be more flexible than previously believed. And as observers, or "dreamers," we have the capacity to "select," by means of our intentions and actions, which of all available states of being we will actualize.

According to Carlos Castaneda, we *Dream* or *Intend* our experience all the time, whether consciously or unconsciously. *Intending* means connecting our will to that of the universe itself. A seer or a person of knowledge, Dr. Castaneda said, possesses *Unbending Intent*. Human beings can *Intend* with a focus and a sustained determination that are unique in our world.

All earthly life remains energetically linked and in harmony. But in spite of our extraordinary capacity for curiosity and creativity, the human consciousness is so often at odds with the natural world. Paired with the likelihood that our particles and those of the natural world are entangled, we can conclude that our diminishing intent is worsening the world around us. For instance, the animal we call the gray wolf is merely a small physical manifestation of that consciousness, but it is also asleep to a certain degree, a mere glimpse of what it could be. Our lack of awareness paired with our untrained intent have downgraded wolves to brute animals. In the process of dumbing ourselves down, we have done this to the wolves, too. We have intended wolves just as we intend ourselves: incomplete and unresolved. The more we see or dream them as beasts, the more they become that.

In my dream download, *Wolf* said that the biological wolf is a physical, sensorial extension of the collective consciousness that is *Wolf*, and is putting on a show to reflect human behavior back at us, to improve our understanding of what we are. A lot of the violence among packs is almost a way for them to show us how ridiculous we are among ourselves.

But this can change. The earthbound wolf—this majestic animal we observe in the wild—is humanity's partner, our counterpart life form on this extraordinary planet. The way in which I understood the message—which led to the clear understanding that I now carry with me in my life and work at Wolf Connection—is that wolves are the only animals who truly care about the precarious future of humanity.

Other high-order animals such as elephants, dolphins, and whales are fond of us, but their primary concern is global natural balance. If humans get with the program and align with that, they are happy to have us; and if not, and we become detrimental to the good of all—as we currently are—then they are perfectly fine with losing us. For most other animals, we are just part of the landscape. Reptiles, for instance, carry a deep and silent wisdom that is millions of years old and they do not even register us unless we become an immediate threat, or match their vibration, which is virtually impossible for most humans. As for insects, they live in another state of reality and speed altogether.

Wolves are the ones deeply connected with helping humanity to evolve, and they want us to succeed.

FURTHER CONVERSATIONS WITH *WOLF*

As I reflected on *Wolf*'s messages in the months that followed, new questions arose that I asked *Wolf* while I was in a state of deep meditation or "dreaming awake."

Wolf said that the consciousness in early humans had plasticity; they were able to conceive and connect on many layers of existence. On the physical level, they were shape-shifters.

What's the purpose of a form if you're going to shift it a lot? I wondered.

Form brings us agreement, *Wolf* said; in form we can be in consensus. For instance, humans vibrate at a different "agreement" than elephants do. The form of elephant gives them a common place, a home to go back to in order to be *Elephant.*

I asked, "Why have humans been allowed to dominate and bring about such destruction to the world?

Wolf explained that only we interpret it as "destruction," but it is not something that really affects them at the level of consciousness. What we call "destruction" occurs at only one level of form. There is no real destruction; the natural order continues to regenerate and come back to center. *Wolf* said that there are other levels of existence where all of Earth's life forms live in balance.

The ones who suffer the most are humans, not the elephants or the trees or anything else. This other level of existence can be described as what Carlos Castaneda called "the second attention," an unseen world of awareness that exists alongside our own, but *Wolf* explained that it is "second" only to us. For them, and for most life forms, it is integrated.

For instance, the biological life form that inhabits the Earth and that we describe as wolf is integrated by a collective, global awareness. The collective being known as wolf is omnipresent, an omniconsciousness. If one wolf is killed, the consciousness of the wolf is not killed, nor does it vanish. Rather, it integrates back into the collective, almost in a transferrable fashion. *Wolf* used the image of a tree to explain this. The trunk is the collective awareness, the branches being the flares of consciousness linking out to all the leaves, which are each individual wolf. You can cut a branch with a bunch of leaves on it, but the consciousness of the tree is still there.

According to *Wolf*, when a wolf dies or is killed, the physical form expires, but the awareness lives on. In fact, it is closer to the rainbow body experienced by accomplished masters of the East, or the process of the burning fire from within described by Carlos Castaneda in his writings, a most sophisticated maneuver that allows the lifelong practitioner to retain the individuality of their consciousness at the moment of death while simultaneously merging with the consciousness of the universe at large.

The way I understood this *Wolf* transmission, wolf and human arrived here sharing consciousness as a single beam of light. They dissociated and went into a duality state. At one point wolves chose a form for its nobility, resilience, and pliability, and because it was somewhat reminiscent of the shape it had at the cosmic place of origin, though not exactly like the wolves of today. The consciousness that became human chose a more apelike shape, with hands, because of their functionality and potential. There was some kind of ape or primitive hominid, as well as wolves, when wolf-human arrived.

Researchers have enough evidence to suggest that the genus *Homo* has been on this planet for roughly 2.5 million years, and wolves have been here for about 1 million years, or 750,000 years in North America. But wolf-human arrived only a few hundred thousand years BP. So, according to *Wolf*, today's human being is not a direct evolution of the ape; instead it is more like the biological configuration was copied and upgraded, into some kind of blend or hybrid.

"What are we doing here?" I asked. "Did we come to learn, to explore? What did we come here to do?"

Wolf said that humans have a need to find meaning and purpose in everything they do but that that is only an emergency measure to find some direction in the fog of oblivion. The way I understood it, our coming here was part of the cosmic plan of expansion of consciousness that is still going on.

It has something to do with our natural environment. Earth is very different from our place of origin. It is very fun with all this green. We had some form of vegetation back home, but it is not the same type. It is a different landscape.

Earth is, or was back then, virgin, unaltered, and innocent. Coming here was simply the next step. It was an energetic flow we just rode without questioning.

Wolf says that we keep ourselves so busy because a fundamental part of us still believes that if we slow down, we will actually cease to be here. But that is an erroneous notion. In the dream vision *Wolf* showed me the time when we conceived or *dreamed* our ego. *Ego* is the Latin word for "I" and, with "me," are terms popularly used to talk about the self. "How do 'I' look?" "Am 'I' cool?" "Do they like 'me'?" "How dare they do [or say] that to 'ME'!" "What's in it for"—you guessed it—"'ME, ME, ME, ME'?!"

We think we are transcending our ego by becoming of service. So we focus on "MY" mission and "MY" purpose, on what

"I" am here to do and contribute; the legacy that "I" will leave behind. Definitely an improvement, but it is easy to see that the pattern is still intact.

Wolf said that our self-reflection is not something that we need to get rid of, kill, or destroy. Some shamans and teachers direct their students to work to achieve the "death of the ego" or the self, but if we misinterpret this, we won't have a healthy relationship with our experience on this plane of existence. Picture a friend you've been ignoring, who is consequently starting to get resentful. Sooner or later you must go back to that friend and make peace. After that, the self can become a very effective resource.

"But how are we wronging the self?" I asked *Wolf.* "Isn't it the self and the ego that are screwing us up and screwing up the world?"

A medicine man I knew once said to me, "If you resist any energy it will chase you . . . like a dog that barks at you, if you run, it will go after you. If you stand your ground and witness it, the dog will likely calm down and leave you alone." Of course, there are dogs that will come after you and attack you no matter what you do, and some do have aggressive energies, so it is important to pick your battles.

The self or ego is not meant to run the show—and people who try to serve it, or get others to do so, risk diminishing their essence or soul to the point that it is almost nonexistent. *Wolf* communicated to me that some people are not humans anymore, they are just the identity. The human *being* in them is actually dormant. They have become just a walking ego, a shell that can be very efficient because it's really good at talking to other shells. Sadly, for many people the shell is the only dependable resource they have. Other tools and abilities are atrophied and need cultivation before they can rely on them again.

Carlos Castaneda and Don Juan Matus talked about a simi- lar concept and a practice they described as "losing the human form," which means shedding our reliance on the shell and its fundamental insecurity.

Wolf said that the insecurity is not ours. It is the result of the ego, or self-reflection spinning into the fog, confused, chasing its own tail, rendering us, in this state, unable to feel or see anything. It keeps us walking in the dark.

I asked, "How can humans dominate the planet with that limited awareness?"

Wolf said that we were not meant to run over all the other species and that the bullying domination that is our defining characteristic is simply a desperate act of overcompensation.

"Why is *Wolf* making such an effort to help human beings, who made this huge mistake so long ago?" I asked.

"Because we are you," *Wolf* responded.

"Yeah, but we really screwed up," I pushed. "It sounds like we are traitors."

"No," *Wolf* said. "You are under siege . . . you are trapped, imprisoned. You are our comrades, we are just trying to free you, to help you break out of this jail to which you have the key."

WHAT'S NEXT?

I propose a new relationship with the wolf, a rekindling of our ancient bond. It is possible for humans to live in harmony not only with wolves but also with all other living beings. It is time for the wolf to assume its rightful place in the world. It is time for us not only to protect and preserve this majestic animal whose existence is critical to ecological balance but also to foster a living legacy that can help us understand where human beings came from and where we could be going. Ancient wisdom contends that activities of animals are signs, messengers for the actions of humans. Much as the polar bear is the image of the need to address global warming, and the dove is the messenger of peace. I propose that we restore the wolf as the teacher and symbol for healing the human heart.

As a species, we've almost gone extinct . . . twice, that we know of. One was an evolutionary event; the other, the result of climate change. Both times we survived by assimilating the wolf ways and by directly partnering with the wolf for survival. The wolf united us not once but twice; it can bring us together again.

Today, however, humans are at odds with the natural world, with each other, and with themselves. If we don't change willingly, other forces will make us change. If we continue to persist with behaviors that pump pollutants into the air and water, and into each other's minds and hearts, we will most likely face a man-made event of cataclysmic proportions.

To top it all off, we are facing socioeconomic challenges of no less magnitude. Our identity and place as members of modern society are at stake with the exponential advancement of infinite computing, robotics, artificial intelligence, and space exploration. Experts predict that in the next fifteen to twenty years, 45 percent of jobs will be taken up by robots. And this is not only factory jobs, but those of teachers, doctors, and law enforcement as well, to name a few. It could mean the end of today's socioeconomic systems as we know them. What if working to make a living is no longer the primary human concern; what will we do? We will still need to eat, clothe, house ourselves, and have access to health care. These will affect all areas of human endeavor, from education and community dynamics to politics and philanthropy. A different social system of value exchange and goods distribution will need to be created, perhaps one in which contribution becomes the currency. But can we do that? As a species, do we have the willingness to create new, sustainable social models and do the deep, personal inner work? *Wolf* says that good intentions are not enough anymore—they must be backed with intelligent, mature, and decisive action.

However, action prompted by current worldviews and beliefs will not suffice.

In fact, I don't believe there is a solution at humanity's present level of consciousness. Any tactic we come up with will utilize the same mental and emotional processes that created the problem in the first place. Just as there was no solution for Neanderthals or for the AMHs at the state of awareness at the time they were facing extinction, and a new level of consciousness had to emerge for survival to occur, it is imperative that we WAKE UP!

I am not talking about unattainable concepts from the top of the Himalayas. I am referring to a gradual and systemic rise of consciousness. With a small hairbreadth increase at the human collective level, the transformation would be so radical that the things that seem irreconcilable today would cease to be issues. Habits such as the obsessive accumulation of stuff (wealth, power, recognition, possessions) would cease to make any sense. Planned and perceived obsolescence would become the stupidest industrial concept ever devised. Competition for unnecessary resources would be abandoned. People's health and education as obscene profit machines rather than birthrights, the manipulation of government and power for the benefit of the few rather than the good of all, the inefficient distribution of survival essentials such as food and clothing, manufacturing processes that deplete natural resources could all become things of the past. We will realize that the way we do philanthropy is more about nuisance management, personal recognition, and self-worth than really solving issues. Most likely, the entire philanthropic sector would be obsolete. For instance, at Wolf Connection we inspire people from all walks of life, and the ranch is designed to demonstrate a higher, more sustainable way of living, but I look forward to the day when Wolf Connection is no longer needed. I aspire to the day when there are no more animals needing protection or rescue, and no more young people being mistreated or forgotten. Some might say this is utopian daydreaming, but I choose to believe that I will see that day in my lifetime, and I will certainly not stop working toward that as long as I have air in my lungs and a beat left in my heart.

Whether you believe such a world is possible or not, the bottom line is, there is no more time to defend our divisive identities and their puny, underpinning views of the world. There is no more time to hide behind our masks—being the smart one, the stupid one, the charmer, the intellectual, the conservationist, the traditional-land-use defender, etc. We must consider including in our lives experiences that are beyond what we know, beyond what we are used to, beyond what we can see and touch.

But it can be confusing. How does one differentiate cheap talk from a true spiritual offering or opening? There are many teachers and gurus, programs and courses. I live in California; you throw a rock in any direction out here and you hit a healer or shaman of some sort, and we all talk about energy, consciousness, and inner guidance.

Here is the kicker: you will never figure that one out, not with your head. You must pay attention to how the message resonates or "feels" in your body. Easier said than done for a lot of people. We are so used to thinking our way through life that *Feeling*, as *Wolf* called it—the one reliable inner compass—has become confusing and unreliable too.

But my experience is that when we stay present and we approach our lives with an open mind and open heart, there is very little to lose and so much to gain. So please, keep believing in yourself and leading your life with questions such as:

- What if the boundaries of my world, our world, are set only by limiting imagination?
- What if the world we live in is truly infinite and filled with possibilities?

- What if my experience could include not only my everyday life, but also the awareness of a global life in harmony with all living beings?

I discuss three consciousness layers with my private students. Imagine these levels stacked, like bands of experience, one on top of the other, exponentially growing in breadth, width, and magnitude as they evolve into each other . . . or imagine them as an ascending spiral with no beginning or end.

At the lower/basic level is what I call the muddy land of misery, of human suffering. A lot of people's life experiences reside at this level and they are trying to survive from day to day. Sometimes the suffering is karmic, sometimes it is rooted in upbringing, the result of a particularly intense event that creates temporary or long-lasting trauma, and looping emotional and psychological processes keep the person reliving that trauma over and over.

Then there is the band that the vast majority of people aspire to: the band of growth, whether it is financial, social, professional, psychological, emotional, physical, or spiritual. This is also the band of self-worth, self-esteem, success, and recognition. Business and life coaching, behavioral sciences, therapeutic modalities, self-help, religion, spiritual practices, time management systems, goal setting, leadership strategies, and all levels of education belong to this band. From the child dreaming of becoming an engineer or firefighter to heads of state and those at the top of their career and field, most of us live in this band of consciousness. While this band has obvious advantages over the lower/basic level in terms of quality of life, they don't differ much from each other in the sense that both are "all about me!" Me and my suffering, or me and my great success. In terms of freedom, both are shackled to the mirror of self-reflection and egomania and consequently are booby-trapped. Furthermore, the intention to move away from a state of fear and acquiring power and gaining freedom, as well as talking about universal, energy principles and sounding like, even believing, that you know what you are talking about also belongs in this band of awareness. Having sporadic "esoteric" or "out there" experiences such as dreams, insights, visions, or expansions of awareness also belong here in the sense that these experiences happen to you instead of our being able to consciously elicit them. Most people get hung up on that one experience they had years ago without ever knowing how to tap into it again.

Why is this broad band of experience booby-trapped? Because this is also the band that contains the energetic configuration of "want," "need," and "more," so no matter how much you do and how much you accomplish, you are never truly fulfilled or satisfied. Most of us know someone who seems to have everything but is not happy. In the case of some very accomplished humans, the opposite is the case: the more they have, the more obsessed they get with acquiring, controlling, or creating, often leading to unhealthy numbing behaviors that can take them straight down to the band of human suffering.

But there is a third band of consciousness and experience. This level is less known and more elusive because it does not carry any points of reference to our everyday life. But once you connect with it, its existence is unquestionably concrete. This band of consciousness and experience differs from the previous two in the sense that it constitutes a complete shift in the direction of the energy flow. Visualize the previous two bands as a funnel focusing the energy of perception and experience on the individual. The self is the end of the line, so it is virtually impossible not to see the world through the me, me, me lens. But if we are able to sustain our focus and resolve, that current of energy can shift direction and flow from self-reflection as the recipient and focus of attention, to self as a conduit of consciousness and expression of something much greater. This is an entirely different ball game that opens up infinite possibilities, not only for humans but also for all other living beings since, as we change our perception, we also shift the reality of the world around us. Power, freedom, mission, purpose, growth, or suffering are no longer central concerns, and there is a pervasive experience of "enough." Paradoxically, the fulfillment at this level is so much greater than anything we can ever imagine from the perspective of the other two bands of experience, and yet it is not about us, not about me, myself, or I.

This is the level *Wolf* is offering for all of humanity, truly heaven on Earth, and it is worth every possible effort—hence, WAKE UP!

REALM SEVEN

The Mythological Wolf

I consider myth a source of knowledge, and emphasize, in the work we do at Wolf Connection, the traditions that depict the ancient connection between wolves and humans, through a wolf-centric lens. Joseph Campbell wrote, "Myth is much more important and true than history."[1]

Myth and science can be reconciled, particularly when we see mythology and traditional knowledge as prescience.[2] Raymond Pierotti, a professor in ecology and evolutionary biology at the University of Kansas, is working to establish the validity of oral history. Pierotti discusses what he calls "indigenous science," a systemic scheme for understanding the world in which the relatedness of all things lies at the core of mythological accounts of phenomena. Myth may not be verifiable, but neither can the explanations passed through oral traditions be disproven.

I believe that modern, evidence-based science neither negates nor replaces ancestral, mythological knowledge, but rather acts as a complementary stream of understanding. At a fundamental level, there is no fixed boundary between science and spirituality; rather it is precisely at their intersection of the provable and the believable that a fuller understanding of the natural world becomes possible. If creation and evolution theories could be unified for humankind today, perhaps we could understand the extraordinary journey that is life on this exquisite planet Earth.

Years ago, other teachers and I facilitated a series of Carlos Castaneda Tensegrity workshops titled "We Were All Shamans," which were *Dreamt* to help participants reawaken their ancestral selves. The practices presented at those gatherings could help us remember a time when, as a species, we looked to the stars and the natural world around us for answers. We encouraged people to reach back to a time when earth, fire, water, and wind were sacred elements with intelligence, conveying meaning and messages—a time when animals were allies and carried powerful medicine. We collectively sought a time when life was simpler and intentional, and our actions had a deliberate purpose.

In those ancient times, we gathered around a fire in a cave, tee-pee, kiva, yurt, igloo, or stone temple. Or we met in the open plains, jungle, forest, or desert, on a mountaintop, or at the bottom of a ravine. We offered tobacco, sage, palo santo, cedar, sugar, cacao, animal or human hair, copal, and even blood. And we bonded. We shared purpose, meaning, and teachings in the form of stories. We were intentional in the transmission of legends. We relived myths through the practice of ancestral ritual.

The wolf-related myths, stories, and legends that I recount here reflect visions and messages similar to the one *Wolf* gave me. As I assembled wolf legends from around the world, I paid particular attention to places and peoples that may have been previously overlooked, including remote areas of Finland and Mongolia, as well as Tibet and China. In many cases, the originating culture we sought had undergone profound changes over the centuries and millennia. Dominant civilizations and cultures throughout history have tried to eliminate the existing ways of the conquered, seeing them as threats. In many Eurasian cultures, the beliefs of the First Peoples have been lost or distorted by the cultures that attempted to replace them. By looking at the myths of related language groups, however, I found relatively intact and unique wolf traditions and stories from eastern and northern Europe, as well as parts of Asia, some of which have not previously been accessible in English texts.

A WESTERNER'S VIEW

At first it was difficult for me to connect with many of the stories, most of which appeared meaningless or even nonsensical to me, like children's simple fables with poor story lines. But I realized that I was reading these stories from the very perspective I so often criticize, that of the Westerner who discards anything that does not match his expectations or preconceived ideas, that doesn't supply enough of an "adrenaline shot" or an entertainment thrill.

My teacher Carol Tiggs shared an article with me titled "When Scientists 'Discover' What Indigenous People Have Known for Centuries," which goes on to say, "When it supports their claims, Western scientists value what Traditional Knowledge has to offer. If not, they dismiss it."[3] This article and a *National Geographic* article[4] discuss the recently "discovered" behavior of three different species of hunting birds in northern Australia that are dubbed "firehawks" because they intentionally carry burning sticks to spread fire, causing rodents and other small prey to flee into an open field, where they can be easily hunted. While this finding attracted great attention in the scientific community, "the behaviors of the . . . hawks have long been known to the Alawa, MalakMalak, Jawoyn, and other Indigenous peoples of northern Australia whose ancestors occupied their lands for tens of thousands of years."[5] These birds are even represented in some of their ceremonial practices, beliefs, and creation accounts. But until now that knowledge was dismissed as myth because neither scientists nor credible academics had documented the behavior.

This begs the question: How many other "mythological" facts from indigenous peoples around the world have been arrogantly dismissed and remain unknown to modern society to this day?

Trudy Spiller, a member of the Gitxsan First Nation and keeper of stories for the Gitxsan wolf clan to which she belongs, told us that wolves shared the wolf way of living with people to help them. She said that wolves embody humility, and that to follow their lead, people must adopt that humility themselves.[6] The irony was not lost on me. There I was, studying ancestral wolf mythology while bringing my own biases and arrogance with me.

But if we are to survive as a species on this planet, we must bring forth something other than self-importance. It is time that we realize—or remember, rather—that we are not separate from the natural world, nor are we all-powerful over it.

In *The Power of Myth*, Joseph Campbell writes that people are not really seeking to find the meaning of life, because meaning, in his view, is in the limited realm of the mind. What we are really seeking, at a conscious and/or unconscious level, Campbell believes, is an experience of being fully alive.[7] I would add that we are seeking an experience of being in this body, in this realm and reality, since there are many ways of being alive that we cannot necessarily see, hear, or touch.

After I stopped trying to find "meaning" in the stories, I was able to perceive that the stories reveal an experience of being alive, in a different time, in a different belief system, and—in Dr. Castaneda's words—beyond our syntax and interpretation. Reaching deep into my training, I closed my eyes and intended my consciousness to "journey" to the time these stories were originally told and focused on the vibration and mood behind the words. In this way, I was able to touch the shaman in me, and read the stories again, allowing them to reach me at a non-logical level.

Now I am asking you to close your eyes and take a few deep breaths to help you slow down. Use the breath to circulate your energy from the top of your head all the way down, six to twelve inches below your feet and into the earth. And call upon your ancestral, wiser self, the part of you that is timeless and ever connected. And as you get there, begin imagining. Feel yourself sitting comfortably by a fire. Visualize the circle of women and men to your left and to your right, all gathered to be with one another, to share and receive wisdom . . . to be.

Here are those stories that speak clearly of a time when our wolf connection was intact. They reveal the nature of humanity's original relationship with *Wolf*. They reveal a time when we all understood that everything is connected to everything else, and that everything is aware, because everything is energy.[8] At a practical level, these stories show that in cultures across the Northern Hemisphere, the wolf was recognized as our greatest teacher, and the old way of seeing our place in the world contained no hierarchy of life forms.

WOLVES OF CREATION

First Nations peoples live in every ecoregion of North America, from the Arctic to the Southwest. Most of these First Peoples are organized within clan systems—or groups of interrelated families— and many have a wolf clan.[9] These clans are based on matrilineal inheritance, which is traced through the maternal bloodline. The clans are also usually exogamous, meaning that one cannot marry a member of one's own clan.

Many myths about wolves are creation stories, often clan-specific, but they can also be about the origin of an entire nation. Though they come from all different regions of the continent, the stories that appear here all share a worldview in which wolves play a central role—they are the ancestors, they are the teachers, they are the beginning point for human development.

THE WOLF PEOPLE
The Kwakwaka'wakw

Some First Nations peoples who live on the Pacific Northwest coast of North America describe themselves as being descendants of wolves. The Wakashan-speaking peoples on the Pacific coast of British Columbia, including the Kwakwaka'wakw, are descended from four wolves who survived a great flood because they were able to get to a high mountain, then shed their wolf-skins to become the first humans.[10] The Kwakwaka'wakw also maintain a wolf clan as part of their social structure, whose members are descendants of the original four wolves. Similarly, the Gitxsan of northwestern British Columbia, though of a different language group, also have a wolf clan as one of their society's four. Members of the Gitxsan wolf clan received their instructions for how to organize their clan and conduct themselves directly from wolves . . . possibly in the way I received my instructions directly from *Wolf*.

The Dene People

Immediately south of the Arctic tundra is the Boreal ecoregion, a landscape of taiga, forest, and lakes. The taiga or "land of little sticks" is a sparse forest of stunted trees that lies along the northern edge of the Boreal Forest. The Dene people, members of the Athabaskan or Na-Dené language–speaking peoples, live across the central and western Boreal ecoregion of Canada, up into Alaska. They are related to the southwestern tribes—the Apache and Navajo—as well as the Hupa and Cahto of California. Dene elder Patrick Robillard says that his people "were always big game hunters depending solely on the caribou for their existence. All aspects of Dene life were wrapped around the idea of survival and dependency on the barren land caribou. Spiritually, the Dene called themselves 'The Wolf' and believed they were the direct descendants of the original wolf clan. The Dene word for 'us' is *nnü*, which is also the word for wolf in Dene. The elders tell us that we lived as one with the land like animals, and we had to in order to survive the long, cold climates of the taiga-tundra of northern Canada."[11]

The Quileute

Farther south along the Pacific coast from the Kwakwaka'wakw are the Quileute people. The Twilight Saga series of novels by Stephenie Meyer fictionalized stories of Quileute youth who shape-shift into oversize wolves. The Quileute people have powerful wolf creation stories, and their name comes from their word for wolf, *kwoli*. Their origin story, as told by Quileute elders and Chris Morganroth III, goes as follows:

"The Changer or Transformer is called Kwati, and he was put on the Earth by the Creator. Kwati was given the task of setting things right in the world, including making the Earth beautiful and abundant. Whenever the times changed, Kwati would be there to set things in balance, to make the transition smooth.

"Long ago, when the animals could talk, they could become people by taking off their skins. In many places along the Pacific Coast, there were no people, because the animals had all chosen to keep their skins on. When Kwati went to Qui-lay-ot land, he saw that it was very beautiful, much too beautiful for there not to be any people. Then he saw two big wolves, and the Changer clapped his hands together and with a loud sound of thunder he made them into human beings. All the things the new people needed were provided for them there by Kwati, and they stayed in that land from that day onward.

"The Quileute people were the first to be made by Kwati, but others followed, also made from animals. For example, when Kwati came to the area where the Quinault reservation is now to visit his brother who lived in that place, he saw a beautiful lake, so clear, but so empty of life. He reached into the water and rubbed his hands together until pellets of skin on his palms came loose, then he rinsed them in the water, and that skin came to life and formed the sockeye salmon. He then summoned two of the salmon, a male and a female, and transformed them into human beings, and they became the first Quinault people.

"As he continued along the coast, Kwati went to each place where there were no people, and transformed pairs of animals into humans—whales, eagles, bears, beaver, and so on. Each pair became humans by leaving their animal skins. This is how the clans came to be. Each clan celebrates their origin in the winter ceremonials, when they remember how they came to be and honor their ancestors."[12]

The Pawnee People

The Pawnee lived in the heart of the American portion of the central Plains. "Wolf Star" describes how the Pawnee were created and became the "Wolf-People."

"The Pawnee creation spirits gathered together where the people lived. The creation spirits were called together by the One, but the One forgot to call on Wolf Star Spirit. He found out about the great council meeting, and he was angry, blaming the trouble on Paruksti, the Storm of the West, whom the spirits sent out to inspect the people's Place to be sure of its completeness. Paruksti carried the people in a whirlwind leather bag. Whenever he was tired, he would set the bag down and the people would come out, set up camp, and have a buffalo hunt. After Paruksti had rested, he would gather the people up in his leather bag and go on his way. Wolf Star Spirit noticed this. He placed Wolf on the Earth to follow Paruksti. One time when Paruksti was asleep with his head on the leather bag, Wolf came. Wolf gently pulled on the bag. He took the bag to the flat lands. The people came out, set up camp, and prepared to hunt for buffalo. Except there were no buffalo. They saw Wolf and invited him to eat their dried meat with them and share in stories. Paruksti awoke. Frightened at the loss of his leather bag and the people, he hurried to the flat lands. When he saw Wolf, he chased him and told the people of Wolf's identity. The people pursued Wolf and killed him. Paruksti did not like this. He told the people that they would have to take Wolf's skin, dry it, make a sacred bundle of it, and always be known as the Skidi, or Wolf-People. Paruksti told the Great Spirits of what had happened. They met with the people, telling them that since they had brought death to the Place, they had also brought death to themselves. . . .

"Just before dawn, the sacred Wolf skin lifted from the ground. Some say that it turned back into the shape of Wolf and ran into the sky to become Tskirixki-tiuhats, or the Star of Wolf-He-Is-Deceived. It is said that it appears in the southeast just before the rising of the Morning Star. Wolf constellation deceives the wolves, who begin howling to greet the morning. Those who had killed first Wolf became wolves themselves. Now they run howling in their sorrow, only to be hunted themselves."[13]

WOLF-HUMAN TRANSFORMATION STORIES
Peoples from the Eastern Region

The forested lands surrounding the Great Lakes are home to the Algonquin-speaking peoples of the Anishinaabe, a group of inter-related tribes that include the Algonquin, Nipissing, Mississauga, Potawatomi, and others.[14] The Anishinaabe peoples place the wolf clan into the Nooke clan group, composed of the Bear, the Lynx, and the Wolf. Members of these clans are responsible for both defense and healing.[15] The Lenape People, also known as the Delaware First Nation, live east and south of the Great Lakes. The Lenape are considered by other Algonquin speakers to be "the grandfathers" from whom the other Algonquin-speaking peoples originated, and their clan system includes the Wolf, Turtle, and Turkey.[16]

The Iroquois Confederacy was originally made up of five nations—the Seneca, Oneida, Onondaga, Cayuga, and Mohawk—with the Tuscarora joining in 1722, all of whom have Wolf Clans. The Seneca story "Granny Wolf" is unique because it describes an aspect of wolf clan membership that is not normally revealed publicly—the gift of wolf transformation.[17]

"Mike Bastine remembers a woman, an old storyteller from Allegany, who knew someone who could shift her shape. It was her grandmother. When she was a girl, she used to like sleeping over with her grandmother, but many a time she woke late at night with the feeling she was alone in the house. When she checked, it was always true. Where had her grandmother gone? When she was older, she tried to stay awake to see her grandmother come back. She never succeeded, though once near dawn she heard someone come in and go straight to her grandmother's room. That afternoon, as she played with the other children, she found wolf tracks all around her grandmother's house. One night when she heard the sounds of her grandmother leaving on the other side of the house, she looked out her window. She believed she saw the form of a wolf lope off through the moon shadows into the trees. One morning a short time later, her grandmother didn't get up. The girl found her in bed with a wound in her leg. There was blood leading from the window to the covers. 'Don't worry, dear, I'll be all right,' said the old dame. 'I just need to rest awhile.' The girl asked about her leg. 'Darn it. I was walking in the woods and there was this sharp stick out. Got me right here. I'll be all right.' The little girl took a breath. 'Uh, Grandma . . . one time when you left at night I'm pretty sure I saw a wolf run into the woods. I've been meaning to ask you about that for a long time.' At first the grandmother dismissed the matter, but the girl wouldn't let it go. 'I always knew you were a smart little girl,' she said. 'Well, I have to tell you something just for you. You're right, honey. There have always been some of us who've gone around like that at night. I'm one of the only ones I know anymore who still does it. But that's how I keep an eye on the neighborhood and make sure everything's all right. You can't go all over the yards and woods like that like a person. I make sure people are treating each other right, and if I have to get involved, well, I do it my own way. Sometimes I wonder why.' She groaned. 'That old Mr. Jamison would just drink all his money away and there'd be nothing left for the family. Somebody has to scare him into keeping home at night. Mary Snow is out at all hours with her boyfriend and just about anything could happen to those little kids of hers if somebody didn't keep an eye out. And if Davey Green ever hits his wife again, he has to know something's coming for him. Now this story is just for you,' she finished. 'If this got out and around in the community'—she shook her head—'it wouldn't be good. It wouldn't be good at all.' She rolled over and groaned. 'That's all for now, honey. I have to get some rest. You run home and tell your mom to come over later. Boy, it's lucky that darn farmer's such a bad shot, or he'd have got me for good.'"

Peoples from Southeastern North America

The Cherokee of the Southeast Forest of North America—one of the Algic language–speaking peoples—describe in "Medicine and the Wolf Clan" how the healing arts came to their clan. This striking wolf medicine–teaching story is rare, as most medicine knowledge is kept secret. Normally only initiates would hear it, and they can only share it with another initiate.[18]

"In the old days, it's said, that back in the very, very beginning times, after the villages were built, it was an old man who came walking out of the woods, and he had sores all over his body, and he came down to the clans of the Cherokee, and he said to the first woman in charge of the first clan, 'Would you take me and make me well?' And she said, 'Oh, you look so terrible, we don't know how to make you well. Go away.' The man goes down to another clan of the Cherokee, it could have been the blue clan, and the woman comes out and says, 'We have children here. Don't, don't bother us, please go away.'

"Again and again he's turned away from these villages, and eventually he comes to the wolf clan of the Cherokee. All the terrible sores on his body, and he says to the woman of the wolf clan, 'Will you bring me in and make me well?' She says, 'I don't know what to do for you. But if you'll come in, we will lay you down upon the bed, and we will do everything we possibly can to make you better.'

"He went in, and he lay down upon the bed, and he sent her out to the forest the first day and said, 'Get the bark of the cherry tree and bring it back and make a tea to let me drink.' And she did. And his cold went away. 'Go back to the willow tree and get some bark and make it into a poultice and wring it and put it upon my sores.' And she did. And the sores went away.

"Again and again, for a long time, he sent her into the forest, telling her every time a certain cure for a certain ailment. After a while he was completely healed. Then one day he got up from the bed and said, 'Since you were good to me, I have taught you, the women of the wolf clan, all the cures of the forest. And from this day forward, you, the women of the wolf clan, will be the doctors of the communities and the reservations.' "[19]

The key feature of this story is the fact that the wolf clan woman, by embodying a principal teaching of her wolf clan—that one must care for the sick and the old with total commitment—receives the gift of medicine plant knowledge.

Winnebago Peoples

Among the Winnebago peoples, each clan has their own creation stories. Each version reveals a different aspect of the tribe's long history and varies according to which clan has kept them. Here is one of the surviving versions of the wolf clan origin story:

"In the beginning of the Wolf clan, people came from the water. Therefore, their bodies are of water—i.e., their sacred possession is water. There were four male wolves and four female wolves, and as they came up from the sea and swam toward the shore, one after the other, they caused waves to go before them. Therefore one of their clan names is *Wave*. They first appeared as wolves, and later on they became humans. After swimming to the shore they lay on their backs to dry themselves; and that also is a name, a female name, *She-who-spreads-herself-out-to-dry*, and another name is *He-who-comes-up-first*.[20]

"When Winnebago tribal expeditions cross a body of water, a wolf clansman may be called upon to still the winds. Water is the sacred possession of the wolf clan, and it is considered impolite for visitors in a wolf clan lodge to look into any container of water."[21]

Huichol Peoples

The Huichol Peoples of the Jalisco, Nayarit, Durango, and Zacatecas regions of Mexico still practice wolf shamanism. This creation story also describes the path for becoming a wolf shaman.[22]

The myth surrounding the origins of the Huichol describes that, in the beginning, men were part wolves, who lived in darkness without yet having acquired the art of hunting. One day, a Deer Person allowed the Father of the Wolves to hunt him. While the wolf was devouring him together with his companions, the Deer Person transformed into a peyote. The wolves ate him and acquired great wisdom. They came out of the darkness and into the sun, which gave them the option to become either wolves or human beings. They chose the second option, and the Father of the Wolves was the first person to construct a temple for the divinities, where a special place was set aside and dedicated to the Kumukemai Uru-yare, the Arrow of the Wolves, so that human beings could always communicate with them.

For the Huichol People, wolves represent their mythical ancestors and are cultural heroes, fast, powerful, cooperative in hunting, carniv-orous, and monogamous, which meant that the shaman who wished to obtain the status of wolf shaman had to observe the same rules.

The account of Ulu Tennay, a wolf shaman who completed this apprenticeship successfully, describes the apprenticeship for those who wish to become wolf shamans. It may continue for five to ten years, during which the candidate must visit six different wolf shrines, dedicated to different-colored wolves: red, yellow, white, blue, multicolored, and gray, and complete a precise ceremonial procedure, making offerings of various types.

Ulu Tennay recounted that during his transformation he contin-ued to see his human form, though others saw only his wolf form. Ulu Tennay's grandfather had also been a great wolf shaman who would often come to the house with his wolf friends.[23]

Peoples of Siberia, Northern Russia, and Finland

The indigenous peoples of Siberia, northern Russia, and Finland have practiced wolf shamanism for thousands of years. Genetically related to the indigenous people of North America, these cultures have retained much of their oral history and traditions. At one time, anthropologists only recognized shamanism as something specific to Siberia, but today it is understood that the practices of hunter-gatherer and nomadic cultures from across northern Europe and Asia are akin to those of the First Peoples of North America.

"In the beginning there lived a man-bear; the dog was also a man. Both of them guarded the creations (*ona-lban*) of Christ (as Seveki had been named) and were his helpers. Satan was Christ's older brother. When Christ went away the dog guarded his house. Once Satan (originally named Khargi) came. 'Open up Christ's house,' he said. 'I will not,' said the dog. However, he did eventually open it. Satan let in all the snakes and worms. He gave fur to the dog. Christ came home. 'What did Satan do here?' he asked. 'Satan dressed the dog.' Christ was angry and said, 'Now you will be a dog, be without speech, eat only bad food, live only ten years, smell with your nose, bark with your mouth.' He said to the bear, 'You sleep in the course of the year together with the chipmunk and do not touch the Evenks.' But to the wolf, who then was also a man, he said, 'You will be a master on the Earth. If you want to eat (man) eat him, one at a time.' And the raven (*oli*) was also a man. To him he said, 'You go thither, and follow everybody.' That is why the raven eats everything that his younger brother (i.e., man) kills, and why he flies."[24]

To kill a wolf is considered a very dangerous act, because when the other wolves learn of this, they seek revenge upon the hunter. To escape the wrath of the wolves, many indigenous cultures in Eurasia perform a ritual to direct the wolves to someone else on whom they are blaming the crime—usually their enemies. "When the Chuck-chees (Chukchis) of northeastern Siberia have killed a wolf, they hold a festival, at which they cry, 'Wolf, be not angry with us. It was not we who killed you, it was the Russians who destroyed you.' "[25]

Note that the Chukchi are not just making a gesture to avoid the revenge of the wolf's relatives; they are also honoring the wolf they have killed.

Tuvan . . . Turkic-Mongol

In the Siberian Tuvan culture, "The wolf is a very powerful sha-manic helping spirit, and in the North there are tales of women turning into wolves to rescue lost souls."[26]

The ancient Tuva tradition is possibly the source of the earliest version of Turkic beliefs. Tuvans view the wolf as a protective entity that can guard people from illness, are beneficial and benevolent to humans, and will not harm them. The wolf is the shaman's helper, not just in healing practices, but also acting as a protective companion. In ancient times, wolves connected the shaman to other worlds. He or she might also transform into a wolf to battle enemies. The practice of wolf transformation can also be found in Turkey itself. "The *kurtadam* of Turkey was considered in lore to be a shaman or benevolent witch, who after very long and difficult spiritual rites could become a werewolf. Contrary to opinions of werewolves throughout the rest of Europe, the Turkish shamans who had the power to become a kurtadam were actually held in great respect."[27]

Tuvans believe that wolves have the power to converse with humans without using words. Their shamans state that wolves can stand against infinity—meaning they can claim their own destiny—being one of only a handful of animals with this ability, in addition to human shamans. Wolves are referred to as "the elevated ones," and their images appear on objects that have special significance in shaman practices, especially drums, which create a connecting link between the two worlds, between which wolves are intermediaries. Tuvans describe how the female wolf is the ultimate leader of a wolf pack, a matriarch that makes the life-and-death decisions for her kin. Significantly, in Tuvan culture, it is women who carry the songs, the musically encoded oral history of the people.[28]

In Turkic-Mongolian mythology, wolves are creatures of changeable nature with transformative powers, which only a handful of uniquely powerful animals have. Tuvan prayers mention a six-mouthed wolf, which may be connected to the ancient Japanese name for their wolf god, Ooguchi no Magami, whose name literally translates as The Large-Mouthed Pure God.[29]

Wolf Peoples of China

The Wu, the founding culture of China, practiced shamanism and, like their Turkic and Siberian neighbors, believed that they were descended from wolves. One of China's oldest origin legends is about A-se-na, a hero descended from wolves:

"The oldest hero of all in ancient China was A-se-na, the founder of the Tujue dynasty, known only through the Chinese transcription of a dubious word. Born of a she-wolf and a young Hiong-nu, he married the daughters of the gods of summer and winter, unknown elsewhere."[30]

This is strikingly similar to the story of Ashina, the founder of the Goturks, whose mother also was a she-wolf. Another ancient hero of the Wu peoples, Kunmo, was rescued by animals, fed by birds, and raised by a she-wolf in the desert.

The Nanai or Goldi, a marginalized culture that has maintained shamanistic practices involving wolf transformation, live in China's Heilongjiang province as well as in the Russian region of Khabarovski Krai. The following account about being chosen by his helping spirit, or *ayami*, is from a Goldi shaman:

Once I was asleep on my sickbed, when a spirit approached me. It was a very beautiful woman. . . . She said, "I am the *ayami* of your ancestors, the shamans, I taught them. . . . Now I am going to teach you." . . . She has been coming to me ever since, and I sleep with her as with my own wife, but we have no children. . . . Sometimes she comes under the aspect of an old woman, and sometimes under that of a wolf.[31]

In the mideastern Han region in the 110s CE, a tiger plagued a southern region and there were also wolf attacks. In an edict, the governor explained that the human intrusion on natural habitats and excessive hunting were the causes of these attacks.

In general, the residence of tigers and wolves in the mountains and forests is like the residence of human beings in cities and markets. *In antiquity, in the age of complete transformation, wild animals did not cause any trouble.* All this originated from the fact that grace and trust were wide-ranging and abundant, and benevolence reached the avian and running species. Although I, your governor, possess no virtue, how could I dare to neglect this righteous principle. (Therefore) when this note arrives, let cages and pit-traps be destroyed, and do not recklessly go trapping in mountains and forests.[32]

The italic text within this quote is a direct reference to the earlier shamanistic culture of the Wu period of Chinese history, when human transformation into animal form occurred and the relationship between humans and animals was harmonic. The governor's insight and compassion for tigers and wolves is remarkable, and stems from his knowledge of history, and his understanding of how people should behave.

By the time Buddhism had taken hold in China, the relationship between wolf and human had changed greatly. The story of the Zongshan Wolf, a popular fable first found in print in the Ming Dynasty of sixteenth-century China, portrays the wolf as deceitful and ungrateful.

A wolf, on the run from pursuing hunters in the Zhongshan area of the kingdom of Zhao, asks a traveling scholar named Master Dongguo if he may hide in the scholar's book bag. After the hunters have left, the scholar lets the wolf out of the bag. However, as soon as it is safely free, the wolf wants to eat the scholar.[33]

The man persuades the wolf not to eat him and ultimately through his own trickery kills the wolf.

Tibetan Wolf Stories

Tibet is a land of extremes—the largest and highest plateau in the world, with an average altitude of more than thirteen thousand feet. Genetic adaptation to high altitude for better oxygen utilization allows Tibetans to perform physical tasks at such high elevations that lowland people cannot. Recent genetic analysis reveals that Tibetans are most closely related to the Yi people of the Hengduan Mountains, immediately east of the Tibetan Plateau, but are not as closely related to Asian populations to the west and south of the Himalayas.[34]

The close genetic relationship between Tibetans and other Asian shamanistic cultures is echoed in the overlap between their belief systems and religious practices. Shamanism still has a strong presence in Tibetan culture, although it is deeply integrated with Buddhist practices.

In the Vajrakilaya cham dance—Dance of the Dagger—ceremony, from the eighth century, the time of Buddha, two lamas representing a wolf (*spyang ku*) and a hawk (*khra*) wear masks to symbolize their transformation into animal form. They dance to round up and destroy the various harmful influences and spirits, which are then led to a fire to be burned. So, at some point in Tibetan culture, the wolf was a protecting spirit animal, as in many other Asian shamanic cultures.[35]

Peoples of Scandinavia

The beliefs and practices of marginalized hunter-gatherer and nomadic peoples of North America and Eurasia have managed to some degree to escape suppression by modern cultures. Connections between Scandinavian and Sami culture are clear in their oldest myths. This creation story of the Norse people, "The Story of Odin and His Companions," has similar themes to other indigenous peoples' origin stories, and includes the incorporation of a wolf clan in their society.

"It was once told that Odin and his brothers created the world. In loneliness while traveling Odin created the First Wolves, Geri and Freki, to accompany him in his travels and to be partners in the hunt. The wolves became Odin's special companions. Wherever Odin went, the wolves went with him.

"Odin traveled all over the world with the wolves. This explains why there are wolves in so many places in the world. As they traveled with Odin, Geri and Freki left their grown offspring behind to enjoy the riches of the New World. Geri and Freki cured Odin's loneliness. The way the wolves celebrated life filled Odin with joy.

"Odin also created two ravens, Hugin and Munin, to help scout ahead as they traveled. Hugin and Munin were very good at finding game and were always hungry. Hugin and Munin were not able to take game by themselves, but teamed with Geri and Freki, they were well fed. To this day, you will often find ravens in the company of their friends the wolves. The ravens still scout out the game for the wolves, and the wolves leave a share of the meal for the ravens in thanks.

"When Odin created the humans Embla and Ask (from whom all humans sprang), he instructed them to learn from the wolf. The wolf could teach them how to care for their family, how to cooperate with each other in the hunt for food, and how to protect and defend their families.

"The wolf gave much wisdom and skill to the early humans. In the old times the wolf was respected. To be wolf clan (Ulfhednar) was a great honor: a wolf brother."[36]

Note the similarities between this ancient Norse creation story and those of other indigenous peoples from Eurasia and

North America, including the practice of incorporating a wolf clan into the social structure.

Medieval Europe

The Old English term *were-wulf* first appeared in written form in England during the reign of King Cnut, a Danish prince who assumed power in England in 1016 and later in Denmark as well.[37] Wolf-positive beliefs were reflected in the given names of the king's advisers and important members of eleventh-century England, such as Werwulf; Ethelwulf, "the noble wolf"; Berthwulf, "the illustrious wolf"; Eadwulf, "the prosperous wolf"; Ealdwulf, "the old wolf"; and many more.[38]

The story of Anglo-Saxon King Edmund tells us that during the ninth century, he was captured by the Danish and brutally tortured to recant his Christian loyalty, but Edmund would not be broken. Realizing that, Ivar, the leader of the Danish army, had Edmund beheaded and his head thrown in the woods. His followers went looking for his head and began hearing a voice guiding them, calling, "Here!" in Latin. When they arrived at the place the voice was guiding them to, they saw a monstrous wolf, stretched at full length on the ground, embracing the king's head with its front paws.[39] Today a statue of a giant wolf guards his grave at the Abbey of Bury St. Edmunds, a place of pilgrimage for centuries.

Prior to Christianization, both the Anglo-Saxons and the Danes had warrior cultures in which wolf transformation was a central theme, when to be wolf-like was to be both noble and courageous.

At the beginning of the medieval period in Europe, werewolves were not seen as people suffering from a disease, but rather as humans who were capable of voluntary transformation into the shape of a wolf. Wolf transformation stories, such as the epic poems of Melion, Bisclavret, and Gorlagon, depict their central figures as heroic and life-affirming, embodying selfless service to others. These men-become-wolves are not overcome by taking on wolf form, do not eat humans, and are in fact the farthest things from cannibals. When these epic poems were written, popular culture in early medieval Europe still held wolves and those who could transform into wolves as romantic figures, not horrible monsters.[40]

Since this act of physical transformation challenged the teachings of the Christian Church, as well as the increasingly rational view being adopted by priests and scholars, the definition of a werewolf changed over time to a human who *believed* he was transformed into a wolf, though no actual change of form had physically occurred. No longer an act of conscious volition, a werewolf was a deluded person and was either himself a witch or warlock, or someone who had been ensorcelled by a witch or warlock to become a werewolf.

In the last two decades of the sixteenth century, widespread war and famine could well have pushed poor people to cannibalism. In this same period, wolves are reported to have become very bold and to have attacked humans with increased frequency. Combine this with the seven-century influence of the Catholic Inquisition, and it is not difficult to see how people committing crimes involving cannibalism came to be accused of being werewolves. This is the point in history when the depiction of werewolves shifts entirely from positive to negative, and the vilification of wolves was complete.[41]

German humanist and cartographer Sebastian Münster wrote in the 1550 version of the *Cosmographia*, which was the earliest German-language geographical description, that "In this land there are many sorcerers and witch-women, who adhere to the erroneous belief—which they have often confessed before court—that they become wolves, roam about, and cause harm to all they encounter. Afterwards they transform back into human shape. Such people are called werewolves."[42]

Münster is referring to testimony collected from people accused of witchcraft living in Livonia during the Inquisition. Of those who were on trial, Thiess the Werewolf stands out. The words of Thiess the peasant were not recorded, but the inquisitor's interpretation of his testimony reads, "men, incited by the Devil, appear in the shape of a cruel wolf and roam the land, and harm both men and livestock."[43] Yet the people accused of being werewolves did not see themselves as agents of the Devil, but rather as agents of God. Thiess claimed that he, as a werewolf, was a "Hound of God" who hunts and fights sorcerers and who was "certain to enter heaven as a reward after his death." In the peasant counterculture, the idea of a "benevolent werewolf" still survived.[44]

Donecker notes, "Common folk were still engaging in wolf-transformation practices in the late 1600s, in spite of persecution by the Church. Tallin wrote, "In what is now north-western Estonia, "there were still some sorcerous peasants capable of transforming themselves into wolves. But fortunately . . . such misdeeds had almost disappeared, thanks to the continuous efforts of the clergy to instruct the peasants in the Christian faith." Wolf practices were expunged by the Church by threats of torture.[45] The only convincing explanations for why people continued practices for which punishment was so severe are great bravery and compassion—for love. Healing the sick, protecting the crops from harm, helping a woman to conceive, reducing her pain in childbirth—for these things, they risked being burned at the stake. They were not evil werewolves; they were practitioners of an ancient art, one that their ancestors had passed on to them, that harkened back to the days when humans and wolves walked together, in harmony, and performed acts of altruism, even in the face of death.

REALM EIGHT

The Ritualistic Wolf

Wolf societies not only believed their myths, they also lived them. Numerous cultures in the Northern Hemisphere still maintain their oral histories and perform rituals to pass on knowledge and affirm their wolf connection. Glenn Schiffman, storyteller and member of the Iroquois wolf clan, shared this simple and powerful depiction of the subtle intricacies of ritual.

This portrayal reminds me of dynamics in the Wolf Connection pack when one of the wolves is particularly intense and the other members move away.

He's tall. Even in that crouch that all the powwow dancers assume, bent at the waist, chest forward, head darting left right, left right—I can see he's tall. He dances alone. None of the other dancers will go near him.

The wolf pelt that hangs loosely from his shoulders bounces as he dances. The head of the wolf tops his head. When the wolf head swings left I can see that the left side of his face is painted black. When the head swings right, that side is painted red. A surround of white paint circles the eyes. He dances alone.

All the dancers stay away. They stay on the other side of the circle. It's the wolf robe. They must all be Southern

Plains dancers. At least he's not wearing a coyote skin. They wouldn't even let him in the circle if that were the case.

He dances past a drum group and they lose the beat. I have to smile. It was the singer with his back to the circle. He lost the beat just as the wolf danced by him. The tobacco the headman put on the drum as a test of their consistency is now bouncing erratically, splayed, not centered. That singer drops out, needs to get the rhythm back, will wait for the next pushup to the song. Amazing energy that Soldier Wolf dancer puts out.

In a spiritual sense, I consider ritual the "enactment of a myth,"[1] as Joseph Campbell put it. Ritual is how mythology becomes alive and anchored in our beings. Ritual is far more than a series of repeated behaviors performed in a prescribed order, the standard definition. True ritual has its roots in a living tradition; a practice that evolves with the culture it belongs to. Ritual has deep meaning to those performing it because it is done with commitment, purpose, and intention—a deep "belief" that becomes the life force behind the ritual in the same way a gracious wind fills the sail that propels the vessel forward.

Ritual is endemic to all human cultures, yet many Western societies have misunderstood and even trivialized traditional rituals, regarding them as irrational and superstitious. A healing ritual, for instance, performed by a wolf society shaman may be viewed skeptically by a Western mind, even if the person's health improves after treatment without pharmaceuticals or medical procedures. Evidently, observation without immersion is enough for the Western mind to formulate an opinion. It is one thing to draw conclusions while observing from the bleachers and eating popcorn, and quite another to act, *get in the game*, and fully engage in the experience.

Fortunately, in the past few decades, the concept and practice of intentional ritual has made a comeback in mainstream Western culture, and is even being recognized as aiding personal development, spirituality, and intimacy. Behavioral science and military, athletic, and business performance theory also incorporate rituals. Commonplace events and behaviors in our lives, from Thanksgiving to our morning routines, are rituals that we enact and maintain vigorously, whether we realize it or not.

Research into ritual efficacy concludes that repetition is a critical component to the use of *simpatia*, a Brazilian ritual act performed to help obtain something desirable such as love, good luck, or a cure for an illness.[2] When more repetition is involved in a ritual, something within us responds with increased confidence and optimism. This is supported by further neuroscientific work that concludes that "ritual buffers against uncertainty and anxiety."[3] Removing doubt is critical to ensure the efficacy of a ritual, and repetition can calm and reassure the mind.

Whatever words, actions, or songs the ritual prescribes for us to repeat are just as important as repetition itself. Sound is a powerful element of ritual, whether in the form of voice or musical instruments. Research confirms what we intuitively know: melodies with certain rising and falling patterns or unusual tone intervals capture our awareness so completely that we find it very difficult to get them out of our heads.[4] The use of these rising/falling or arching melodic structures and particular rhythm patterns are common in rituals around the world.[5]

Repetition also engages movement and breath. If we surrender, as a child would, to the natural impulse to move to these sounds, whether by simply stomping or clapping to a beat; twirling; doing energy circulation movements such as tai chi, qi gong, or Tensegrity; or doing animal-inspired dances or intricate, choreographed performances, physical movements and breath help to focus our awareness on the present moment. In *The Body's Recollection of*

Being, David Levin writes, "With the creation of the universe, the dance too came into being."[6]

Recent genetic research leads scientists to believe that we have evolved to be social movers, engaged in ritualistic communication. This is something wolves constantly demonstrate. Bonds among pack members are their lifeline, and they constantly elicit and react to each other's rich repertoire of body movements and expressions.

Visual spectacle is also important in an effective ritual. Our brains are wired to focus on visual stimuli that are shiny, brightly colored, luminous, or reflective, moving and changing in appearance.[7]

Picture the opening ceremony for the Olympic Games—the national teams march with their uniforms and flags with lights, performers in their fabulous costumes, music, songs, and the carrying and lighting of the Olympic torch, which will burn for the duration of the games. This fire has been rekindled since the time of the ancient Greeks, in a similar fashion to the fire that is kept alive at the center of a First Nations ceremony.

At Wolf Connection we employ ritual as a tool for immersing participants into program experiences. The program leaders first teach these rituals, and later students conduct them themselves. We use the wolf howl as a way to establish the bond among participants and as the symbol for the authentic calling in their hearts. We hike the mountains with the wolves to bond with the pack, train the participants' minds, and anchor the experiences in their bodies. For instance, at the beginning and end of each day we gather around the medicine wheel at the center of the wolf compound. We enter through the east and move around it in a clockwise fashion, mimicking the journey of the sun. Once the entire group is standing around the medicine wheel, we close our eyes, take a few deep breaths, and clear our minds to shift our attention to the effect of the earth beneath our feet, the warm sun on our bodies, the gentle caressing of the wind on our skin. Through this experience we become grounded, pay our respects to the wolves and to the land, and ask permission to be there. The wolves, witnesses to this human ritual from a short distance, often howl as we stand in reverence.

On the first day in the program, students receive a stone. They will carry this with them for the duration of the program. We call it the "journey stone," and it symbolizes their presence and their growth. As we gather at the beginning of the day, students place their journey stone in the medicine wheel to say "I'm here," and they retrieve it before they leave the ranch, keeping it with them at all times until the next program day.

Program students doing the Medicine Wheel practice. *Photo by Chris Perry's Wildside Galleries.*

After placing the stone in the wheel, students reflect on the stages of their lives and their journeys, as symbolized by its four directions. The east signifies birth, the rising sun, the crescent moon, spring, and morning. South represents development, youth, midday, when the sun is burning highest in the sky, summer, and the full moon. West characterizes maturity, adulthood, afternoon, sunset, waning moon, and fall. And north denotes the time of elder wisdom, night, new moon, and winter. These stages exemplify daily, monthly, yearly, and life cycles and we use them not only to help students understand the past, present, and future periods in their lives but also their paths through school, aspirations, and career, issues with their family or the law, the journey through substance recovery, or a short-term school or work project.

This clearly demonstrates an undeniable truth that ritual, be it conscious or otherwise, has the power to shape our perception of reality. But such immersion requires the courage to put one's beliefs on the line while simultaneously carrying the alchemical power to transmute "belief" into "knowing."

RITUAL FORMS AND ENHANCED BONDS

As social animals, we humans find that the power of ritual is amplified when performed with others. At Wolf Connection we call this "the pack effect," whether it is among wolves, wolves and humans, or a purely human pack. Every single circumstance in life is a collaborative situation involving other people, which is an invitation for connection. In her book *The Bond*, journalist and author Lynne McTaggart discusses the powerful and intrinsic desire individuals have to pursue wholeness by connecting with others.[8] We feel intuitively that participation in ritual is driven by the desire to be attached or bonded to one another. In rituals, individuals are invited to relinquish their boundaries and to be transformed by the bond with others. McTaggart writes, "The world essentially operates, not through the activity of individual things, but in the connection between them . . . *in the space between things.*"[9]

At my first Carlos Castaneda Tensegrity workshop in the late nineties, more than four hundred people came together over three days to learn and practice the Tensegrity movements or Magical Passes, the body positions and breath patterns discovered in a state of dreaming by seers of ancient Mexico and passed down from generation to generation for thousands of years in secrecy, and then made available by Carlos Castaneda for anyone to practice.

I had never experienced anything like it. All we did was practice those movements—so many of them, in fact, with new ones being introduced every session, that my daily cognition became overwhelmed and my inner dialogue simply stopped. Without self-doubting thoughts, everyone at the Tensegrity event, experienced and novice, young and old, kinesthetically inclined and otherwise, was fully connected with each other and moving in unison.

My physical vitality increased and my perceptions were sharpened by the movements. I was completely clear and had no thoughts, only laser-focused direction. The light and colors in the room were heightened to an incredible detail. At night I realized I could see in the dark, as I imagine a wolf would.

Since then I've had the privilege of facilitating many events and witnessing the waves of energy moving through the crowd as the ritualistic Magical Passes are performed. I know that is the type of energetic connection and sense of belonging wolves feel within a pack. Chemists describe a bond as the strong attractive force that holds atoms and molecules together, resulting from the sharing or transfer of electrons.[10] When two atoms share electrons, they share energy. As research demonstrates, the bonds that form between humans—or humans and animals—as we share energy with each other actually hold us together well after the fact.[11] When we come together again to perform the ritual, those bonds are reaffirmed.

This type of transcendent practice, once a common part of human experience, has largely been lost to modern Western cultures. The few Western rituals that survived, however, are still meaningful— those that celebrate birth, naming, puberty, coming of age, marriage, and death. Celebrations of time and calendar-oriented rituals honor the phases of the moon and the changes of the seasons, as well as specific annual events and occasions marked at a particular time of year, such as Easter, Hanukkah, and Diwali. Others take place in secular settings and may include pregame rituals performed by members of a sports team, military exercises on a parade square, or a meeting of twelve-step program members.

Our predisposition for ritual, however, can also be misused to foster oppression, confrontation, and greed. One need only watch a film of a Nazi rally, or read about trophy hunting and poaching practices, to know this. Thus we must choose with wisdom and compassion what we include in rituals. If we do not examine the motivation underlying our actions, we may be swayed to act at the expense of others rather than in life- and community-affirming ways.

What we do together, the experiences we share and the things we celebrate with each other, can contribute greatly to the quality of our lives. When we don't have opportunities to experience rituals that enhance connection with others, we suffer. When they are introduced, well-being quickly follows. A 2012 study looked at how survivors of domestic violence could be helped[12] through the practice of rituals that fostered self-reclamation and healing, followed by a ritual that publicly marked their change in status, opening them to well-being and connectedness in themselves and with others. Participants experienced a shift from perceiving themselves as victims, to a state of what they referred to as "incorporation," described as "thriving" and "joyful." This is the foundation behind every activity we do at Wolf Heart Ranch. The individual wolves and the pack as a whole serve as gateways to healing for people with trauma caused by abuse, neglect, abandonment, separation from their families, or perhaps incarceration or substance abuse.

ANIMALS AND RITUAL

Our beautiful bonding rituals at Wolf Heart Ranch cross the species divide. Every morning when we enter the wolf compound, and every evening when we leave after evening feeding, the wolves give us a howling serenade. It is very cheerful, high-pitched, and upbeat in the morning and with long, mournfully low tones at sundown. Feeding is also a powerful ritual, one staff and volunteers train to perform for months, since it requires complete awareness of one's own as well as the wolves' emotional and energy states, focus on the task at hand, and confidence that we have the situation handled no matter what.

Rituals performed by animals can help us understand our affinity for them. Zoologists define ritual as a "set of actions that an animal performs in a fixed sequence, often as a means of communication."[13] Wolves demonstrate ritual with exquisite creativity and flexibility. Kira Cassidy, a wolf biologist with the Yellowstone Wolf Project, has observed wolves holding a "rally," usually during or before a howl. Sometimes it is howling back and forth between two packs. At other times it is a pack bonding experience. She said that the furiously wagging tails make it seem that there are more tails than there are wolves, with everyone jumping up and down on each other and whining and yipping with each other. Then they'll break out into the actual howl, their typical, iconic, long, low sound. Time slows and, for a few moments, every wolf stops moving and puts their whole heart into this song. And then some kind of spell will break and they'll go back to the rally, jumping on each other and yipping.

I felt Kira's passion and admiration for the wolves as she shared this. The rally motivates them, somehow, perhaps to go hunting, or to cross the road together when they're nervous. They rally to build each other up. Kira likened it to a ritualistic bonding experience that has been practiced for millennia by tribal hunting or war parties, and in modern times by sports teams and sports fans.[14] This may be another demonstration that we have memories encoded within us, that we remember things such as rituals that are not taught directly to us.

We see rallies at the ranch all the time. The wolves live in separate but nearby habitats and do not hunt, but they still use their communal howl to support each other and synchronize their mood. The howl can end a fence fight, for instance, which is the equivalent of a heated argument between people that disrupts the harmony of the social group. Without physically stepping in, other people begin singing— it would probably be opera, since that's how I see the wolves, as the opera singers of nature. Feeling the pull of hundreds of thousands of years of ritualistic evolution, those involved in the confrontation immediately drop the argument and join the song. It is a sophisticated and highly evolved peacemaking ritual.

Understanding more about ritual as we now do, we can see how the ritual behaviors that help wolves to survive would have been apparent to our human ancestors, who were keen observers of the natural world and who spent a great deal of time watching their wolf neighbors. Watching the joyful interactions of a thriving wolf pack as they demonstrate their collaborative hunting technique, their sharing of risk, their performing acts of altruism and consistently displaying loyalty to packmates, all would have had a tremendous impact. One could argue that it was only a matter of time before the rituals of wolves became the rituals of humans.

THE ANCIENT WOLF RITUALS

One of the most powerful rituals we perform at Wolf Connection is "hiking with the pack," where we hit the trails of the national forest that surrounds Wolf Heart Ranch. Traveling on foot in silence, feeling the impact of nature on our being while moving next to a wolf is a profound, transformative experience. It awakens our primal connection with these magnificent animals, and an ancestral memory from a time when we were much more alert, clear, and plugged into the energy flow of the natural world. Our visitors rarely have the words to describe their experience, since it predates language, but the hike is invariably their favorite activity.

Only a handful of cultures maintain the ancient oral histories and wolf rituals they received from our ancestral teachers. What would it be like to live in a society like this, one that has kept its wolf connection alive, where social practices learned from wolves are woven into the very fabric of the culture? Glimpses of this perspective are available to us thanks to the collaborative efforts of First Nations elders and anthropologists. Here is an excerpt describing the Wolf Dance songs of the Arapaho people.

"The Arapaho, who speak an Algonquian language, are from the Northern Plains region. During the early nineteenth century they lived in Wyoming and eastern Colorado, but in the 1850s they split into two bands: members of the northern band now live on the Wind River Reservation in Wyoming, while members of the southern band settled in Oklahoma (Fowler 2001). Prior to the twentieth century, Wolf Dance songs were a significant part of the Arapaho repertory. The literature on Arapaho culture mentions a Wolf Dance only occasionally, and identifies it as a ceremony of one of the men's societies, which had certain duties in social life and warfare. Frances Densmore describes Arapaho Wolf Dance songs as focused on preparations for warfare, and explains that these songs were performed at communal dances prior to the departure of a war party."[15]

At Wolf Heart Ranch, program participants report that the howl of our wolf pack saying good-bye at the end of the day remains recorded in their bones and hearts. It has given them the strength to face the problems in their lives, as well as a sense of hopefulness because they know that the wolves will be there waiting for them to come back.

Some First Nations cultures continue to practice wolf-centered rituals that connect the entire community to this day. The story of the origin of the wolf ritual of the Nuu-chah-nulth people (formerly known as the Nootka) is remarkable. In the early 1900s, ethnographers studying indigenous cultures in British Columbia for the Anthropological Division of the Geological Survey of Canada became aware of the wolf ritual of the Nuu-chah-nulth. At that time, Edward Sapir, Canada's first professional anthropologist and a student of Franz Boas, the father of American anthropology, believed that the cultural practices of the Nuu-chah-nulth were in grave danger of being lost if not recorded,[16] and sought to preserve them. He may have been acting with the best of intentions, and we don't have the version from tribal members at the time, but his intrusion may have created instability within the community, both tribal and scientific. Nonetheless, Sapir's actions may have salvaged an invaluable piece of cultural history that not only maintained cultural continuity in Nuu-chah-nulth communities but also provided a significant resource for linguistic scholars, preserving a legacy of global significance.

The Tlo:kwa:na (or wolf dance) is the most important cultural ceremony of the Nuu-chah-nulth as well as for many other indigenous people of the Pacific Northwest. Sapir worked closely with

Alexander Thomas, whose traditional name means Turning-into-Wolf-at-Intervals, to transcribe a detailed description of four rituals practiced in Ucluelet, British Columbia, in the early 1900s and later recorded in the book *The Origin of the Wolf Ritual.*

The ritual was intended to occur mainly in winter, when people were more geographically concentrated in traditional times. Winter is also the most energetically intense time of the year for wolves, since it is their breeding season. The seven-to-ten-day-long ritual was supposedly secret, and in some versions, only the supernaturally endowed or initiated members were allowed to see the parts of the ceremony where dancers acted as wolves.[17] Planned well ahead of time, it had three stages, and in the first, villagers are invited to potlatch but not told that the wolf ritual will occur. During the feast, wolf society members dressed as wolves with crawling wolf masks on their upper faces capture and abduct the novices, who are seven years of age or older. These masked wolves are paid by the chief of sponsors to take the initiates to the ancestral lineage house, deep in the forest, to learn his or her ceremonial wolf songs and dances to be displayed upon return to the community.

In the third stage, the novices return to the village wearing standing wolf masks to perform the songs and dances of the wolf ritual. At this point they are considered to be carrying the power of the wolf, and are fully reborn into their clan through the transformation of gaining this ancient knowledge and practice. There is a celebratory feast.

The ritual recognizes the fundamental equality of all people and all living beings. The Tlo:kwa:na is a primary vehicle for passing on hereditary rights and maintaining social organization. The Nuu-chah-nulth maintain that they were taught this ritual by wolves, who taught humans the right way to live, so it is not surprising that the ritual recognizes the fundamental equality of all people and all living beings.

THE POWER OF DREAMING

Much as I received the wolf message during a dreaming vision, the accounts in Sapir's text describe dreaming experiences in which the dreamer is given specific wolf ritual instructions to remember and then teach to the wolf people in the waking state. Receiving instructions in dreaming is a common feature of many indigenous cultures. For example, the Yuma people—or Quechan, as they call themselves—of the Southwest region have maintained their oral history this way for thousands of years and employ *dreaming*, among other practical applications, to recall and bring to conscious memory ancestral stories that are no longer stored in their physical bodies.[18]

John Peabody Harrington, an anthropologist, wrote about the significance of dreaming among the Quechan people based on his work among them in the early 1900s. In his first published article on the Yuma origin accounts in 1908 Harrington stated, "Every individual can dream vivid dreams, and whatever is dreamed is believed either to have once happened or to be about to happen. Only a few people, however, dream proficiently and professionally." These powerful few have the ability to visit the mythic past of the Quechan—and in particular the scene of the creation—in dreams, which would be corroborated by the elders. A Quechan man born in the 1860s once told Harrington that all he knew about his people's traditional ways and origins was knowledge he gained through dreaming. Joe Homer said that he would dream a little bit of the creation stories at a time and would tell it to the elder. "The old men would say, 'That is right! I was there and heard it myself.' Or they would say, 'You have dreamed poorly. That is not right.'"[19]

In cultures with shamanic and oral history traditions, dreaming is the means by which myth is engaged; dreaming is how myth becomes ritual. Experiences that occur during dreaming are considered to be as real as wakeful and lived experiences, though they take place in a different realm or state of awareness. Dreaming is therefore an active rather than a passive state, in which the storytellers, healers, and shamanic practitioners may receive stories, curing procedures, or messages from other worlds and that may be incorporated into their culture.

The Nuu-chah-nulth wolf ritual is an example of the focus and discipline of dreaming in action. The Tlo:kwa:na were given to participants in at least three different dreaming "installments." Each dream takes the dreamer into a different story, allowing for new details to come forward to be incorporated into the ritual. This variation in context allowed the wolf ritual to become a richly layered ceremony, into which other formerly discrete ceremonies were incorporated. The result is a ritual that is densely packed with meaning and intentions that are woven in a sequence of dances, songs, and actions that capture every aspect of the original dreams the wolf ritual is based on.

Each of the wolf ritual dreams contains references to entities called *topa:ti*, a Nuu-chah-nulth word that translates variously into "supernatural thing," "crystal being," "forest spirit," or "ghost." These entities are described in loose detail, and their roles are variable, but they appear during the ritual's second, teaching stage, and upon arrival the topa:ti are acknowledged and interacted with because they confer the power on participants. The topa:ti also can express displeasure, enforcing "taboos"—such as killing a wolf—and may bring about the death of those who are not properly prepared to encounter them. The story line of the first dream takes place prior to European contact in an area of Vancouver Island where the present-day community of Ucluelet is found. The people of this region, the Hitats'o:ath, have been repeatedly attacked by other tribes and "are down to a handful as they take refuge on a high cliff. In desperation they seek help from the wolves, selecting an emissary through a physical trial where volunteers are dragged naked over sharp barnacle-covered rocks and must endure without calling out to end the pain, to be chosen as the one who will go to the wolves for aid. A young man named Hasa:as is chosen and placed inside a large seal carcass set on the beach to be found and carried off by the wolves to their house deep in the forest, where the chief of the wolves gives him what he seeks: a war club of heavy whalebone to combat the attacking tribes. He is also shown the wolves' Tlo:kwa:na ceremonial performances, particularly dances imitating those of several other creatures. Taken back to the human world, the hero reenacts the ceremony on the house roof to attract passing canoes. Word spreads and a fleet of canoes gathers to watch the dances. The hero then displays the war club, which is so magically powerful that just the sight of it kills the visitors." Not only the source of the Tlo:kwa:na but also the origin of the military might of the Yo:lo:ilzath are accounted for mythically.[20]

There are several important elements to this dream. The trial of physical pain endurance in which young men allow themselves to be dragged across barnacle-covered rocks establishes their ability to maintain self-control. Additionally, the request made to the wolves for help is of central importance. Their response is to give Hasa:?as two things: the wolf ritual, and a magical weapon to destroy their enemies.[21] By repeating the wolf ritual, his people will always continue to remember how the wolves saved them from certain demise.

At Wolf Connection we also guide students through a sacrificial and renewal ritual we call the Weight That Can Bring Us Down, or the Rock Activity for short. The wolves are present throughout the activity as witnesses to the struggle and transformation. In it we ask participants to gather a number of rocks from fist-size to watermelon-size . . . and we hand out markers. Then we begin naming heavy feelings and emotions that are part of the typical human experience, things that can hold us back, such as fear, anger, resentment, vindictiveness, sadness, guilt, shame, victimhood, self-loathing, and self-doubt. As we name them, we ask students to write those words on the rocks; if that feeling or emotion is present in their lives once in a while, we direct them to choose a small rock; if it is a frequent occurrence, use a midsize rock; and if it is overwhelmingly present all the time, we ask them to write it on a large rock. Once complete with that part of the ritual, each student ends up with a pile of rocks of different sizes at their feet.

Here is where it gets interesting. At that point, we take out backpacks we kept hidden and ask them to put them on and, with each other's help, they put all their rocks in their packs. Once packs are loaded we lead them on a hike up the mountain. After twenty minutes of moaning effort, with broken backpacks and blistered hands and feet, the hike culminates at the edge of a cliff, where one of our ancestor wolves is buried. With the valley at their feet, students get to stand at the edge of the cliff, remove the rocks from their packs, spend a moment in silence, expressing their gratitude to each of the heavy feelings and emotions for the lessons learned, and throw the rocks into the ravine below. The purpose of this ritual is for students to gain a kinesthetic experience of the weight of these feelings and emotions, of how they hold them down in their lives, and the deep feeling of release and liberation when they are able to let them go.

The second dream pertaining to the Nuu-chah-nulth wolf ritual tells the story of a man who has gone hunting but is led by wolves to their forest home, where they show him the ceremony he must take back to his people. The man in this story is Hi:-xwa:qmi:k, and he is from "a less prominent Yo:lo?il?ath group."[22] After teaching him the Tlo:kwa:na, the wolves transform themselves into killer whales, the other physical form that wolves may take when hunting, and bring him home to his people. In this dream, as in the others that describe the origin of the wolf ritual, wolves and other animals as well as humans change form at will.

Program students carrying and releasing rocks representing their life burdens.
Photo by Chris Perry's Wildside Galleries.

The third dream is the longest and most elaborate that Edward
Sapir was able to record. It was told by Sa:ya:ch'apis in 1916 to
his colleague Alex Thomas: "It speaks of a high-born Hitats'oʔath
girl, Haw'ilmaʔotl, the chief's daughter.[23] While out digging clo-
ver roots she sees a wolf with four cubs, including one that is very
attractive, and she wishes that he was her husband. That night
when she is back home she is fetched by him in human form and
taken to the house of the wolves. He is the son of the wolf chief,

and the couple are married. Renamed Li:?i:k, the girl is initiated into the Tlo:kwa:na with its attendant performances. Described at length, the ritual doings of the wolves are given in well-detailed, ideal form, a blueprint for staging the Tlo:kwa:na. The heroine has two boys, returns to Hitats'o?ath, and teaches the people the ceremony. The second half of the account is another detailed how-to description. It is followed by a description of how Li:?i:k helps one of her sons to win the daughter of a chief."

This last account, in which the young woman Li:?i:k is married to the son of the chief of the wolves and has two sons with him, contains the most detailed description of the ritual itself, but it also contains many other fascinating details. The wolves give Li:?i:k a set of precise instructions for how to perform the wolf ritual, and in addition they give her the ability to calm a storm at sea, which she does near the end of the account, as part of a test by which Li:?i:k's son is given the right to marry a woman from another tribe. This prematrimony testing ritual is one that, by good fortune, was carried forward within this particular account of the origin of the wolf ritual.

Today, for the Pacific Northwest First Nations communities who take part every year in the ten-day wolf ritual it provides a practical opportunity to come together, recognize and value everyone for their contribution to the community, and reaffirm connections that will keep the spirit of the wolf songs, dances, and rituals alive in their hearts, minds, and culture until they gather again a year later.

Agnes S. W., an artist, outdoor guide, and member of the Kwakwaka'wakw Thunderbird clan, works with traditional Kwakwaka'wakw symbols and myths. When she is guiding groups on sea kayak adventures, Agnes takes kayakers to places where her people used to live, reinforcing the ancient view of those locations, seen through the eyes of her ancestors. And when she goes out into the wilderness, she does so consciously, opening herself and connecting with the plants and animals that live there.

Every morning, Agnes takes a spoonful of oolichan oil to establish a direct physical connection with her ancestors. She sits in silent meditation to cleanse and connect with the wolf, the killer whale, the salmon, and all her relations. When she hears a wolf pack howling, those are the voices of ancestors that have passed on, and when she sees a pod of orcas, or "sea wolves," she is encountering her ancestors swimming next to her kayak.[24]

Through these rituals she has reached a deeper awareness of herself and a way to guide others to do the same. As she celebrates her lineage, embracing the strengths and vulnerabilities, she has found her humanity and become able to connect with people of any cultural background and welcome them. Agnes demonstrates what the wolves have taught her—how to meet with other humans the same way that she is when she meets wolves—with gentle strength, free of judgment, and listening.

At Wolf Connection, we tell our students that, in the end, it is not only what ritual is or what it can do that matters. It is also what we decide our rituals will be. The ritual that we create and practice is for each of us to decide upon. But we guide our students to ask themselves, *Will you choose to follow a life-affirming path from now on?* Will you become the hero in your dream, or continue to be the victim in your nightmare? To the extent that we achieve our goal and help them do this consciously and sustainably, our world will change for the better.

Long ago, we lived and thrived alongside wolves. This is not a romantic tale, created out of longing; it is fact. Wolves invite us to walk with them again, to listen to the heartbeat of the Earth and commune with the life of the Earth. To pay attention to our dreams, to bring the heart to our choices, and share, in awe, the responsibility of stewarding this extraordinary Spaceship Earth, as R. Buckminster Fuller called it, not from a position of self-delusional superiority, but in collaboration and harmony with all living beings.

REALM NINE

Your Own Wolf Practices

The Nine Realms are not only nine ways to talk about wolves, but also nine bodies of comprehensive knowledge, and nine ways to think about humans as well. I pray that the *Wolf* energy and message has transcended the limitations of this flawed writer and humble messenger, to touch your heart and awaken the primal being within. I intended this book as a journey of initiation, and the purpose of this chapter is to bring together all that I've presented.

My teacher Carol Tiggs said to me years ago, "Never forget that the vast majority of consciousness is nonhuman—that is an energetic fact." That simple statement had a profound impact on me. It brought humility to my life and provided a means to focus my energy outside of myself.

Indeed, we humans are the overwhelming minority on the planet, but we behave as if we own the place. We are not using our perceptual and creative abilities in ways that support our long-term sustainability on this planet. In other words, it is not the planet we are destroying, it is our chance to be part of it. *Wolf* can bring us together and help us create an extraordinary future, one where heart-centered contribution is the currency.

The Ninth Realm is about applying *Wolf*'s lessons in the world to fundamentally change our behavior and raise our consciousness, which is the only viable way to a sustainable future in planetary harmony. Every other living being on the planet focuses their actions and efforts on moving their species forward in balance with the natural world. It is time humans got onto that program, too. It's about evolving from "me first," "me against you," and "us vs. them" to "we first," "me AND you," and "us WITH them." I propose that we integrate tradition, nature-based wisdom, and cosmic knowledge with our advanced technologies, in the service of all living beings. *Wolf* can guide us on this path and first help us to reconnect with our true nature.

Once *Wolf* has facilitated the reset of our primal hearts, energy, and focus, we must add the human dimension back into the equation. We must recalibrate our unique, frontal cortex ability for discernment to reflect and evaluate our thoughts, words, and behavior. We possess the capacity to visualize and imagine a specific path of action out of nearly infinite possibilities. Once our true nature is reclaimed and freed, these capabilities can make us truly magical beings, with the power to manifest and achieve anything imaginable. Our creative life force will no longer be at the service of the insecure self-reflection or ego, but in alignment with the cosmic flow of purpose and intent.

When we purposefully and deliberately immerse ourselves in ritual, we can interrupt the frantic momentum of our thoughts and fully engage in the now. This inner silence can lead to a state of focused intent that can bring about an enormous expansion of our daily perception and a redefinition of reality.

ELUCIDATING THE TWELVE WOLF PRINCIPLES

In this final section I want to offer more context and practical applications of the twelve Wolf Principles used in Wolf Connection's eight-week Education, Empowerment, and Life Re-direction Program. I strongly encourage you to take your time working your way through the twelve practices. And keep a journal of your experiences and insights. The more deliberately you pursue this, the more powerful the outcomes, so please don't rush, there is nowhere to be but here, there is no time to be but now.

Annie, standing fierce and strong. *Photo by Chris Perry's Wildside Galleries.*

WOLF PRINCIPLE 1:

Wolves are okay with who they are.

We all make mistakes, and many of us are brutal with ourselves when we do. Mistakes are inevitable, and hopefully we learn and grow from them. What we can avoid is our habit of self-criticism.

In the Wolf Connection pack is a three-legged wolf named

Annie. While she could be viewed as "disabled" compared to her four-legged companions, Annie carries on as part of the pack, unencumbered by any self-doubt or lingering judgments. She is whole as she is, which can be seen in both her cheerful, energetic, and loving demeanor and in the way the rest of the pack treats her. Nobody pities her or gives her any special consideration—for when we accept ourselves fully and completely, we give others permission to do the same. Being okay with who we are is more than self-acceptance, which is a human construct. The wolf, on the other hand, lives in a state of being with what is, flowing with the natural course of energy. This is an extremely simple concept and yet nearly impossible for us to emulate.

For humans, being okay with who we are doesn't mean that we necessarily need to like who or where we are at a given time in our lives. It means that we take our circumstances as they are without wasting time and energy in self-judgment and internal conflict.

HOWL TO ACTION
PART 1: FREEWRITE

On a piece of paper or notebook, draw a vertical line down the middle, or use two blank pages side by side. On the left side write the things that are working well in your life, the things you are happy about, proud of. This is a freewriting practice, so don't worry about chronological order or organization of any kind; write things as they come, big or small, without judgment. On the right side list what is not working in your life right now. It doesn't need to be elaborate; a few bullet points will do.

When you are done, put your pen down and read the lists on both sides of the line.

Ask yourself: Am I okay with all of this? If so, to what degree? Give your level of okay-ness an intuitive number from 1 to 10.

This first part of the exercise is not about trying to fix or change anything in your life. It is about slowing down and interrupting unnecessary judgments.

Being okay with both lists doesn't mean you necessarily like all of the elements in them; it means you are not wasting energy and time judging yourself and others and can refocus that energy and time into supporting what you want to see expanding and growing.

PART 2: MOVE YOUR BODY

Dance, jump, go for a walk or swim, perform a Tensegrity, yoga, tai chi, or qigong movement. It doesn't matter if you don't do any of this perfectly; this is about being okay, remember? In fact, I recommend some form of movement in combination with all the other practices in this chapter. To learn the Tensegrity (shamanic) movements, you can visit the home practice library at www.Castaneda.com.

If you have a dog or access to one—perhaps you can help care for a friend's dog or offer to walk dogs at a local shelter—play with the dog. Or go to a park and observe dogs at play. Playing with any animal you may have in your life—a cat, hamster, rabbit, or bird—will also work, since they, too, can facilitate a link to the natural world.

If there are no animals in your life, connect with a tree or your favorite plant, or simply close your eyes and take a few moments to focus on a story about a wolf in this book that affected you.

How do you feel in your body now?

Read your lists from part 1 of this exercise while keeping this mood and noticing the fluctuations of your breath patterns.

Ask yourself again: Am I okay with all of this, with the items on both sides of the line?

Notice if the number you gave before changes.

Repeat the breaths and the question as many times as you want. Look for a distinct "feeling" in your body—true expansion of your breath, a relaxation of your muscles, or a simple moment of peace. The self-questioning and breathing actions are a fluid practice and I recommend revisiting them often.

Write your insights for two or three minutes. Keep your hand moving; don't stop to censor or edit your thoughts or notes.

WOLF PRINCIPLE 2:

In order to be okay with who they are, wolves first know *who* they are.

Wolves in a pack are each at ease with themselves, their capabilities, and their role within the group. There are alpha leaders (the breeding pair), the betas, hunters, trackers, nannies, and omegas or peacemakers. All these wolves fully embody themselves without hesitation, knowing at a deep and instinctual level who they are and why they are present. This deep knowing allows them to contribute powerfully to the pack and to show up as the best possible version of their wolf self.

HOWL TO ACTION
PART 1: WHO ARE YOU, REALLY?

Have you ever sat down and asked yourself, *Who am I, really?* It's time to take a deep look at your defining core characteristics, unique traits, and makeup.

The question "Who are you, really?" is about purpose and mission. Who are you in the pack and in relation to it?

It's a lifelong, deep, existential, and philosophical question, the power of which is not so much in the answer but in the question itself.

Who are you, really? What are the gifts, strengths, experiences, and perspectives you are here to share? What are your natural, energetic tendencies? What are you here to learn?

More often than not, the truth of who you really are is staring you right in the face. It just takes time and attention to see this, sitting down and taking inventory of your surroundings, the things you do every day, and what you give your attention to. If you want to know yourself, look at where you put your time and your focus, where you apply yourself and where you don't. This is not about who you "think" you are. This is about who you are.

Miko, for example, discovered that she was a being who came to share love with those who needed it most. She showed humans their own light to the very end; even when she was crippled by a tumor in her spine, her purpose never wavered.

What have you discovered? Take a few minutes to write your insights.

PART 2: FIRST GUT INSTINCT

What role do you think you naturally have a tendency to play in your life?

- Alpha, the leader
- Beta, the enforcer, going by the rules
- Hunter, the closer, the go-getter
- Tracker, the detailed information and resource gatherer
- Nanny, the caretaker
- Omega, the peacekeeper

Now split your page into three parallel columns and list the various packs you belong to in the first column—for example, nuclear family, extended family, work, school, sports team, sports fan, car club, music band, high school friends, college friends, spiritual community.

Beau gave life another chance and became one of Wolf Connection's most prominent ambassadors. *Photo by Chris Perry's Wildside Galleries.*

Read down the list of "packs" you belong to and write, in the second column, the pack role you think you play in each of them. There's a good chance you don't play the same role in each pack.

Read the list of packs once again, and this time write, in the third column, the role other people would believe you play in each of those packs. You can take your best, most honest guess.

Are there any discrepancies? Take a few moments to write your insights.

If you wish to take this deeper on a second round, you can actually explain this practice to your family and closest friends, and ask them what roles they believe you play.

WOLF PRINCIPLE 3:
Wolves let go of the past and make room for new things in their lives.

Beau was one of the most abused animals we'd ever received— malnourished and beaten, with open wounds showing through his fur. He didn't trust anyone for a year and a half after coming to Wolf Connection, and would just hide behind his shelter, chuffing at anyone approaching.

But with time, as his physical and emotional wounds healed, he started to connect with people again, because his natural state is one of trust and bonding. He didn't hold on to past trauma. He didn't create permanent stories for himself about how all people are bad and can't be trusted. Instead, his natural state of curiosity and connection overcame the resistance, and his defensive stance eased. He took risks to trust people again, as his natural desire to play and interact in the present moment guided his behavior. Today Beau is one of the most well-adjusted animals we have, an amazing ambassador. He is loving, safe, gentle, and welcoming to everyone.

HOWL TO ACTION

Unlike many humans, wolves are not defined by their past. Instead, their past is a point of reference that provides knowledge and experience to be applied in the present, in order to avoid repeating mistakes or putting themselves in harm's way. We can say the same about most, if not all, animals, but because of the close kinship we share with wolves, they are in the best position to teach us this.

Ask yourself: What events of my past do I continue referring to over and over to reinforce my limitations? What are you using as an excuse to avoid living fully in the present?

If you have a dog or any other animal in your life who has a gentle, loving temperament, you could invite him or her to be with you as you uncover the real you—expansive and free. Or you could imagine Wolf Connection's gentle giants Rocky, Zimba, or Logan coming to sit with you. Take your time. There is no rush. Let yourself be.

Breathe, and when you exhale, visualize the assumptions, judgments, and attachments to past events that you no longer need gently and quietly leaving as your breath goes out. And new sun, moon, or starlight coming in as you inhale and replenish your lungs and the rest of your body.

Imagine the heavy chains that kept Chance and Koda tied to posts for the first few years of their lives. Or go for a hike carrying heavy rocks, representing the weight from your past. At home you can try this with a stack of books or some other weight—walk around the room with it for a moment. Ask yourself, "How much longer do I want to carry this pain, judgment, or guilt?"

When and if you are ready to let this go, say the words "Thank you for what you've taught me. I release you now."

Note any new thoughts or steps that come to you to take.

WOLF PRINCIPLE 4:
Wolves are open to learning new things.

Wolves explore all the time, and they don't begin with judgments and preconceived ideas. Experiencing the world like a wolf means maintaining a sense of openness and curiosity, presence rather than previously established notions.

Even when they are familiar with the territory—such as when we hike the same trails with the pack around Wolf Heart Ranch—the experience is always new for them. They keep their ears up, senses alert, nose and eyes constantly scouting ahead, ready to face whatever comes next.

Keeping an open mind requires humility; if we look at the vast amount of knowledge on this planet alone, not to mention in the rest of the cosmos, it's impossible to pretend to even know a small portion of what's out there. The true state of existence for any living being is a state of constant discovery.

Wolves embody this and train their young to be alert and curious. Curiosity is creativity, and offers the biggest chance for survival, growth, and expansion. Humans, on the other hand, train their young to "know." We give kids a good grade if they know the "right answer" to a question and penalize them if they don't. For some of us, knowing became a matter of personal survival, so we learned to do whatever was needed to look like we knew, even if that meant faking or denying anything we didn't know.

Curiosity is confidence-based. It is the way of the powerful predator. Knowing-as-safety is fear-based, the way of the weak prey.

HOWL TO ACTION
PART 1: REFLECT

At the ranch, we ask program participants to observe the alertness that wolves display while on the trail. At home you can watch the documentaries *In the Valley of the Wolves* by Bob Landis or *Living with Wolves* by Jim and Jamie Dutcher and pay attention to the wolves' attentiveness and curiosity.

Now move your body to circulate energy and breath, and reflect on the following:

Using a scale where 1 is the most difficult and 10 is no problem, rate how easy it is for you to say, "I don't know." Does it energize or debilitate you when you say it?

When was the last time you learned a new skill; a new, meaningful piece of information; went to a place you hadn't been before; ordered a meal—or cooked food— you hadn't tried before?

PART 2: LEARN SOMETHING NEW

In the next week, purposefully try three new things, big or small, that you can explore and learn. Perhaps you can watch a video in a language you don't speak and try to understand what it is about; read an article on a topic that would not typically interest you; attend a lecture or sign up for a dance, pottery, archery, or singing class . . . just one class.

PART 3: CHANGE A HABIT

In the next week following that, change one pattern of behavior, such as going to work using a different route, even if it takes a bit longer, or don't watch television (or watch it) while having dinner, or use your other hand to brush your teeth, or avoid checking your phone first thing in the morning or last thing at night.

Be creative and look for the routines that you don't even realize you have, and make sure to bring humor into this practice of reevaluating your habits.

Jot down your discoveries as you go.

WOLF PRINCIPLE 5:
Wolves give 150 percent to everything they do, so they choose carefully what they agree to do.

You may say, "Wait a minute: how can someone give 150 percent? It is mathematically impossible!"

You can give only 100 percent, right? That's all anyone has! But most of us quit before we reach that edge, and we give up before leaving everything on the field.

Watch National Geographic's *Yellowstone Wolf Dynasty* series—first aired in August 2018—and notice that when they hunt, wolves give every last drop of energy to the chase. If the hunt is fruitful, they eat as if there is no tomorrow. They "wolf it down." Then they sleep like the dead, and they play until they drop, and they are down for the count again. They protect their pack and defend their territory with everything they've got.

Humans, on the other hand, rarely give themselves so fully. Those who do are seen as charismatic, inspirational, exceptional, or even crazy! The 150 percent principle is about tapping into resources you don't know you have. It means that when you think you've given everything, there is more you are capable of. So keep going. Push past what you *think* is your edge, your perceived limitation. Find that extra reserve in the tank to truly give it all. This practice is extremely liberating because it frees us from regret, from wondering what could have happened. It clears the air of all the could'ves and should'ves.

For anyone practicing this principle, we must be extremely careful about what we agree to do. You can't say "yes" to everything in front of you and expect to give 150 percent. On the other hand, if you stay in the comfort zone, you'll never have the chance to truly apply yourself. You'll be looking at the game from the bleachers instead of the field. This principle is about creating clear priorities, making the decision, and following through all the way to the end.

Giving 150 percent includes having the wisdom and sobriety to know when you are not up to an endeavor, task, or relationship, either because you know you don't have the energy, or the skill.

Passion is at the core of what being a wolf is. They have an intensity in their eyes that says, "I am fully here!"

In contrast, have you ever found yourself dragging your feet around? Or seen someone else trudging reluctantly or resentfully? That's a luxury only humans think they have. But in reality, the cost of not living passionately and playing to the fullest is incalculable. Wolves are deeply connected and in harmony with the cycles of life and death, so they live each moment to the fullest. Humans, on the other hand, live a lot longer than wolves do, which can be both a blessing and a curse. We can take things for granted, fall into an apathetic routine. Wolves' decisions are deliberate and final because they know their lives are on the line at each turn. Humans hesitate, behave cautiously, and play safe. The next thing we know, we are at a crossroads or on our deathbed with "what ifs" torturing our mind and regrets in our hearts.

HOWL TO ACTION

For wolves, the priorities are clear, and they are extremely focused on them. Number one is to survive as a pack. Second is to thrive. This includes having a safe, protected territory, cultivating and maintaining a strong bond with each other, hunting efficiently, mating at the proper time, having the proper nutrients in their bodies to produce healthy pups, and taking care of those pups to forward the species.

PART 1: WHAT IS IT FOR YOU?

On a sheet of paper, write the top five or ten things that are most important to you. You could choose one area, such as family, career, health and fitness, financial security, or spiritual growth, or several areas.

PART 2: WHY?

Why do you want each of those things? Write it down.

PART 3: HOW?

What are one or two decisive steps you can take to move those priorities forward? Make it real and give each of those actions a timeline. Commit to completion.

Take a walk with your dog, or go watch dogs play at the park, write your insights, and get to work. Give it your utmost—as if your life depended on it!

WOLF PRINCIPLE 6:

Wolves live by the power of their bond. They care deeply for each other without giving in to drama and pity.

Humans have an extraordinary capacity for empathy, solidarity, and goodness. That's who we really are. But we live in a busy world. There is so much to do and so little time, endless demands pulling our attention in every which way. We can easily gloss over our relationships and interactions and fail to comprehend the real purpose and meaning behind our actions. As a consequence, we can confuse pity and self-indulgence for empathy and compassion. Instead of truly supporting each other, we may join in blaming, complaining, and gossiping. We feel sorry for ourselves and for those going through hardship and need, enabling us and others to become smaller and weaker.

Wolves, on the other hand, thrive in the strength of their bond. They are about full support and empowerment, in almost a tough-love kind of way. They often play rough, and one of them will take a tumble, go over a log or rock, and fall on his face or back on the other side. The others immediately come to check on his well-being. They sniff him a couple of times, and when they realize that he is fine and will soon get up, they walk away and resume their play or lie down. They don't spend any time reminiscing about the bad luck of the one who fell, or who is to blame, who pushed him or her, or who put that log or rock in the middle of the way, worrying about looking stupid to their friends during the fall, or ridiculing the one that is down. Of course, these are unrealistic scenarios in the animal world, but easy to imagine among humans. In the wild, accounts of wolves that continue hunting and traveling with the pack after getting injured are common. The rest of the pack checks on them from time to time, but they keep going.

HOWL TO ACTION

During the Wolf Connection program, we gather in council, a traditional practice that brings people together, in a circle, to develop community and heal. During this practice, students often feel safe to share their stories and poems about their challenging lives. The council practice is about listening to each other with presence, without judgment, and pausing before reacting to another's emotional process. This is a practice that can be extremely powerful for anyone, during any interaction.

PART 1: REFLECT

This principle is an invitation to reflect in writing on the following questions: Who matters in your life? How do you demonstrate that you care about them? Who are the people you interact with daily? Perhaps the members of the different *packs* you belong to at home, at work, etc.? How present are you during your interactions with them? How would you know you are present? How would they know?

PART 2: PRACTICE

In the interactions you have with other people over the next days and weeks, make a conscious, deliberate effort to *stop, look, and listen* to them. Take your time, notice their breathing, body language, and expressions, as well as their *growls*, *howls*, *yips*, and words.

Is your family member, dog or pet, friend, partner, boss, or neighbor trying to tell you something? Are they trying to send a message? Observe. Listen. Breathe.

Mirror their mood back to them if you can, or respectfully paraphrase what they said, to let them know you are paying attention and to make sure you understood what they said.

PART 3: REFLECT

After having a few more conscious interactions, reflect on the following: What part do you have in the creation and maintenance of drama in your life?

Do you notice when you fall into the socially accepted pity for yourself (poor me) or another (poor them)?

Do you feel you need to "be rescued" or "save" them?

What is a new action you could take to lower drama and increase joy?

Take a few moments to write your thoughts and insights.

Students gathered in a circle at a spring Wolf Connection program. *Photo by the author.*

WOLF PRINCIPLE 7:
Wolves use their individual gifts and talents for the benefit of all.

The effectiveness of a well-rounded pack depends on the ability of each pack member to perform his or her function. It is usually the same group of wolves within the pack that does all the hunting and protecting against other packs. The breeding female does most of the leading, making important decisions such as where the den is going to be during breeding, gestation, and puppy season, where and what to hunt, and whether to engage in a particular fight with a neighboring pack. The adolescent and elder wolves often help raise the pups. Captive packs also have the role of the peacemaking omega, which diffuses tension. Wolves celebrate being different, knowing that the skills and talents of others will benefit the whole pack.

HOWL TO ACTION

During the Wolf Connection program, we ask students to bring their innate and developed gifts and talents to different collaborative expression projects, such as murals, spoken word, carpentry, or filmmaking.

PART 1: GIVING

Answer the following questions: What gifts or talents, natural or developed, are you bringing to the various "packs" you belong to? How do you put your gifts forward?

Some gifts can be part of your innate personality—a calm demeanor, the ability to inspire others, a big heart, fire in your belly, etc. Others can be more practical—a good organizer, listener, team player. And, of course, your training—healer, administrator, animal trainer, mountain climber, teacher, artist, dancer.

On the other hand, are you withholding your gifts from your community?

PART 2: RECEIVING

How easily can you accept gifts from others? Are you comfortable about asking for help? Is any fear or pride getting in the way?

Notice what's going on in your body and write your insights as you process these questions.

WOLF PRINCIPLE 8:
Wolves communicate effectively. They keep it honest and real.

Wolves don't mince their "words." They have a rich verbal and nonverbal communication system with sounds, body movements and posturing, facial expressions, and energy expressed in a clear and direct way. You never have to guess what a wolf is trying to communicate. If they are happy and playful, you can tell. If they are assertive or aggressive, you can certainly tell!

Lucas, one of the founding wolves at Wolf Connection, had one of the most contagious happy faces, and the gnarliest growl, that would give you an adrenaline rush every time.

Most animals are not easy to understand. Humans tend to struggle to "figure out" how to say what we want to the point of often becoming very confusing and manipulative. *Well, this is what I think I want to say, but if I say that, then they're going to think this, so I'm going to say this other thing instead . . . and I'll hope they can just get my point . . . or not say anything at all and hope they read my mind.* Sound familiar?

Lucas with the author. *Photo by the author.*

This principle is all about effective communication, honesty, and directness. This doesn't mean being blunt or disrespectful, but being truthful and straight up with what you mean. It is definitely an art in its simplicity and may take years to master.

Think how our lives—and the world—would change if we developed the skills to clearly and simply say what we need to when we need to.

HOWL TO ACTION

During the program at the ranch, we coach students to speak in full, clear sentences and to articulate their questions and collaborative instructions.

PART 1: WITHHOLDS

On paper, reflect on the following: Is there a relationship or area in your life in which you are delaying, possibly for too long, saying what you need to say? Perhaps they are words of love and appreciation that have been withheld, needs and desires that could be expressed, or a situation that needs addressing.

PART 2: CREATE FLOW

Move your body, take your dog to a dog park—or go and watch the dogs there—and observe how they communicate with you and with each other.

Did your observations give you any insights? Jot them down.

PART 3: SHIFT

What small shifts can you make in your communications, in a caring, respectful way, to begin to put your life and relationships on a more harmonious, authentic track?

WOLF PRINCIPLE 9:
Wolves know how to lead and how to follow. You can't lead if you don't know how to follow.
In the wild, a wolf pack is typically led by the breeding pair, the parents. In captivity, alphaness is a function of presence in a balanced pack, or just plain dominance in a maladjusted one. Nevertheless, every role in the pack is equally valuable. Leadership for a wolf is a function of individual disposition, energetic group agreement, practicality, and efficiency. It is not a unilateral decision, or a function of an individual's identity.

Maya, a majestic Arctic wolf and the founding matriarch of the Wolf Connection pack, led the pack from 2009 when I found her and the original pack until she died in May 2017. She was one of the gentlest, most well-adjusted, and loving wolves we've ever had the privilege to care for, and she held a sense of presence that was never challenged by any of the other pack members. Her leadership was so balanced because, for the first three years of her life, her parents raised her. She was taught to be a wolf by wolves.

In contrast, the majority of the wolves we rescue are bred in captivity, sold as pets when they are only weeks old, and grow up somewhat "confused" about who they are. The same can be said about many humans.

Leading and following are two sides of the same coin. Young wolves are raised by the pack, and they naturally follow the older, more experienced wolves as they gain the skills they need to become well-adjusted members of the pack. They are guided and supported by their mentor wolves while learning to model their leadership skills.

Wolf 21, the powerful and benevolent alpha "super wolf" who is part of Yellowstone National Park's mythology, is said to have never lost a battle, and have never killed a defeated opponent. This was a trait he is believed to have learned as a yearling from his adoptive father, Wolf 8. Leadership for wolves is simple, straightforward, and heart-centered.

Humans, on the other hand, are not as clear as wolves about leadership. We seem to believe that being a leader is better than being a follower. Many of us want to be "leaders" at all costs, and even elbow others out of the way to lead, rarely stopping to contemplate whether we even have the skills, knowledge, stamina, and mental and emotional disposition to do so. We often lack awareness of the burden that comes with true leadership. Personally, I don't trust those who are eager to lead. For the most part, they are just looking to prove themselves. On the other hand, the one who sees the need for vision and direction and reluctantly answers the call has the potential to become a true leader in the service of those who follow. Leadership for wolves is not about self-validation. It is about functionality and efficiency. Following is also about functionality and efficiency.

In our society, we are obsessed with teaching kids to become leaders. *Leadership* is a catchphrase in most grade schools, just like *more jobs* is a sound bite in politics. But this man-made concept is not in line with the natural world. Just look at the animal kingdom and tell me if you can find a pup, cub, chick, calf, foal, or any young member of any species leading anything. Asking kids to step into leadership without having yet developed the capabilities and the skills is essentially setting them up for failure. Young humans haven't fully developed their mental, emotional, and psychological equipment for critical thinking, ownership, discernment, empathy, and emotional processing, not to mention life experience or the ability to even recognize if they want to lead in the first place.

This dead-end game causes a lot of stress and tension for young people, often creating the conditions for coping mechanisms such as violence, substance abuse, social withdrawal, and crime to release the pressure to be a leader when they aren't ready for it.

The results? People grow up with confusion in their minds and hearts, and go on to become parents and teachers . . . passing on the confusion to the next generation, which will repeat the cycle.

By first following, without any pressure or need to become leaders, young people have the chance to gain skills and confidence through the guidance of a leader. Experiencing how it feels to be led by a seasoned and balanced leader will teach them the best ways to become a leader themselves.

Leaders who have been followers can step into a leadership role understanding the impact their decisions have on the ones they lead. Some cultures historically lived in support of this idea. Children stayed with their mothers and helped with domestic chores such as fetching water or firewood. Puberty was acknowledged though a rite of initiation, and through allowing the youngsters to have more responsibility, such as tending a fire, following the hunters, training with the warriors, or learning how to use tools. Leadership started with being responsible for one's own life and having concerns for the well being of the whole pack. Later, as they reached adulthood, they would become responsible for providing for and protecting the family and village through hunting, warfare, commerce, learning how to use medicine, and practicing the sacred arts, such as healing and divination. Most of them would become family leaders; some, community leaders. With the passage of time they would earn the honor of becoming community or tribal elders.

That's the way of the wolf, a way that we humans learned a long, long time ago.

HOWL TO ACTION

During our program we teach students to follow and trust our leadership. Hike behind a Wolf Connection program leader, for instance, as a yearling wolf would do.

PART 1: EXTERNAL

Think of some leaders you respect and admire—current or from history—and note the qualities they exhibit. Write your reflections.

Students and wolves hiking, learning to follow and to lead. *Photo by Chris Perry's Wildside Galleries.*

PART 2: INTERNAL

What is leadership? Do you appoint yourself alpha when you may or may not have expertise? Or do you hold back and play low-ranking when you actually have the most skills and experience in the group?

PART 3: THE HUMBLE LEADER

Are you able to admit when you have made a mistake? Try admitting a mistake to a trusted friend or colleague.

Do you acknowledge other people's contributions? See what happens when you specifically acknowledge or thank someone you normally don't, someone who is helping you or your community.

WOLF PRINCIPLE 10:
Wolves collaborate and work together. They know that together they will succeed.

Wolves have their work cut out for them when it comes to hunting. The sheer size of an elk, some five hundred to eight hundred pounds of muscle and hooves, is enough to thwart many an attacker, but they also have antlers that weigh up to forty pounds and span four feet. That weapon, along with brutally strong kicking power and all the adrenaline of a life-or-death moment, make that ten-foot-tall beast terrifying to take down.

How do seventy-five-to-one-hundred-pound wolves do it? Teamwork.

Wolves hunt prey many times their size—bison, elk, and deer—using evolved and coordinated strategies. In a systematized form of teamwork, some of the wolves separate the prey, then tire them out until they are slow and weakened so other wolves can take them down ambush-style, sharing the risk.

They even show teamwork in the way they move through fresh snow, usually taking turns being in the front doing the hard work of plowing a path for the others. The wolf in front doesn't complain when it's his turn. He assumes the role required of him purely because it will help the pack. This is a great lesson to put into play whenever we're called into a position that's not our ideal. How can we set aside our personal interests in the moment, to benefit the greater good?

Collaboration is the instinctive default for wolves. Wolves trust each other implicitly; humans don't.

But none of us gets to operate in a vacuum, ever. We can be part of a group and boss people around or follow others' directives mindlessly, but while that would still appear to the onlooker like a group of people working together, it is far from true collaboration.

True collaboration is a graduate-level topic because it includes the embodiment of the previous wolf principles: being okay with ourselves, clear and effective communication, being vulnerable and willing to learn, and the ability to lead and follow with the project's and group's best interests in mind. Ultimately, if you have a dream or a mission you can accomplish by yourself, your dream or mission is not big enough.

HOWL TO ACTION

At Wolf Heart Ranch, we practice trust and teamwork through collaborative expression projects. After students bond with the wolves, they work with other students on various creative projects such as photography, a mural, a short film, or woodwork to express that bond.

This principle is simple yet challenging, since it requires students to go out in the world and seek true collaboration with others.

PART 1: CREATE A COLLABORATIVE PROJECT

What are you, or could you be, working on at work, at school, or at home? Pick a project—or a portion of one—that is small enough to be completed within a few weeks, but big enough to require a team where members interact with each other. Describe the processes, tasks, and objectives on a piece of paper. A few sentences will do.

Now write down the next three to five steps needed to move the project, or portion of the project, forward. What do you need to complete those steps?

PART 2: ENVISION THE TEAM

Who can collaborate on, or contribute to, the project at hand? This is not about you giving others a to-do list, it's about seeking their contribution to make the project better than you could make it by yourself.

PART 3: ENROLL YOUR TEAM

Now present your project to those people, enroll them on its purpose, engage them in conversation, and elicit their feedback and ideas.

Relax and listen.

Any significant decision must be made through consensus. In other words, once there is a team, the project is no longer yours exclusively but belongs to the group.

Keep notes not only on the progress of the project but also on your reactions and responses during the collaborative process.

WOLF PRINCIPLE 11:

Wolves understand they are part of everything around them.

Wolves are a function of the world around them. They are aware of their environment and recognize their intrinsic participation in its natural balance. For instance, wolves won't overkill or kill for fun. They are efficient and kill only what they need to eat. And even in the violence of the hunt there is gentleness and reverence, which Joseph Campbell referred to as the ritual of hunting.

We are hard-wired for integration the same way wolves are, but we have created an artificial, *un*natural environment to live in, made out of concrete, cars, processed foods, smartphones, and financial concerns. Most people go through life without regard for the impact our consumption has on the environment and the Earth. What might our world look like if we all began listening to that innate awareness of our environmental impact and began behaving from a place of integration and responsibility for the immediate and global ecosystem?

HOWL TO ACTION

Daniel Smachtenberger, a friend and thought leader, once said to me, "The world economy is eighty trillion dollars a year. There isn't a single product or service that doesn't produce damage at some level."

Taking that as a premise, I challenge each and every one of you.

PART 1: RESEARCH

Without political, religious, or emotional bias, inform yourself about the environmental impact of modern life. Learn about how consumer products and services are created. Inform yourself on the importance and sustainability of key global ecosystems, and conservation of animals from large mammals to insects. Don't just believe the news media or watch a YouTube video. Read the research, and look into who conducted the studies to make sure they don't have a bias. Think for yourself and draw your own conclusions.

PART 2: MAKE IT REAL FOR YOURSELF

Take an inventory of your footprint and make your best effort to reduce it. You can start by looking at the obvious things, such as the vehicle you drive; the products you purchase and the services you use; the way you dispose of your waste; the amount of fuel, power, and water you use in your home; the sources of that power and water; and the sources of the foods you eat. Put it all down on paper.

PART 3: TAKE IT DEEPER

Take inventory of the less obvious aspects of environmental pollution, such as the attitude you bring to your family, friends, or place of employment; the trash you put out with your thoughts, words, and actions; and the impact the news and social media you give your attention and time to has on your psychological and emotional states.

Do you spend your time and attention on things that excite and invigorate you, or things that bring up anger, resentment, complaints, and criticism? Do you seek to promote dialogue, collaboration, and kinship, or resistance, conflict, and separation?

I encourage you take a hard look on paper at your thoughts, words, and actions in the past days and weeks.

PART 4: DO SOMETHING

Move your body with or without an animal companion.

Based on your discoveries, create a simple, thirty-day action plan to decrease your environmental impact and waste.

WOLF PRINCIPLE 12:
Wolves are into being, not into doing.

Because humans are trained from childhood to pay attention to fast-paced action, most wildlife films and documentaries focus on the conflict, the chase, and the bloody hunt. But there's a lot of time in the life of a wolf to just *be*. They spend a great deal of time just sitting and looking out at the vista, feeling the wind on their face, and watching their young play. They simply observe the day, closing their eyes at times, or watch the leaves falling from the trees.

Wolves aren't worried about rushing around "doing wolf things" to feel worthy of being. They aren't defined by what they do, but by who they are. What this means is that a wolf just focuses on being a wolf, doing the things that come most naturally to her or him.

Essentially, wolves are into the experience of life, not the doing of life.

Human beings have turned into human doings, and we have much to learn from this. We often define ourselves by what we do and how busy we are, feeling like the more we do, the more we are. How many times do we feel like we haven't done enough, earned enough, become enough, or achieved enough to feel worthy and loved for who we are? So you need to hear this:

YOU ARE ENOUGH!
YOU ALWAYS HAVE BEEN . . .
AND YOU ALWAYS WILL BE!

Wolves don't need to be told this. For them, it's much simpler: the more they are, the more they are. There are no "checkpoints" to cross that will give the right to feel worthy. They are worthy simply because they exist.

Being is not something we need to earn. Being is a divine right we all have. The wolf fully embodies their divine right to being, and every single one of us, no matter what, where, or when, have every right to be the same.

HOWL TO ACTION

At Wolf Heart Ranch, we teach our students to *be* in the simplest way. We hike to a mountaintop with the wolves, pick a spot with a vista, sit, clear our minds, and just *be* for fifteen or twenty minutes. There is nothing to do or to think about.

I invite you to do the same. Find a beautiful place, sit . . . and *be*.

Do this as often as you can, and once you can feel that you have recovered and built up your beingness, take it to others, to your loved ones, to your colleagues at work.

Being is an inner state that can be sustained through all your levels of doing. In other words, *being* first, *doing* second.

If you have read this far, it means the wolf message has spoken to you. But the principles presented in this book are worthless if not practiced. Our modern-life inertia and complacent nature may still try to lure you into treating this life-transforming technology as mere intellectual entertainment rather than as an opportunity for practical action.

Succumbing to that temptation would carry the assumption that humans still have time to continue behaving as they currently do . . . disconnected, clueless, idiotic. Therefore, before you put this book down, I *challenge* you, on behalf of the wolf and every other living being on this Earth, whose lives will be impacted by your growth, to make the commitment to yourself, and to your loved ones,

become aware that you are in a dream, and you can act.

To take this exploration further, go to WolfConnection.org, WolfConnectionAcademy.org, or visit us on our social media pages to ask your questions, share your progress, and connect with other like-minded pack members. I look forward to hearing from you.

EPILOGUE
Stories for My Daughter

Every wolf we rescue spends the rest of their lives with us, and we come to love them like our own children. When a wolf dies at Wolf Heart Ranch, we express our gratitude, honoring their lives and service with a burial ceremony. We invite staff, board members, and donors to join us for a wake, during which we spend the night with the body in a space lit by candles and present stones and feathers.

At dawn or sunset the following day, we gather at the ranch and do a short council to set the intention. Together we carry the body, wrapped in a blanket, to a predetermined place, usually on a hilltop overlooking a section of the ranch. We dig the grave out of hard desert ground together and carefully place the body in it. After that, everyone places an offering in the grave and says a few words. Some people share their sadness and love for the departed four-legged sister or brother, but most attendees recount stories about how lives have been transformed by that wolf, and how they witnessed the ambassador in action. Crying turns to laughter, and back to crying.

Chance—the wolf featured on the cover of this book—was rescued from a roadside show in Alaska. He came to us traumatized and mistrusting, but the loving care he received from the Wolf Connection staff allowed him to heal and shine the light emanating from his huge heart over everyone that met him. Years later, he contracted an aggressive cancer. When he died, more than forty people showed up for his burial, and we spent nearly two hours telling stories and saying good-bye. I was very moved and couldn't help thinking, *I hope this many people come to my funeral.* Of course, I will never know and thus won't care, but what I was witnessing went beyond my desire to be loved after death. I was witnessing the impact of a profound legacy. Chance never said a word, never traveled, and didn't have social media accounts, but the legacy of his big heart lives on in the people whose lives he transformed. When the time came to close the grave, his body was covered with stones, jewelry, photographs, feathers, and an array of personal items. His body rests at Chance's rock, and his story of love, resilience, and redemption continues to inspire our program participants.

To be honest, I didn't know what I was signing up for when I founded Wolf Connection. We've buried dozens of wolves since then, and it does not get any easier. In fact, it is a constant practice of a heart broken open, deepening and healing.

Shima (Navajo for mother) was the most precious being. Her energy was so clean, clear, and innocent that we loved her from the first moment she arrived at the ranch. Rescued from an alleged fur farm, Shima was about two years old, and she was pregnant when she came to Wolf Connection. She lost her pregnancy, perhaps due to the stress of the rescue and transport across the country.

Shima was with us for only four months, but it felt like a lifetime. My wife, Renee, was Shima's primary caretaker, and even though she was untouchable, Shima opened up and showed her sweetness to Renee. Seeing them playing hide-and-seek, wolf and woman as a pack, was heartwarming. During a spaying operation, an unforeseen complication caused internal bleeding. By the time Renee got home with Shima that evening, she was laying in a pool of blood. We rushed her to the emergency vet, where she had two blood transfusions and emergency surgery. She was saved by a hair that night, but Shima never really recovered. She stopped eating and was losing weight. A few weeks later, her habitat partner attacked her. We are not sure what happened but presume Shima was ill or weakened and her mate had a reaction to it. Perhaps she was absorbing or recycling some negative energies; we will never know. Her wounds were not life-threatening, but her weakened immune system couldn't withstand the assault and she died. Our students see themselves in the lives of the wolves, and Shima's case was no different. As we put her to rest, I couldn't help thinking about the many youths whose lives are full of promise and are cut short by life circumstances.

Shima on the day she arrived at Wolf Heart Ranch. *Photo by the author.*

Shima's blinding but short-lived light, and the great potential that would never be realized, left a deep sadness in Renee, me, and the rest of the Wolf Connection team. As I finished this book, we buried her with reverence and placed a spotlight on her grave, so she can continue shining through the nights.

"Mommy, Shima is with Mother Earth now," our daughter told Renee after the burial.

Every night, my wife or I put our daughter to bed with a story. She often picks the book she wants us to read to her, but we've carefully curated her library, making sure we include books that expand her imagination while fostering curiosity, compassion, inclusion, and the awareness of all the living beings that inhabit this breathtaking planet. At the time of this writing, she is into unicorns; dinosaurs; wolves, of course; and superheroes—her favorite is Wonder Woman.

It has been difficult for us to find well-written children's books with a positive message and a heightened awareness with regard to animals. They are usually either stupid and downgraded in their meaning and message; the animals behave like humans with human concerns, or they have negative, divisive vibes, in a big-bad-wolf sort of way.

With time, I've realized that we are actually reliving ancient wolf stories and creating new *Wolf* mythology every day at Wolf Heart Ranch. Stories of resilience, courage, and hope. Stories that validate the greatness of the wolf-human bond and spirit and reclaim our true place in this marvelous world.

Those are the stories I will be telling my daughter every night.

ACKNOWLEDGMENTS

Saying thank you to those who have graced me with their care is not something that has ever come naturally to me. I guess I got too much, too easily. In a time of blazing-fast information and never-ending stimuli, when many borrow without asking and take the gifts they receive for granted, acknowledgment is falling out of fashion. There is a cultural shift that relegates gratitude, honesty, and integrity to mere liability management and transactional currency.

I have been blessed to have countless people in my life who have served and loved me on my journey. Many have walked the trail next to me for many years—some continue to do so—and others came into and out of my life at the perfect times, together, in service of one another's journeys. It would be impossible to mention everyone here, but, as I complete the present work, I wish to turn around and yell my thanks from a hilltop, as Carlos Castaneda's teacher had him do.

To all my ancestors, from the time of those hunting and traveling alongside wolves. My deepest thanks to the peasants and the royals, the prudent and the deviant, the ignorant and the educated. To the warriors, the merchants, the hunters, the farmers, and the immigrants. To the teachers, the factory workers, the lawmen, both conservative and revolutionary. To the mothers and fathers, daughters and sons, the proud and the shameful, the courageous and the cowardly, the honest and the false, the realized and the wasted.

To all the dreamers and the *Dreamt* that came before me, I carry a small piece of you in me.

To my mother, Nidia, who showed me how to care for others no matter what, and how to be of service in mud streets and marginal schools. To my father, Alberto, who taught me the value of hard work and how to love as a man, how to stare adversity in the eye, and how to contemplate nature in the backyard of a South American suburb. My parents gave me my life, and I owe them everything. To my sisters, Laura and Veronica, my lifetime best friends whom I could always count on. To my wonderful grandparents, aunts, uncles, cousins, nieces, and nephews, who have supported my choices whether they understood my unconventionalities or not.

To Carlos Castaneda, thank you for the writings that shook my being and inspired a journey from which I never returned. To my beloved teacher Carol Tiggs, for believing in me when all I presented was hot-headedness, entitlement, and lack of awareness. Your unwavering love and guidance made the life I have today possible.

To Nyei Murez and Renata Murez, thank you for the many voyages and the many lessons you've taught me. To Bruce Wagner, for your friendship and for generously sharing your experience as a successful writer. To Darien Donner and Tracy Kramer, thank you for your support and your help in navigating the legalities of publishing.

To Yamin Chehin, for your unconditional love, trust, friendship, and support both in sleeping and waking dreams. You were there in the brightest and darkest moments and saw in me what I myself couldn't see.

To Howard Wills, thank you for your healing and your prayers. You are a constant reminder to continue accepting the gifts, whether I understand them or not.

To the late Rafael Bejarano Rangel, for venturing into the shamanic realms with me. And to Gabriela Bejarano Rangel, for your deep love and support. You have shown me powerful light practices that I will never forget.

I extend my gratitude to the worldwide Tensegrity community, the Association of Transformational Leaders and Social Venture Partners.

To the brothers in my men's group—John Wineland, Rich Litvin, Keith Kegley, Stephen Bochner, Mark Thornton, John Baker, Nicolas Sage, Rod Wunch, and James Price—for the many years of fierce depth and presence. You became my tribe when I needed it most, and I would not be the man I am today without you. To Michaela Boehm, for helping me refine what it means to be a man.

To my friend Diego Lopez, for the many climbing and skiing adventures. To Marcelo Chimienti, for the endless Pink Floyd *Wall* sessions in your attic bedroom. And to David Kwak, for bringing me Tala and for your role in supporting my family.

To Patti M. Hall, thank you for seeing me as a writer long before I did, for your fierce nanny-ing, and for the innumerable hours of editing and project managing. I could never have written this book without you. To Sheila Archer, for your incredible passion in the pursuit of knowledge; this book would not have the depth and flair it has without your help. To Claralynn Schnell, for your unyielding support throughout the process.

To Zhena Muzyka and Enliven Books, for believing in this book from the moment it was only an idea in my head, and to Sarah Pelz at Simon & Schuster/Atria, for shepherding it when it became a tangible promise.

To the human pack of fellow wolf lovers and watchers at Yellowstone National Park, especially Linda Thurston and Nathan Varley, who ushered me through a life-changing experience. To Laurie Lyman, for her infectious love for the wolves. To Doug Smith, Rick McIntyre, Dan Stahler, and Kira Cassidy at the Yellowstone Wolf Project, who were extremely generous with their time and knowledge. Our conversations expanded my awareness and understanding of these majestic beings.

To all the scientific researchers, First Nation elders, and Keepers of Stories who also graced me with their time and knowledge during the writing of this book, I offer my sincere gratitude and acknowledgment. Especially to Glenn Schiffman, Trudy Spiller, Wolf Wahpepah, Agnes S. W., Dr. Bridgett vonHoldt, Wolfgang Schleidt, and Michael Shalter. Additional mention must be made of the contribution of the work of Raymond Pierotti and Brandy R. Fogg (*The First Domestication*); the coauthors of *Wolf Conflicts*, Ketil Skogen, Olve Krange, and Helene Figari; and Edward Sapir and the many contributors and editors of *The Origin of the Wolf Ritual*. To the master's and doctoral degree program students at Claremont Graduate University Psychology Department—Piper T. Grandjean Targos, Courtney Koletar, Devin Larsen, Rae Perlman, and Adam Markey—for the study that gave credibility to the Wolf Connection and Wolf Therapy methodologies.

Last, I extend my acknowledgment to the Wolf Connection family of staff and volunteers, for being storytellers and caregivers of the highest order. Especially to Chief Operating Officer Giulia Cappelli, for holding down the fort and leading the team while I was in the cave writing, and for contributing ideas and feedback to the manuscript. To Director of Development Cate Salansky and Head of Partnerships Kyle Baker, for keeping the revenue flowing while I was writing, and to Director of Programs Amanda Beer, for her support and feedback on the manuscript. To Renee Alfero, for keeping the pack healthy and happy, and to Dave Aubry, for taking care of the ranch like no other. To the rest of the team that makes Wolf Connection possible every day—Brenda Aubry, Doris Glassberg, Ree Merrill, Elena Albanese, Julie Avila, Michelle Lima, John Calfa, Genevieve Mariani, Valerie Fresh, Jennifer Thompson, Jen Carey, Stephen Rivera, Bianca Naranjo, Dona Whiteley, Siv Flick, Lance Hearing,

Ana Harrison, Annette Golden, Kylie Taylor, Sophie Clerico, Cindy Starry, Dustin Fleischmann, Jess Stone, Crowley Coriell, Laurie Cousins, David Sanches, Matt Thoms, Tamara Marwah, Ken and Lauri Nakashima, Micha Thomas, Myriam Guerci, Natasha Dolgushkin, Ember Pell, Anita Wischhusen, Heather Mentzer, Amanda Maas, Bella Cavalheiro, Isa Mercado, Steve and Jacky Andrews, Karen Levi, Saumia Ramakrishnan, Tara Bruner, Taylor Meade, Jacinta Williams, Harvey Price, Quentin Dunne, Terry Lyman, Toni Heebner, Stacey Nivic Hanov, Paula Ficoro, Steve Wastell, Chelsea Schaefer, Shea Perez, Wesley Keith, Donny, Drew, and many more who have been part of the team over the last ten years—thank you from the bottom of my heart. A special mention to Chris Perry for the artistically deep and magically moving photographs of the Wolf Connection and Wolf Therapy programs in action.

There is a small group of individuals without whom Wolf Connection would still be a grassroots organization trying to make a difference. These bighearted and generous people have, at one time or another, contributed their resources, relationships, and genius to creating a quantum leap in Wolf Connection's reach, longevity, and impact. For that, I will be forever grateful to Tia Torres, Tonya Littlewolf, Roseanne Ziering, Christopher Henrikson, Susan Reiner, Erol Spiro, Caroline W., Charlie Weingarten, Peter Sprecher, Gilbert and Lynda Hale, Deborah Addicott and Anjali Ranadive, Tamar Teifield, Ashton Charles, Palo Hawken, Daniel Tresemer, Christopher Marsik, Briana McGrath, Jan Medema, and Robert Davis. Additional thanks to Daniel Amir, Stephen McAndrew, Miguel Rivera, Vernon Wells, Grace Kono-Wells, Ken Ferber, Steven Golightly, and Jeremy Richards.

My deep thanks to the administrators and teachers who have put their faith and trust in a once-outrageous proposition and brought their students to the Wolf Connection program. And to our students, for showing up, playing full out, and applying the wolf ways in your lives.

To my wife, Renee, I love you with all my heart. Thank you for loving and embracing all of me. I know I don't make it easy at times.

To my daughter, you are the light of my eyes. My life stopped being about me the day you were born.

I wish to close this section by expressing my gratitude to the wolves in the Wolf Connection pack, whose names are listed below, without whom none of us would be here. I especially thank Tala, for choosing me, giving me a vision, and teaching me about a fierce heart; Maya, for her example of impeccable leadership; and Lucas, for teaching me how to be a wolf. To the wolves I have mentioned in stories in the book—the Original Pack and those who share their lives and hearts with everyone who visits Wolf Heart Ranch in person and online today—I offer my eternal acknowledgment, because they have changed my life forever.

Finally, I express my gratitude to the Wolf Spirit that has guided my steps since before I even realized it.

Abeka	Luna	Sage	Lobo
Annie	Maggie	Shade	Logan
Anora	Malo	Shadow	Lucas
Ayasha	Max	Shima	Maya
Bandit	Mazi	Taboo	Miko
Baron	Merlin	Willow	Misha
Beau	Mikey	Wolfee	Moonshadow
Bella	Misha	Wyoh	Ozzy
Charlee	Nali		Rezzie
Gemma	Neo	**Ancestors**	Rocky
Jacy	Nova	Abeka	Sissy
Kenai	Omak	Chance	Smokey
Koda	Ozma	Cloud	Tala
Leo	Rafa	Dakota	Zimba
Liwanu	Ranger	Kyra	
Lobo	Ryder	Liwanu	

NOTES

Realm One: The Wolf Heart Awakens

1. Carlos Castaneda, *The Teachings of Don Juan: A Yaqui Way of Knowledge* (Berkeley: University of California Press, 1968), 76.
2. Carlos Castaneda, *The Eagle's Gift* (New York: Simon & Schuster, 1981), 122.

Realm Three: The Ancestral Wolf

1. Mark Roberts and Simon A. Parfitt, "Boxgrove: A Middle Pleistocene Hominid Site at Eartham Quarry, Boxgrove, West Sussex," *Geoarchaeology* 15, no. 8 (2000): 819–22.
2. Juliet Clutton-Brock, *A Natural History of Domesticated Mammals* (London: Natural History Museum, 1999), 3.
3. Ibid.
4. Wolfgang Schleidt and Michael Shalter, "Co-evolution of Humans and Canids: An Alternative View of Dog Domestication: Homo Homini Lupus?," Conference Proceedings, *Evolution and Cognition* 9, no. 1 (2003): 57.
5. Kira Cassidy (biologist) in interview with the author, May 2018.
6. Juliet Clutton-Brock, *The Domestic Dog, Its Evolution, Behaviour and Interactions with People*, ed. J. Serpell (Cambridge, UK: Cambridge University Press, 1995).
7. Mary Elizabeth Thurston, *The Lost History of the Canine*

Race: Our 15,000-Year Love Affair with Dogs (Kansas City, KS: Andrews & McMeel, 1996).

8. F. Sanchez-Quinto and C. Lalueza-Fox, "Almost 20 Years of Neanderthal Palaeogenetics: Adaptation, Admixture, Diversity, Demography and Extinction," *Philosophical Transactions of the Royal Society of London. Series B, Biological Sciences* 370, no. 1660 (2015): 20130174.

9. K. Prüfer, F. Racimo, N. Patterson, F. Jay, and S. Sankararaman, "The Complete Genome Sequence of a Neanderthal from the Altai Mountains," *Nature* 505 (2014): 43.

10. L. S. Weyrich, "Neanderthal Behavior, Diet, and Disease Inferred from Ancient DNA in Dental Calculus," *Nature* 544, no. 7650 (2017): 357.

11. C. Finlayson et al., "Late Survival of Neanderthals at the Southernmost Extreme of Europe," *Nature* 443, no. 7113 (October 19, 2006): 850.

12. C. J. Van Meerbeeck, H. Renssen, and D. M. Roche, "How Did Marine Isotope Stage 3 and Last Glacial Maximum Climates Differ? Perspectives from Equilibrium Simulations," *Climate of the Past* 5, no. 1 (March 5, 2009): 33.

13. K. Harris and R. Nielsen, "Q&A: Where Did the Neanderthals Go?" *BioMed Central Biology* 15, no. 1 (2017): 73; I. Juric, S. Aeschbacher, and G. Coop, "The Strength of Selection Against Neanderthal Introgression," *PLoS Genetics* 12, no. 11 (2016): e1006340.

14. S. H. Ambrose, "Late Pleistocene Human Population Bottlenecks, Volcanic Winter, and Differentiation of Modern Humans," *Journal of Human Evolution* 34, no. 6 (1998): 623; W. Amos and J. I. Hoffman, "Evidence That Two Main Bottleneck Events Shaped Modern Human Genetic Diversity," *Proceedings, Biological Sciences* 277, no. 1678 (2010): 131.

15. M. Kuhlwilm, "Ancient Gene Flow from Early Modern Humans into Neanderthals," *Nature* 530, no. 7591 (February 25, 2016): 429.

16. T. Higham, K. Douka, and R. Jacobi, "The Timing and Spatiotemporal Patterning of Neanderthal Disappearance," *Nature* 512, no. 7514 (August 21, 2014): 306.

17. M. W. Schmidt et al., "Impact of Abrupt Deglacial Climate Change on Tropical Atlantic Subsurface Temperatures," *Proceedings of the National Academy of Sciences of the United States of America* 109, no. 36 (2012): 14348; R. S. Bradley, *Paleoclimatology: Reconstructing Climates of the Quaternary,* 3rd ed. (Amherst: University of Massachusetts–Elsevier, 2013).

18. Patrick Robillard, Dene elder, http://www.sicc.sk.ca/archive/heritage/ethnography/dene/territory/prereserve.html.

19. Schleidt and Shalter, "Co-evolution of Humans and Canids."

20. Sheila Archer, "Indigenous Peoples of the Northern Hemisphere: Wolf Clan Survey" (unpublished, 2018).

21. M. Tomasello, J. Call, and B. Hare, "Five Primate Species Follow the Visual Gaze of Conspecifics," *Animal Behavior* 55, no. 4 (1998): 1063.

22. P. Gardenfors and M. Lombard, "Causal Cognition, Force Dynamics and Early Hunting Technologies," *Frontiers in Psychology* 9, no. 2 (2018).

23. Sayoko Ueda, "A Comparison of Facial Color Pattern and Gazing Behavior in Canid Species Suggests Gaze Communication in Gray Wolves (*Canis lupus*)," *PLoS ONE* 9, no. 6 (2014): e98217.

24. H. Valladas et al., "Paleolithic Paintings: Evolution of Prehistoric Cave Art," *Nature* 413, no. 6855 (2010): 479.

25. Trudy Spiller (Keeper of Stories, Gitxsan Nation) in discussion with Sheila Archer, October 20, 2017.

26. F. Range, C. Ritter, and Z. Viranyi, "Testing the Myth: Tolerant Dogs and Aggressive Wolves," *Proceedings, Biological Sciences* 282, no. 1807 (2015): 20150220.

27. S. Marshall-Pescini et al., "Importance of a Species' Socioecology: Wolves Outperform Dogs in a Conspecific Cooperation Task," *Proceedings of the National Academy of Sciences of the United States of America* 114, no. 14 (2017): 11793.

28. Ibid.

29. Linda Thurston in interview with the author, February 2018.

30. Kira Cassidy in interview with the author, May 2018.

31. Laura R. Botigue et al., "Ancient European Dog Genomes Reveal Continuity Since the Early Neolithic," *Nature Communications* 8, no. 16082 (2017), DOI: 10.1038/ncomms16082.

32. M. Hofreiter and J. Stewart, "Ecological Change, Range Fluctuations and Population Dynamics During the Pleistocene," *Current Biology* 19, no. 14 (2009): R584; D. H. Mann et al., "Life and Extinction of Megafauna in the Ice-Age Arctic," *PNAS* 112, no. 46 (2015): 14301.

33. Z. Fan, "Worldwide Patterns of Genomic Variation and Admixture in Gray Wolves," *Genome Research* 26, no. 2 (2016): 163.

34. Glenn Schiffman in interview with the author, March 30, 2018.

35. Range, Ritter, and Viranyi, "Testing the Myth."

36. Lee Alan Dugatkin and Lyudmila Trut, *How to Tame a Fox (and Build a Dog)* (Chicago: University of Chicago Press, 2017).

37. Pat Shipman, *The Animal Connection* (New York: W. W. Norton, 2011).

38. Raymond Pierotti and Brandy R. Fogg, *The First Domestication: How Wolves and Humans Coevolved* (New Haven, CT: Yale University Press, 2017).

39. Bridgett vonHoldt, "Structural Variants in Genes Associated with Human Williams-Beuren Syndrome Underlie Stereotypical Hypersociability in Domestic Dogs," *Science Advances* 3, no. 7 (2017): e1700398.

40. V. Maurino et al., "The Elfin Face: Craniofacial and Dental Aspects of the Williams-Beuren Syndrome," *Journal of Biological Regulators and Homeostatic Agents* 31, 2 Suppl. 1 (2017): 105.

41. Darcy F. Morey, "Size, Shape, and Development in the Evolution of the Domestic Dog," *Journal of Archaeological Science* 19, no. 2 (1992): 181.

42. C. Schubert, "The Genomic Basis of the Williams-Beuren Syndrome," *Cellular and Molecular Life Sciences* 66, no. 7 (2009): 1178.

43. Nick Jans, *A Wolf Called Romeo* (New York: Houghton Mifflin Harcourt, 2014).

44. Bridgett vonHoldt in interview with the author, 2018.

45. Z. Fan, "Worldwide Patterns of Genomic Variation and Admixture in Gray Wolves," *Genome Research* 26, no. 2 (2016): 163.

46. Ibid.

47. P. C. Cross, E. S. Almberg, and D. W. Smith, "Energetic Costs of Mange in Wolves Estimated from Infrared Thermography," *Ecology* 97, no. 8 (2016): 1938.

48. D. R. Stahler et al., "The Adaptive Value of Morphological, Behavioural and Life-History Traits in Reproductive Female Wolves," *Journal of Animal Ecology* 82, no. 1 (2013): 222.

49. P. W. Hedrick, D. W. Smith, and D. R. Stahler, "Negative-Assortative Mating for Color in Wolves," *Evolution* 70, no. 4 (2014): 757.

50. Kira Cassidy in interview with the author, February 2018.

51. B. M. vonHoldt, P. J. Pollinger, D. A. Earl, et al., "A Genome-

Wide Perspective on the Evolutionary History of Enigmatic Wolf-like Canids," *Genome Research* 2, no. 8 (2011): 1294–305.

52. Schleidt and Shalter, "Co-evolution of Humans and Canids."

Realm Four: The Wild Wolf

1. Rudyard Kipling, *The Second Jungle Book* (London: Macmillan, 1895).

2. Daniel Stahler in interview with the author, February 2018.

3. Sheila Archer in interview with the author, February 2018.

4. Celal Beydili, *The Encyclopedic Dictionary of Turkish Mythology*, trans. Tolga Yenilmez (Istanbul: Yurt Kitap Yayin, 2005), 350.

5. Daniel R. MacNulty et al., "Body Size and Predatory Performance in Wolves: Is Bigger Better?," *Journal of Animal Ecology* 78, no. 3 (2009): 532; R. M. Schweizer, A. Durvasula, and R. K. Wayne, "Natural Selection and Origin of a Melanistic Allele in North American Gray Wolves," *Molecular Biology and Evolution* 35, no. 5 (2018): 1190; G. Liu, H. Zhang, and X. Yang, "Characterization of the Peripheral Blood Transcriptome and Adaptive evolution of the MHC 1 and TLR Gene families in the Wolf (*Canis lupus*)," *BMC Genomics*, 18, no. 1 (2017): 584.

6. Douglas Smith in interview with the author, February 2018.

7. R. M. Schweizer, B. M. vonHoldt, and R. K. Wayne, "Genetic Subdivision and Candidate Genes under Selection in North American grey Wolves," *Molecular Ecology* 25, no. 1 (2016): 380.

8. Astrid Vick Stronen, E. L. Navid, and C. T. Darimont, "Population Genetic Structure of Gray Wolves (*Canis lupus*) in a Marine Archipelago Suggests Island-Mainland Differentiation Consistent with Dietary Niche," *BMC Ecology* 14, no. 11 (2014).

9. J. B. Foster, "The Evolution of Mammals on Islands," *Nature* 202, no. 4292 (1964): 234.

10. Stronen, Navid, and Darimont, "Population Genetic Structure of Gray Wolves."

11. M. Hindrikson, J. Remm, and U. Saarma, "Wolf Population Genetics in Europe: A Systematic Review, Meta-Analysis and Suggestions for Conservation and Management," *Biological Reviews of the Cambridge Philosophical Society* 92, no. 3 (2017): 1601.

12. J. K. Brown and A. K. Lee, "Bergmann's Rule and Climatic Adaptation in Woodrats (*Neotoma*)," *Evolution* 23, no. 2 (1969): 329.

13. J. A. Allen, "The Influence of Physical Conditions in the Genesis of Species," *Radical Review* 1 (1877): 108.

14. Sven Erik Jørgensen, "Explanation of Ecological Rules and Observation by Application of Ecosystem Theory and Ecological Models," *Ecological Modelling* 158, no. 3 (2002): 241.

15. Klaus-Peter Koepfli, J. Pollinger, and R. K. Wayne, "Genome-Wide Evidence Reveals That African and Eurasian Golden Jackals Are Distinct Species," *Current Biology* 25, no. 16 (2015): 2158.

16. Richard Estes, *The Behavior Guide to African Mammals Including Hoofed Mammals, Carnivores and Primates* (Berkeley: University of California Press, 1991), 400.

17. G. Werhahn, H. Senn, and D. W. Macdonald, "Phylogenetic Evidence for the Ancient Himalayan Wolf: Towards a Clarification of its Taxonomic Status Based on Genetic Sampling from Western Nepal," *Royal Society Open Science* 4, no. 6 (2017): 170186.

18. Ibid.

19. L. E. Painter et al., "Recovering Aspen Follow Changing Elk

Dynamics in Yellowstone: Evidence of a Trophic Cascade?" *Ecology* 96, no. 1 (2015): 252.

20. Chris and Dawn Agnos, dir., *How Wolves Change Rivers*, https://www.imdb.com/title/tt3776154/.

21. Brenda Peterson, *Wolf Nation* (New York: Da Capo Press, 2017), 80.

22. Thurston interview.

23. Smith interview.

24. Barry Hulston Lopez, *Of Wolves and Men* (New York: Simon & Schuster, 1978).

25. Rudolph Schenkel, "Expression Studies on Wolves: Captivity Observations," *Zoological Institute of the University of Basel* (1947): 1.

26. L. D. Mech, "Alpha Status, Dominance, and Division of Labor in Wolf Packs," *Canadian Journal of Zoology* 77, no. 8 (1999): 1196.

27. Nathan Varley in interview with the author, February 2018.

28. Mech, "Alpha Status," 1197.

29. Kira Cassidy in interview with the author and Sheila Archer, May 2018.

30. Ibid.

31. Kira Cassidy and Rick McIntyre, "Do Gray Wolves (*Canis lupus*) Support Pack Mates During Aggressive Inter-Pack Interactions?" *Animal Cognition* 19, no. 5 (2016): 939.

32. Ibid.

33. J. Morris and E. Brandt, "Specialization for Aggression in Sexually Dimorphic Skeletal Morphology in Grey Wolves (*Canis lupus*)," *Journal of Anatomy* 225, no. 1 (July 2014): 1.

34. Cassidy and McIntyre, "Do Gray Wolves," 939.

35. D. R. Stahler, D. R. MacNulty, and D. W. Smith, "The Adaptive Value of Morphological, Behavioural and Life-History Traits in Reproductive Female Wolves," *Journal of Animal Ecology* 82, no. 1 (2013): 222; K. A. Cassidy, L. D.

Mech, D. R. MacNulty, D. R. Stahler, and D. W. Smith, "Sexually Dimorphic Aggression Indicates Male Gray Wolves Specialize in Pack Defense Against Conspecific Groups," *Behavioural Processes* 136 (March (2017): 64.

36. Daniel Stahler in interview with the author, February 2018.
37. Schenkel, "Expression Studies on Wolves," 1.
38. E. Zimen, "On the Regulation of Pack Size in Wolves," *Zietschrift fur Tierphysiologie, Tiererahrung und Futtermittelkunde* 40, no. 3 (1976): 300.
39. Cassidy interview with author and Archer.
40. Ibid.
41. Ibid.
42. M. Lazzaroni, S. Marshall-Pescini, and S. Cafazzo, "Post-Conflict Opponent Affiliation Reduces Victim Re-aggression in a Family Group of Captive Arctic Wolves (*Canis lupus arctos*)," *PLoS One* 12, no. 11 (2017): e0187450.
43. Ibid.
44. Varley interview.
45. Smith interview.
46. Cassidy and McIntyre, "Do Gray Wolves," 939.
47. Daniel R. MacNulty et al., "Influence of Group Size on the Success of Wolves Hunting Bison," *PLoS One* 9, no. 11 (2014): e112884.
48. Ibid.
49. MacNulty et al., "Body Size and Predatory Performance," 532.
50. Rick McIntyre in interview with the author, February 2018.
51. E. S. Almberg, P. C. Cross, and P. J. Hudson, "Social Living Mitigates the Costs of a Chronic Illness in a Cooperative Carnivore," *Ecology Letters* 18, no. 7 (2015): 660.
52. Cassidy interview with author and Archer.

53. Ibid.

54. Doug Smith in interview with the author, February 2018.

55. McIntyre interview.

Realm Five: The Human Wolf

1. Aldo Leopold, *A Sand County Almanac* (London: Oxford University Press, 1949), 137.

2. Ibid., 138.

3. Spiller, interview with Archer.

4. Public domain.

5. Schiffman, interview with the author.

6. Ketil Skogen, Olve Krange, and Helene Figari, *Wolf Conflicts: A Sociological Study* (New York: Berghahn, 2017).

7. Ibid., 3.

8. Christopher Solomon, "Who's Afraid of the Big Bad Wolf Scientist?" *New York Times*, July 5, 2018.

9. Skogen, Krange, and Figari, *Wolf Conflicts*, 6.

10. Ibid.

11. Ibid., 80.

12. Paul Hawken, YouTube talk, https://www.youtube.com/watch?v=uSW-gjjoAcw.

13. Skogen, Krange, and Figari, *Wolf Conflicts*, 85.

14. Ibid., 130.

15. Ibid., 176.

16. Brett L. Walker, *The Lost Wolves of Japan* (Seattle: University of Washington Press, 2005), 132.

17. Carl Gustav Jung and Aniela Jaffé, eds., *Memories, Dreams, Reflections*, trans. Clara Winston and Richard Winston (New York: Vintage, 1989).

18. Laurie Lyman in interview with the author, February 2018.

19. Skogen, Krange, and Figari, *Wolf Conflicts*, 112.

20. Cassidy interview with author and Archer.

21. Skogen, Krange, and Figari, *Wolf Conflicts*, 109.
22. Carl Gustav Jung, *The Archetypes and the Collective Unconscious* (Princeton, NJ: Princeton University Press, 1980).

Realm Six: The Cosmic Wolf

1. Carlos Castaneda, *The Art of Dreaming* (New York: Harper Collins, 1993), ix.
2. Carlos Castaneda, *The Fire from Within* (New York: Simon & Schuster, 1984), 28.
3. Werner Heisenberg, *The Physical Principles of the Quantum Theory*, trans. Carl Eckart and F. C. Hoyt (New York: Dover, 1949).
4. Brian Clegg, *The God Effect: Quantum Entanglement, Science's Strangest Phenomenon* (New York: St. Martin's Press, 2009).
5. Wolf Wahpepah in interview with the author, May 2015.
6. Mohan Sarovar, Akihito Ishizaki, Graham R. Fleming, et al., "Quantum Entanglement in Photosynthetic Light-Harvesting Complexes," *Nature Physics* 3, no. 1 (2009): 462.
7. J. McFadden and J. Al-Khalili, "A Quantum Mechanical Model of Adaptive Mutation," *Biosystems* 50, no. 3 (1999): 203.

Realm Seven: The Mythological Wolf

1. Joseph Campbell with Bill D. Moyers, *The Power of Myth* (New York: Doubleday, 1988).
2. Robert A. Segal, *Myth: A Very Short Introduction* (Oxford, UK: Oxford University Press, 2015), 13.
3. George Nicholas, "When Scientists 'Discover' What Indigenous People Have Known for Centuries," *Smithsonian Magazine*, February 18, 2018.
4. Michael Greshko, "Why These Birds Carry Flames in Their Beaks," *National Geographic*, January 8, 2018. https://news.national geographic.com/2018/01/wildfires-birds-animals-australia/.

5. Nicholas, "When Scientists 'Discover.'"

6. Trudy Spiller in discussion with Sheila Archer, October 20, 2017.

7. Campbell with Moyers, *The Power of Myth*.

8. Carlos Castaneda, *The Active Side of Infinity* (New York: HarperCollins, 1998), 139.

9. Sheila Archer, "Indigenous Peoples of the Northern Hemisphere: Wolf Clan Survey" (unpublished, 2018).

10. Karen R. Jones, *Wolf Mountains: A History of Wolves Along the Great Divide* (Calgary: University of Calgary Press, 2002), 6.

11. Patrick Robillard,"Pre-reserve," http://www.sicc.sk.ca/archive /heritage/ethnography/dene/territory/prereserve.html.

12. Manuel Jose Andrade and Leo Joachim Frachtenberg, *Quileute Texts: Columbia University Contributions to Anthropology*, vol. XII (New York: Columbia University Press, 1931).

13. Teresa Pijoan, "Wolf Star," in *White Wolf Woman: Native American Transformation Myths* (Atlanta: August House, 1992), 65.

14. William Whipple Warren, *The History of the Ojibway People*, 2nd ed. (St. Paul: Minnesota Historical Society Press, 2009), 19.

15. Ibid.

16. Alvin M. Josephy Jr., ed., *The American Heritage Book of Indians* (New York: American Heritage, 1961), 180.

17. Michael Bastine, "Granny Wolf," in *Iroquois Supernatural: Talking Animals and Medicine People*, eds. Michael Bastine and Mason Winfield (New York: Simon & Schuster, 2011), 201.

18. Barbara R. Duncan and Davey Arch, eds., "Medicine and the Wolf Clan," in *Living Stories of the Cherokee* (Chapel Hill: University of North Carolina Press, 1998), 202.

19. Ibid.

20. Paul Radin, *The Winnebago Tribe* (Lincoln: University of Nebraska Press, 1990), 190.

21. Ibid.

22. Susana Eger Valdez, "Wolf Power and Interspecies Communication in Huichol Shamanism," in *People of the Peyote: Huichol Indian History, Religion and Survival*, eds. Stacy B. Schaefer and Peter T. Furst (Albuquerque: University of New Mexico Press, 1996), 267.

23. Mariko Namba Walter, Fridman Neumann, and Eva Jane, eds., *Shamanism: An Encyclopedia of World Beliefs, Practices and Culture*, vol. 1 (Santa Barbara, CA: ABC-CLIO, 2004), 256.

24. Glafira Makarevna Vasilevich, "Early Concepts About the Universe Among the Evenks," in *Studies in Siberian Shamanism*, ed. Henry N. Michael (Toronto: University of Toronto Press, 1963), 57–59, 72–76.

25. James George Frazer, *The Golden Bough: A Study in Magic and Religion*, vol. 8 (New York: St. Martin's Press, 1912), 221.

26. Kira Van Deusen, *Singing Story, Healing Drum: Shamans and Storytellers of Turkic Siberia* (Montreal: McGill-Queen's University Press, 2004), 16.

27. Barb Karg, *The Girl's Guide to Werewolves* (New York: Simon & Schuster, 2009).

28. Beydili, *Encyclopedic Dictionary of Turkish Mythology*, 350.

29. Yves Bonnefoy, ed., *Asian Mythologies* (Chicago: University of Chicago Press, 1993), 337.

30. Roel Sterckx, *The Animal and the Daemon in Early China* (Albany, NY: SUNY Press, 2012), 152.

31. Christina Pratt, *An Encyclopedia of Shamanism*, vol. 1 (New York: Rosen, 2007), 16.

32. Sterckx, *The Animal and the Daemon*, 141.

33. Tian Yuan Tan, "The Wolf of Zhongshan and Ingrates: Problematic Literary Contexts in Sixteenth-Century China," *Academia Sinica, Asia Major*, 3rd Series, 20, no. 1 (2007), 105.

34. Binbin Wang et al., "On the Origin of Tibetans and Their

Genetic Basis in Adapting High-Altitude Environments,"
PLoS One 6, no. 2 (February 28, 2011): 1–10.

35. Paul Waldau and Kimberly Patton, eds., *A Communion of Subjects: Animals in Religion, Science and Ethics* (New York: Columbia University Press, 2006).

36. Matthew Beresford, *The White Devil: The Werewolf in European Culture* (London: Reaktion, 2013), 81.

37. Montague Summers, *The Werewolf in Lore and Legend* (New York: Dover, 1933), 178.

38. Ibid.

39. Lord Francis Hervey, *Corolla Sancti Eadmundi: The Garland of Saint Eadmund King and Martyr* (Edinburgh: T & A Constable, 1907), 192.

40. Leslie A. Sconduto, *Metamorphoses of the Werewolf: A Literary Study from Antiquity Through the Renaissance* (Jefferson, NC: McFarland, 2004).

41. Carlo Ginzburg, *Ecstasies: Deciphering the Witches' Sabbath*, trans. Raymond Rosenthal (Chicago: University of Chicago Press, 1991), 172.

42. Stefan Donecker, "The Werewolves of Livonia: Lycanthropy and Shape-changing in Scholarly Texts, 1550–1720," *Preternature* 1, no. 2 (2012): 295.

43. Ibid., 303.

44. Ibid., 309.

45. Ibid.

Realm Eight: The Ritualistic Wolf

1. Joseph Campbell, "The Wisdom of Joseph Campbell," New Dimensions radio interview with Michael Toms, tape I, side 2.

2. Christine H. Legare and Andre L. Souza, "Evaluating Ritual Efficacy: Evidence from the Supernatural," *Cognition* 124, no. 1 (2012): 1, doi: 10.1016/j.cognition.2012.03.004.

3. Nicholas M. Hobson, Devin Bonk, and Michael Inzlinct, "Rituals Decrease the Neural Response to Performance Failure," *PeerJ* 5 (2017): e3363.

4. Kelly Jakubowski et al., "Dissecting an Earworm: Melodic Features and Song Popularity Predict Involuntary Musical Imagery," *Psychology of Aesthetics, Creativity and the Arts* 11, no. 2 (2017), 122–35.

5. Patrick E. Savage et al., "Statistical Universals Reveal the Structures and Functions of Human Music," *PNAS*, 112, no. 29 (2015): 8987.

6. David Michael Levin, *The Body's Recollection of Being: Phenomenological Psychology and the Deconstruction of Nihilism* (London: Routledge & Kegan Paul, 1985), 201.

7. S. L. Franconeri, D. J. Simons, and J. A. Junge, "Searching for Stimulus-Driven Shifts of Attention," *Psychonomic Bulletin and Review* 11, no. 5 (2004): 876.

8. Lynne McTaggart, *The Bond* (New York: Free Press, 2011), xxv.

9. Ibid.

10. Peter W. Atkins, "Chemical Bonding," http://www.britannica.com/science/chemical-bonding.

11. P. Reddish et al., "Collective Synchrony Increases Proscociality Towards Non–performers and Outgroup Members," *British Journal of Social Psychology* 55, no. 4 (2016): 722.

12. D. F. Wozniak and K. M. Allen, "Ritual and Performance in Domestic Violence Healing: From Survivor to Thriver Through Rites of Passage," *Culture, Medicine and Psychiatry* 36, no. 1 (2012): 80.

13. "Ritual," *Your Dictionary*, accessed June 28, 2018, http://www.yourdictionary.com/ritual.

14. Cassidy interview with author and Archer.

15. Michael Tenzer and John Roeder, eds., *Analytical and Cross-Cultural Studies in World Music* (London: Oxford University Press, 2011), 293.

16. Edward Sapir et al., *The Origin of the Wolf Ritual: The Whaling Indians, West Coast Legends and Stories*, part 12 of the Sapir-Thomas Nootka texts (Ottawa: University of Ottawa Press, 2007), 2.

17. Ibid., 146.

18. Barry M. Pritzker, *Native Americans: An Encyclopedia of History, Culture and Peoples* (Santa Barbara, CA: ABC-CLIO, 1998), 90.

19. John Peabody Harrington, "A Yuma Account of Origins," *Journal of American Folklore* 21 (1908): 324, 327.

20. Sapir et al., *The Origin of the Wolf Ritual*, 27.

21. Ibid., 43.

22. Ibid., 50.

23. Ibid., 85.

24. Agnes S. W. in interview with the author and Sheila Archer, May 2018.